A Mother's
Ordeal

A Mother's Ordeal

The Story of Chi An

ONE WOMAN'S FIGHT AGAINST CHINA'S ONE-CHILD POLICY

Steven W. Mosher

WARNER BOOKS

A *Warner* Book

First published in the United States
by Harcourt Brace in 1993
First published in Great Britain
by Little, Brown in 1994

This edition published by Warner in 1995
Reprinted 1995 (twice), 1997

A CIP catalogue record for this book
is available from the British Library.

ISBN 0 7515 0807 1

Printed in England by Clays Ltd, St Ives plc

Warner Books
A Division of
Little, Brown and Company (UK)
Brettenham House
Lancaster Place
London WC2E 7EN

Contents

Author's Note

*M*Y INTRODUCTION to family planning Chinese-style came long before I met Chi An, the mother whose ordeal I recount in this book. The year was 1980. One of the first American social scientists allowed to do research in China since the founding of the People's Republic in 1949, I was living in rural Guangdong and was engaged in a study of an agricultural commune. One day several hundred young commune women, all pregnant with their second or third children, were ordered to attend family planning meetings. Inquiries revealed that the provincial government had secretly ordered a 1 percent cap on population growth for the year. Local officials were complying the only way they could—by launching a family planning "high tide" during the month of March to terminate as many pregnancies as possible.

The rules governing this high tide were simple: No woman was to be allowed to bear a second child within four years of her first, and third children were strictly forbidden. Furthermore, all women who had borne three or more children by November 1, 1979, were to be sterilized.[1]

Over the next few weeks I became an eyewitness to every aspect of this draconian campaign. I went with young women to family planning "study sessions" (similar to those later organized by Chi An and recounted herein) and saw them harangued and threatened by senior Party officials. I followed them as they were taken under escort to the commune clinic and watched—with the permission of local officials who were eager to demonstrate their prowess in birth control to a visiting foreigner—as they were aborted and sterilized. I spoke with anguished husbands and heartbroken grandparents and interviewed the poker-faced officials in charge. I left China a few months later with women's pleas for help still ringing in my ears and first told their story in *Broken Earth: The Rural Chinese*.[2]

The demands of China's family planners escalated as the eighties unfolded. The one-child policy, first adumbrated by Deng Xiaoping in a 1979 speech, was in place nationwide by 1981. The "technical policy on family planning" followed two years later. Still in force today, the technical policy requires IUDs for women of childbearing age with one child, sterilization for couples with two children (usually performed on the woman, although the law is not specific as to sex), and abortions for women pregnant without authorization.[3] By the mid-eighties, according to Chinese government statistics, birth control surgeries—abortions, sterilizations, and IUD insertions—were averaging more than thirty million a year.[4] Many if not most of these procedures were performed on women who submitted only under duress.

Published provincial and local guidelines for the enforcement of the one-child policy are usually cloaked in euphemisms, but sometimes the real intent comes through loud and clear:

1. From "Junan Commune Family Planning Measures," a directive signed by the Junan Commune Revolutionary Committee, dated March 7, 1980 (copy in my possession).
2. New York: Free Press, 1983.
3. *Nanfang ribao* (Nanfang daily), May 15, 1983, p. 3.
4. *Zhongguo weisheng nianjian 1986* (Public health yearbook of China, 1986) (Beijing: Renmin weisheng chubanshe, 1986), p. 475.

The husband or the wife of a couple that have two or more children should be sterilized. . . . We should implement thoroughly our policy on sterilization in those areas and resort to remedial measures [abortions] when dealing with pregnancies that do not comply with planning.[5]

Birth control should be enforced. . . . Measures to reward good and punish evil should be implemented.[6]

All newly married couples who are expecting must show their planned birth certificates. Those who are unable to produce a permit will have to undergo birth control measures [abortions followed by IUD insertions].[7]

The Sichuan provincial government demands that all areas truly stop early marriages, early births and births out of wedlock to control population growth. . . . Illegal relationships [early marriages] which should be dissolved must be dissolved. . . . Those who are pregnant out of wedlock and have not reached the legal marriage age must undergo remedial operations [abortions] within the prescribed period.[8]

If an unauthorized baby is the second, third, or subsequent child in a family and sterilization has not been accepted, the family will be denied permission to build a dwelling, their water and electricity will be cut off . . . grain coupons will not be issued, [and] driver's licenses and private business licenses will be revoked.[9]

The above passages are taken from a recent book by Dr. John Aird, the dean of China demographers, called *Slaughter of the Innocents: Coercive Birth Control in China.*[10] Dr. Aird, who formerly directed the China Branch of the U.S. Bureau of the Census, sifted

---

5. *Shaanxi ribao* (Shaanxi daily), January 11, 1985.
6. *Jiankang bao jihua shengyu ban* (Health gazette family planning edition), April 18, 1985, pp. 16–19.
7. *Jiankang bao jihua shengyu ban* (Health gazette family planning edition), May 17, 1985, p. 3.
8. *Zhongguo jihua shengyu bao* (China population), September 13, 1987.
9. *China Spring Digest*, vol. 1, no. 5, September–October 1987: 60–62.
10. Washington, D.C.: AEI Press, 1990.

through literally thousands of Chinese family-planning documents for evidence of widespread coercion. His blunt, unequivocal conclusions are worth quoting at length:

> *The Chinese family planning program is being carried out against the popular will by means of a variety of coercive measures. Despite official denials and intermittent efforts to discourage some of the more extreme manifestations, since the early 1970s if not before, coercion has been an integral part of the program. . . . Mandatory IUD insertions, sterilizations, and abortions continue. The national family planning journal has issued thinly disguised injunctions to get the job done by whatever means necessary . . . the emphasis is on "real action," "effective measures," and "practical results." For the first time, articles in the Chinese media are openly advocating coercion in family planning. . . . The Chinese program remains highly coercive, not because of local deviations from central policies but as a direct, inevitable, and intentional consequence of those policies.*[11]

While most China watchers would agree with Dr. Aird's assessment, Western media coverage of Beijing's family planning program has been spotty at best. Some of the social consequences of the one-child policy, such as the "little emperor" syndrome displayed by many of China's only children, have been the subject of numerous articles. Human rights abuses, on the other hand, have received scant play. The problem here is primarily one of access, since Beijing has placed much of the program off limits to foreign correspondents in recent years. Interviews with the minister in charge of the State Family Planning Commission are readily scheduled, but questions about abuses are met with carefully scripted answers about "improving work styles" and "voluntarism." Requests to observe a study session in progress, or to send a camera crew into a government-run clinic during a family planning high tide, are routinely denied.

Insider accounts of China's family planning program have been

11. Aird, *Slaughter of the Innocents*, pp. 88–89.

rare—and are always published under pseudonyms—no doubt for fear of government reprisals. Those that have appeared provide independent confirmation of the kinds of abuses that will be described here. For instance, a Chinese journalist ("Liu Yin") was allowed to accompany the members of a family planning "task force" on a village raid whose mission was to arrest eleven women who had become pregnant without authorization. Her account, which was published in a British newspaper, describes how five of the women were forcibly dragged from their homes in the middle of the night and taken to the county hospital. The other six had fled, but their families were warned that "if [the women] did not go to the abortion center within a week their houses would be pulled down. This was no bluff. On the way back from the raid, I saw six collapsed houses. No family in the village is allowed to provide shelter for the people whose houses have been destroyed."[12]

Later the journalist visited the hospital itself, where she saw "hundreds of women—some more than six months pregnant— . . . packed in dark corridors and makeshift tents, waiting to be operated on in the 'abortion center' in the hospital courtyard. Next to it was a public toilet. I went in: there was simply nowhere you could put your feet; it was filled with blood-soaked toilet paper. Behind the toilet stood a line of waste-bins: the aborted babies—some as old as eight months—were put there, then dumped somewhere else."[13]

In recent years several exposés of the family planning program have been published in Chinese dissident journals. For example, in the premiere issue of the *China Spring Digest*, a Chinese doctor ("Bao Fu") recounted his experiences performing late-term, forced abortions. His brief article, "Massacre of the Innocents in China," is every bit as chilling as anything Chi An witnessed.[14]

When Chi An and her husband first asked for my help, in San Diego, in 1987, I knew little about her past. It was enough for me to know that she had been ordered by Chinese officials to get an abor-

---

12. *The Independent*, September 11, 1991.
13. Ibid.
14. Vol. 1, no. 1 (January–February 1987), p. 45.

tion. The idea that officials from that country would try to enforce the one-child policy on a Chinese couple living in the United States rankled me. To help Chi An and her family win political asylum, I recounted how they were being threatened in articles for the *Washington Post* and the *Reader's Digest*.

The more I learned about Chi An's past, however, the more I came to realize how unique her story was. She had been trained as an abortionist, yet had been forced to have an abortion herself. She had been bullied into signing a one-child agreement, yet had gone on to work as a population control enforcer. She had been both victimizer and victim and now faced victimization again. Here was the ultimate insider's account of China's family planning program, a stranger-than-fiction story so dramatic that it simply begged to be told. I urged Chi An to allow me commit her experiences to paper.

The idea appealed to her, for she was eager to call attention to the kinds of government abuses that she had witnessed. We set to work in July 1991. From the outset we resolved to take every possible precaution to ensure that our account did not cause unpleasant repercussions for her family and friends still in China. Most of the individuals who figure in this book, beginning with Chi An and her husband, Wei Xin, have been carefully disguised by giving them fictitious identities—that is, by altering their names and other unimportant details of their lives. These changes in no way affect the substance of Chi An and Wei Xin's experiences with the family planning program or with each other. Considerations of confidentiality also dictated a change of venue: Chi An did not grow up in the city of Shenyang, but in another city not too many miles distant. It was there that she was trained in family planning procedures and went to work in a large, state-owned enterprise I have called the Liaoning Truck Factory.

I spent hundreds of hours interviewing Chi An. Initially a bit shy, she turned out to be an inspired storyteller. Important events in her life—her father's death, the birth of her son, Tacheng, the one-child agreement she had signed, the little boy who wouldn't die—came alive as she recounted them. Chi An's mother as well as Wei

Xin and Tacheng helped to confirm and amplify many details of her story. Wei Xin, who returned to the Village of the Three Brothers after the first draft of this book was completed, was able to double-check the accuracy of the stories that dealt with his family, such as sister-in-law's harrowing escape from the population control police.

The letters reproduced at various points in the book are quoted verbatim from the originals. Where the originals were in Chinese, as with the series of threatening letters that Chi An received from her factory, I am responsible for the English translations and have copies of the originals. Statements by major Chinese leaders regarding the population control program were verified by reference to public documents of the time. Many of these are also cited by Aird, including Deng Xiaoping's population control ultimatum: "Use whatever means you must to reduce the population, but do it!"[15]

I wanted to present Chi An's story to the reader in as direct and unfiltered a way as possible, so I chose the rather unconventional approach of writing in the first person. Often this involved little more than translating Chi An's words into English (our conversations, which were taped, were entirely in Chinese). Like many Chinese she proved to have an excellent memory and could recall incidents and even conversations in great detail. Indeed, I had to condense or leave out entirely many of her stories, particularly those involving her early years. Her accounts of the Great Leap Forward and the Cultural Revolution are worth a book in themselves. In other cases, especially where Chi An's own work in performing abortions was concerned, I had to draw her out. Finally, although my own experience with China's family planning program proved helpful in understanding and conveying to the reader what Chi An had been through, what the reader will find here is her story, not mine.

15. Aird, *Slaughter of the Innocents*, p. 92.

A Mother's
Ordeal

Prologue

MY HAND was trembling as I opened the letter from the Liaoning Truck Factory, my work unit in China. Its contents would determine the fate of the child I was carrying.

July 1987

Comrade Chi An:

Your news that you had accidentally become pregnant caught me by surprise. I have made some inquiries about whether the one-child limitation applies to Chinese living abroad. . . .

I am afraid that I do not have good news for you. When you left for America three years ago, the birth control policy in our country was already very strict. The "one-couple, one-child" policy is now even stricter, especially since [Chinese Communist Party Central Committee] Directive Number Seven was announced last year. Party General Secretary Zhao Zhiyang recently ordered officials to redouble their efforts to enforce the technical policy on birth control [mandating IUD insertion after one child, sterilization after two, and abortion for women pregnant without authorization, that is, those who do not have a quota to give birth].

In the last few months, some women pregnant with "illegal" children have been forced to have abortions during the eighth or ninth month of pregnancy, or even at the time of birth. Some women claim that they heard their babies cry but were told later by birth control officials that the infants had been stillborn. Officials have used physical force, dragging or pushing pregnant women to the abortion clinics for the operation. Even in extreme cases like this, higher officials have supported them, saying the birth control policy cannot be violated.

Regardless of where you are living now, you are still officially attached to the Liaoning Truck Factory. If you come back at the end of this year pregnant, even if you are eight or nine months along, you will absolutely not be allowed to have your baby. If you really want this baby, stay in America until the child is born. How the Party will treat you when you come back with a second child I cannot say with certainty. There will be fines and probably other punishments as well. But at least you will have your baby.

Please think carefully about our country's one-child policy and how much you want this baby before making a decision. Don't come back until you do.

Wishing you and your family health and happiness, I am,

> *Your friend,*
> *Gong Chang*
> *Population Control Office*
> *Liaoning Truck Factory*
> *Shenyang City, Liaoning Province*
> *People's Republic of China*

I had written to Gong Chang several weeks before, informing her that I had accidentally become pregnant with my second child. I was not sure whether she would be sympathetic to my plight, but I was certain that she would be as surprised as I had been. Before I left China we had worked together in the population control office at the

Liaoning Truck Factory, enforcing the one-child policy among its thousands of workers and their families. If anything, I had been even more zealous than Gong Chang in tracking down and aborting women pregnant with "illegal" children.

"I am a responsible cadre," I had written carefully. "I have not deliberately violated the birth control regulations. I became pregnant accidentally after losing my IUD. I will abide by whatever the Party secretary decides in my case. If possible, however, I would like to keep this child. Could you find out whether the one-child limitation applies to couples living outside China?"

It had not been necessary to remind Gong Chang that, like most women in China, I had been forced to sign a one-child agreement following the birth of my first child. Or that I was now living in the United States, where my husband Wei Xin was a visiting research scholar. Surely my special circumstances spoke for themselves and warranted an exception.

It would be dangerous for me, and lethal for my unborn child, to return to China without permission to carry my child to term. Gong Chang's letter, with its litany of abuses, reinforced what I was hearing from Wei Xin's friends, who hailed from widely scattered parts of China. All knew of instances in which local population control officials had used physical force on women, dragging or pushing them to an abortion clinic. None had heard of a single official being disciplined for such actions. A young man from Siquan told a horrifyingly familiar tale of government doctors dispatching "illegal" newborns with an injection of formaldehyde into the soft spot of the infant's head. In parts of rural Zhejiang, the home province of another friend, strangulation was said to be the preferred method.

I was glad I was no longer a party to such crimes. Instead, in a complete reversal of my earlier role, it was I who was carrying an "illegal" child. When General Secretary Zhao insisted on remedial measures for women pregnant outside the plan, he was talking about me. The frightened, troubled faces of the women I had hounded in the past were about to become my own.

I read again the letter I held in my hand. Permission for a second child would not be forthcoming. If I really wanted this child, Gong Chang warned, I should wait until it was born before returning to China.

Do I really want this baby? I asked myself for the hundredth time. *Do I really want this baby?*

1

"Only a Daughter"

MY MOTHER always doted on my older brother, Liang-yue. With his birth in 1948, after she had been married for one year, my mother fulfilled the greatest duty of a Chinese wife: to perpetuate her husband's line. This was especially important to my grandparents, for my father himself was an only son. Up to this point they had treated their daughter-in-law as little more than a serving girl, not because they were being deliberately cruel to her—although many daughters-in-law were mistreated, some to the point of suicide—but because she was seen as a means to an end, the continuation of the family line, rather than a person in her own right. Now that she was the mother of the next generation of Yangs, her status in the household had risen sharply. My grandmother insisted on personally caring for her during the thirty days of postpartum bed rest dictated by custom, bringing her hot water for washing in the morning and her meals throughout the day.

Custom also decreed that my brother neither be named, nor his birth publicly celebrated, until thirty days had passed, lest heaven be jealous of my family's happiness and unexpectedly call him home. My grandparents spent these weeks preparing for my brother's "full month," as the feast to welcome a newborn son into the family was called. My father, who had not been present for his son's birth, took a leave of absence from his engineering studies at the University of Shenyang for this event. When the "full month" came, it was of a size and splendor that our poor village had seldom seen. Two hundred relatives and neighbors—most were both, since almost everyone in our village was surnamed Yang—sat down to tables piled high with food. Kaoliang whiskey flowed freely, and my father and grandfather were toasted again and again on their good fortune in having a descendant. Each guest received a hardboiled egg dyed a festive red, the color that symbolized new life. The expenses of the feast, coming on top of those of the wedding the year before, left my grandparents in debt for several years. But it could not be helped; nothing was more important than properly welcoming the latest shoot of their family branch into the Yang clan. Nothing less would please the ancestors.

By contrast, my arrival twenty months later caused scarcely a ripple. My father remained at his studies. There was no "full-month" feast, no red-colored eggs. So uneventful was my coming into the world that no one remembers the exact date on which it happened. My mother, who has a clear memory of the day my older brother was born, has forgotten the circumstances surrounding my birth. She knows that it was in October, and she thinks that it was a week or so after the founding of the People's Republic of China, but she is not sure of the day. Later, when I grew old enough to feel the lack of a specific birthday, I decided that I would celebrate mine on October 8, 1949. My family, mother included, never paid too much attention.

October 1, 1949, does stick in her mind, however. This was the date that Mao Zedong announced the creation of the New China. "China has stood up," he declared from a reviewing stand high atop the Gate of Heavenly Peace in the center of Beijing. The Communists had gained control of the ancient capital of the Qing and Ming empires, but much of the rest of China was still in the grip of civil war. The South and Southwest remained in the hands of retreating Nationalist armies, while bandits roamed the south Manchurian countryside where we lived, terrorizing the population. While my mother was not particularly enamored of the Communists, she was relieved at the prospect of an end to a decade of war. After the prescribed wait of thirty days, she named me Chi An, which means "the dawning of peace."

Neither I nor my grandiose-sounding name impressed my grandmother, who to her death called me *yatou*, which means simply "girl." To her way of thinking, only grandsons were important enough to have names. She was also unhappy about allowing my mother a month off from her household chores for giving birth to a mere *yatou*. In fact, my grandmother grumbled so much about it that my mother arose from her bed after only three days of rest and resumed her work around the house. Caring for both a newborn and a toddler, and exhausted by the constant round of chores, her milk soon went dry.

We were far too poor to hire a wet nurse or to buy expensive cow's milk. The meager scholarship my father received as a university student scarcely covered the cost of his meals and books. Under the new regime, university students were not expected to marry, much less have children. My grandparent's fields that year had produced a good crop of Kaoliang—a kind of coarse Chinese sorghum—but much of it had had to be sold to pay debts. They had kept just enough to see us through the winter. My older brother by now had enough teeth to eat steamed Kaoliang. I had to survive on Kaoliang juice, locally called *jiao budz*, or "chew cloth," because it was prepared by the mother, who chewed Kaoliang kernels and strained off the resulting juice using cheesecloth.

It took hours to prepare enough *jiao budz* for a single feeding, so that providing me with enough to eat became a full-time job for my mother. *Jiao budz* remained the mainstay of my diet for several years, even after most of my baby teeth had come in, since my stomach could not tolerate steamed Kaoliang. Later, when I studied nutrition in nursing school, I realized that *jiao budz* must have been little more than sugar water, containing almost no protein, fat, or calcium. It was a wonder that I survived infancy.

I grew into a sickly child and often came down with a cold or the flu. My poor diet affected me in more serious ways as well. I was three years old before I could walk, so weak and bowed were my legs from rickets. It was only after my father graduated from the university in 1952 and obtained a regular teaching position that my parents could afford to feed me better. On a diet of rice congee, soybean milk, and dry biscuits I began to get stronger, but I remember it was a slow process. Even after I found my legs, they remained unsteady under me for two years, and I could not run, skip, or hop. While other children played, I could only sit and watch, a spectator's role that I sometimes resented.

As soon as my father was appointed lecturer in the mechanical engineering department of the Shenyang Institute of Science and Technology, my mother took us to join him. She was eager to join her husband, from whom she had been separated all but a few months of their five-year marriage, and equally keen to set up her own household away from the constant scrutiny of her domineering mother-in-law. University officials, who had expected to be able to put my father up in a residence hall for junior faculty, were none too happy to discover that their new lecturer was not only married but already had two children with a third on the way. The housing the university assigned us was its least desirable: a second-floor apartment in a three-story building located on the other side of Shenyang, a full twenty miles away from the campus. We were the only family of a faculty member in the building; the heads of neighboring households were all university cooks, janitors, and office workers. It took Father an hour and two bus transfers to get to the institute.

The apartment itself—if one overlooked its distance from the university—was quite nice, having been built by the Japanese in the late 1930s. It certainly impressed my mother as a great improvement over the ramshackle house of cracked bricks and mud that we had left in the countryside. Instead of a few warped boards on a crosspiece, held shut by a wooden latch, it had a proper door with a brass handle, brass hinges, and a brass-covered mail slot. She was delighted to discover that it had all the modern amenities: a water closet, a bath, and a kitchen—all indoors. The toilet was a mere porcelain slit in the floor, but a tank was suspended above it, and it flushed with the pull of a cord. The bath was a Japanese *ofuru*, a deep tub made of wood and equipped with a gas water heater. The tiny two-burner range in the kitchen also used natural gas, which was piped into the building. All these were, to my mother, small miracles of convenience.

Later we came to realize how fortunate we were to have been assigned to this particular apartment building, for it was luxurious by Shenyang standards. Most of the apartment buildings in the city, including those on the university campus itself and even those newly constructed by the government, were not supplied with indoor plumbing or kitchens—despite the extremes of a brutally harsh climate, which lurched from subarctic winters to sweltering summers, with only a few weeks of spring or autumn in between. Makeshift cookstoves migrated depending on the season: In the summer, when the temperature could reach nearly a hundred degrees Fahrenheit at midday, they were set up on roofs or sidewalks; in the winter, with temperatures as low as minus forty degrees Fahrenheit, they were moved indoors to windowless hallways.

Bathing habits, too, cycled with the season. In the summer, people took frequent sponge baths in their apartments or on their roofs; in the winter, when daytime temperatures seldom rose above freezing, they kept their padded cotton clothes on day and night, going for weeks without bathing. There was usually only one water closet per floor, so that even in the dead of winter people were forced to leave their apartments and run down the hall to relieve themselves. Our new apartment actually had a garbage chute, located in the kitchen; this, too, seemed a great boon, especially in the winter, since it meant that we did not have to go downstairs and out of the building to dump our trash. (In fact, after my father had built up sufficient seniority to transfer to on-campus housing, my mother prevailed on him to stay where we were. She was to live there for the next forty years.)

What pleased my mother most about her new quarters, however, were its two bedrooms. In the village we had all—children, parents, and grandparents—slept together on a *kang*, a raised brick platform heated only fitfully by the cookstove. But the apartment's bedrooms were furnished with Japanese *tatami*, thick rice-straw mats resting on raised wooden flooring, which were not only more comfortable than the unyielding brick of the *kang*, but warmer in the winter and cooler in the summer as well. My mother allotted to Father and herself the large of the two bedrooms, leaving the smaller—in which we were joined by our younger brother, Ming-yue, the following year—to my brother and me. For the first time in their married lives, my parents would have a bedroom to themselves and a chance to talk to one another in private. They had scarcely known one another when they were married, my mother later confided, because in those days it was regarded as immoral in the village for unwed men and women to date. It was during that first winter in Shenyang, after five years of marriage and three children, that she first felt a deep affection for, and in the end fell in love with, my father.

My older brother and I enjoyed tumbling about on the tatami mats in our bedroom, but our sport ended abruptly a year after we moved in. The cook's family next door had taken up their mats to air them out and had discovered a Japanese officer's sword hidden in the space under the wooden framing. That evening the cook had brought the sword over to show my father. "I wonder how many Chinese heads it has cut off," my father remarked, taking a few swipes in the air with it. "You'd better turn it in to the authorities tomorrow." I was terrified. My parents never talked much about the Japanese period, but I knew that many atrocities had been committed. That night I refused to sleep in my bedroom, fearing that there was a sword that had cut off Chinese heads under my tatami mats as well. I was so upset that my parents finally allowed me to sleep in their room. Not that it made much difference to my state of mind. As soon as I fell asleep, I saw a Japanese officer, sword drawn, crawl out from under the mats and move menacingly toward me. He raised his sword and was just about to cut off my head when I woke up screaming.

The local authorities soon solved my problem, however. They ordered a detachment of police to search the apartment building for weapons and other contraband. Though no other swords were discovered, the tatami mats and their wooden frames, which had been taken up, were permanently removed. Once the bare concrete floors of my bedroom were exposed, my nightmares stopped. Thereafter my brother and I slept on a mattress on a simple wooden frame. Some time later our Japanese-style bathtubs were also removed, not because any weapons had been found but because the municipal utility company decided that heating the water consumed too much gas. Thereafter my mother used the bathroom for storage, and we began taking sponge baths like everyone else. We still counted ourselves fortunate, though, because in the winter we could heat water in the kitchen and quickly scrub ourselves down and rub ourselves dry there, where it was slightly warmer than in the rest of the apartment.

For my mother, who spent her formative years in abject poverty, thriftiness was a way of life. She had lost both her parents in a cholera epidemic just after her fourth birthday. Her two older brothers had been taken in by her relatively well-to-do paternal grandparents, but she herself had been sent to live with Nainai, her maternal grandmother. A poor widow, Nainai depended for her livelihood on the sewing she took in and on two small fields she rented out to sharecroppers. The fields were "thin," and the harvest was never good.

My mother's circumstances were scarcely improved by marriage. Father's college years were prolonged by the chaos of the civil war and its aftermath, and he was unable to send us any money. Mother felt uncomfortable around his parents, whom she felt begrudged us even the food we ate.

Once Father graduated in 1953 and started teaching at the university, his salary was fifty-seven yuan a month, about what our working-class neighbors made. But habits long formed are not easily broken, and my mother continued to pinch every penny. Fruit was an unaffordable luxury, and our meals often consisted of nothing more than Kaoliang cakes or cornbread muffins, with a small side dish of bok choy. Nor were we allowed to eat as much as we wanted. My mother would carefully divide the food she had cooked between us, and there were no seconds. It didn't help that the neighbor children, some poorer than we were, had the occasional slice of watermelon to eat or cherry lollipop to suck. Even though such treats sold for only a penny each, my mother insisted that we could not afford them. I soon learned not even to ask, because doing so always led to a lengthy scolding.

Mother was strict with us in other ways as well. We were not allowed to jump or run inside the apartment. When we spoke, we had to keep our voices low—except at mealtimes, when we were not allowed to speak at all. Back talk of any kind was strictly forbidden. When Mother asked us to do a chore, we were expected to say, "Yes, Mother," and do it without a word.

When I was five years old, I hated the way she dressed me. My everyday clothes were worse than hand-me-downs. They were my mother's old clothes, which she ripped apart at the seams and re-sewed to my size. They were baggy and old-fashioned, the style in my mother's rural village. The colors, drab to begin with, were badly faded from the sun and countless washings. Worst of all, strips of unfaded color ran through them at odd angles, where the cloth had originally been part of a seam or lining. The other children on the block, whose parents dressed them in pretty, colorful blouses and pants that fit, all laughed at me. "*Tu-bao-dz,*" they would call out mockingly. "Country bumpkin."

In the winter they laughed even louder. Rather than spend money on shoes, my mother made my shoes by hand out of black cloth, as she had done in the village. She made them large on purpose, so that cotton wadding could be stuffed inside to keep my feet warm. In their inflated state, my feet took on the appearance of great black balls. Never fast on my feet, I was slowed down even more by these clodhoppers. My winter hat—also handmade by my mother—was equally odd. It was conical in shape, with a little peak that arched up over my head like a dunce cap. Fifteen years before the Cultural Revolution, when Communist Party officials were forced to wear dunce caps and parade through the streets of China's cities, I was crowned by my very own mother. The neighborhood children invented a special nickname for me, by which I was known for several years: *Laosan-guai*, "old-triple-weird," they called me, on account of my hat, my shoes, and my clothes.

I had only one outfit—a soft cotton print with red and white flowers, which my father had bought for me as a New Year's present —that I considered presentable. I was very attached to it. Had it been up to me, I would have worn it every day, but this was not permitted. I was allowed to wear this dress only on Sundays, when my parents took us three children on outings. My mother even kept the dress in her wardrobe so that I would not be tempted to wear it.

Not that she was any harder on me than on my brothers. If she had ever had the traditional attitude of my grandmother that "boys are precious and girls are worthless," she lost it soon after moving to the city. My mother neither spoiled her sons nor piled all the household chores on her daughter, as so many Chinese women did.

Unlike my mother, who never smiled much, my father had an open, sunny temperament. He was as patient and affectionate with me as my mother was short and distant. His homecoming each day at six o'clock was marked by a ritual as fixed as a baptism. I would be waiting by the front door of our apartment. He would come bounding up the stairs, sweep me into his arms, and give me a big hug. Then he would carry me in to the washbasin, pour some warm water into it, and wash my face and hands. After this he would comb my hair until every stray wisp was neatly in place. Finally, he would sit down in the mahogany chair that was his alone and take me onto his lap, stroking my head while he talked to my brothers and me.

At bedtime he would even carry me to bed, tucking me gently in for the night. At the time I took this special treatment as my due, convinced that I was his favorite, but perhaps he had gotten used to nursing me because I had been sickly for so long. Whatever the reason, I thrived under his care. My mother would occasionally protest against what she called this "coddling," murmuring that he was going to spoil me, but she never became angry over it. She was always more relaxed when my father was home; his presence created a sanctuary that her fear of famine and abandonment could not penetrate. Whether my father sensed the transformation he wrought in her or not, he rarely spent an evening away from us. In the summer most of the men in our neighborhood could be found in the alleyways, smoking and playing chess; in the winter the games would move indoors, and they would fortify themselves against the cold with a glass of Kaoliang whiskey: If they stayed home it was to nap. My father spent his free time with us.

At this time the street on which we lived swarmed with children. The one-child-per-family program was many years in the future, and couples were even being encouraged by the government to have large families. My mother did not agree with this policy. When we were small, before we were able to help much, she often complained out loud about how much work it was to take care of us. "You children are a burden," she would say to us. "Two children are enough. Just keeping you three clean and fed takes all my energy. What a bitter fate I have. Why did I have so many children? How am I going to feed you all? And what am I going to do if I get pregnant?" On hearing this my younger brother, Ming-yue, and I would look at each other out of the corners of our eyes, wondering which one of us was unwanted. He was third in line, but I was a girl.

In late 1954 my mother suddenly decided to go back to school and become a teacher. The timing of this move was not entirely her idea. The early fifties saw wave after wave of propaganda encouraging women to "make a contribution to the revolution." Staying at home to take care of children was constantly portrayed in the government press not only as meaningless drudgery but as practically para-sitical on the larger society. Women were to be liberated for their own good. The newspapers quoted Friedrich Engels's dictum that "to emancipate women and make her the equal of man is and remains an impossibility so long as the woman is shut out from social productive labor and restricted to private domestic labor." With the same excess of zeal that would mark later political campaigns, women were forced to abandon the home—regardless of their wishes—to go to work for the state. Street committees, the lowest level of urban administration, were encouraged to set up both primitive factories and day care cen-ters, and to enlist local homemakers as laborers.

Long tempted by the additional security that a second income as a teacher would offer, my mother had wanted to wait until her chil-dren were older. She changed her mind when the head of the local street committee paid her a visit. He told her that the committee had just set up a new workshop to recycle light bulbs and asked her to take a job changing the filaments in burned-out bulbs. My mother did not want to alienate this powerful individual, the eyes and ears of the party in the neighborhood, by rejecting his offer outright. So she politely thanked him for thinking of her and, improvising rap-idly, went on to tell him that she could not accept his kind offer because she had already made plans to attend a teacher's training school that fall.

So it was that in late 1954 my parents enrolled me and my younger brother, Ming-yue, in a boarding nursery at my father's university. Every Monday our father took us with him on the bus and dropped us off at the nursery, where we remained until Saturday noon, when he came to fetch us home. I found the teachers strict, the regimen daunting, and the other students aggressive. I especially missed the comforting presence of my older brother, who had been spared this banishment because he had just started first grade. Desperately un-happy, I cried myself to sleep each night.

Fortunately, I stayed in the nursery for only one year. Shortly before my seventh birthday I came home to enroll in elementary school. After I left the nursery, my younger brother became more and more withdrawn, especially toward my mother. One weekend, when my father brought Ming-yue home, he refused to have anything to do with Mother. He would not even look up when she called his name but remained resentfully standing at the far end of the room. After this incident my father made arrangements for the janitor's wife who lived in the basement of our building to care for Ming-yue during the day.

We were all relieved when Mother graduated. By a stroke of luck she was assigned to teach at the same elementary school my older brother and I attended, just down the street from our apartment.

In the fall of 1958, when I was in third grade, our principal, who was also the school's Party branch secretary, announced to us at a school assembly that China was embarking on a Great Leap Forward. "Chairman Mao says that steel is the commanding general of industry!" Principal Gao shouted. "He has called upon us to overtake Great Britain in the production of iron and steel within fifteen years. No longer will China be a backward nation. We will build steel smelters everywhere. We will build a steel smelter right here in our own school! We will be the first school in Shenyang to heed the chairman's call!" His excitement was contagious. When he ended the assembly by chanting, "Everyone, make steel!" we all joined in enthusiastically. For many months to come, "Everyone, make steel!" would be the watchword by which we lived.

Principal Gao, whose ambition was to be the first Party branch secretary in all of Shenyang to produce pig iron, was elated when my mother suggested that perhaps my father, an engineer, could supervise the construction of a smelter. It took only a day for my father to obtain the permission of his university department head and Party secretary for a temporary leave of absence, and he set to work in the schoolyard the following morning. Initially overjoyed that my father had come to our school, thinking that I would now be able to spend more time with him, I failed to reckon with our principal's desire to impress his Party superiors. So that the teachers would not be distracted from their work of building the smelter, classes were cancelled and we students were sent home. For the next few weeks I hardly saw either of my parents.

Gao pushed his work force to the limits of exhaustion. A day and a night crew were organized and alternated twelve-hour shifts, so that the work would continue around the clock. When the walls started to go up, the sixth graders were called back to school to help carry bricks and mix mortar. As for my father, he lived, ate, and breathed the smelter for the better part of a month.

Ours was not the first smelter to be fired in the city but, thanks to my father's expertise and our ample supply of building materials, it was one of the first. On the day chosen for its inaugural firing, a number of officials from the municipal department of education were present for the ceremony. Principal Gao made an impassioned speech in which he attributed the school's achievements to the thoughts of Chairman Mao and the enlightened leadership of the Party. "Today, in the era of Chairman Mao Zedong, heaven is here on earth," he crowed. "Once the Party calls, tens of millions of the masses leap into action." He never once mentioned my father, an omission that rankled me for years afterward. Still, I burst with pride when Principal Gao cried, "Make steel!" for it was my father who ignited the coal in the smelter. Brownish yellow smoke began to draft out of the chimney into the chill autumn air. Then it was time to chorus, "Everyone make steel!" and "Long live the Great Leap Forward!" In my childish pride and exuberance, I tried to outshout the others.

Despite my father's best efforts, however, we were never able properly to smelt even a single load of iron ore in our new smelter. The only available fuel was soft brown coal, which burned at too low a temperature. Principal Gao quickly resorted to chicanery. In order to meet the school's quota of iron and steel, he ordered us students to collect scrap metal, which could then be melted with relative ease into ingots for the authorities. Each student was assigned a monthly quota of scrap metal, adjusted by grade.

So began our great scavenger hunt for scrap iron. It was fun at first, but as the months passed our quotas grew more and more difficult to fill. Liang-yue and I scoured muddy back alleys, haunted the neighborhood bicycle repair shop, and even crawled along the floor and under the workbenches of the street committee's light bulb factory late one evening. We came up with only a few screws. It was as if a plague of iron-eating locusts had moved through the city before us, consuming everything ferrous.

Our lessons were hit or miss, taught by tired teachers who had been up all night. Although the smelter was being used only to melt down scrap metal, it still required around-the-clock tending. Someone was always being burned, either on the hands from wrestling with the red-hot wok or on the feet or calves from flying drops of molten metal. My parents took to wearing their quilted cotton clothes, shoes, and gloves early that fall, for the protection they offered.

It was quantity that Mao had asked for, and it was quantity that he got. Roughly six hundred thousand ramshackle smelters were built nationwide, and nearly all, like the smelter in our school, were kept working twenty-four hours a day. The real output of this massive effort quickly mounted into the millions of tons—and was probably inflated by two or three times that amount in official reports by overzealous cadres. So encouraged was Mao by the figures he was shown that he set ever-higher targets. Fifteen years would not be needed to overtake England in steel production, he declared. China could do it in five. A few months later he shortened even this estimate to a breathtaking three years. "Three years of suffering; a thousand years of happiness," exulted one slogan. It was only a shimmering mirage, but in its pursuit Mao led the entire country on a forced march into a wilderness of hunger and want.

Chairman Mao also fixed on the idea that sparrows eat too much grain and launched a nationwide campaign to exterminate all birds from China's skies. Twice a week our teacher would form us into a column of twos and, holding high a red banner, lead us out into the countryside. Every member of our troop carried something with which to make noise. I had a washbasin and a stick, while other children carried whistles, wok lids, and pans. Whenever we came on a flock of birds, we would set up a tremendous din, blowing our whistles and beating on our washbasins and woks with all our might. The startled birds would take flight. Whenever they tried to land, we or another group of noisemakers would run to the spot and drive them away. Finally, after several hours of wheeling and circling in confusion, birds would begin to drop from the sky in exhaustion, falling dead on the ground.

I looked forward to these outings into the green countryside, walking along dirt paths in the warm sunshine. And what child doesn't like to make noise? Our teacher, who insisted on absolute silence in the classroom, now encouraged us to make more noise. As for our efforts to decimate the sparrow population, millions of birds did die throughout China, but the outcome was not what Mao had imagined. The resultant infestation of insects caused grain losses far in excess of what the birds would have eaten.

Busy making steel, our mother was rarely home until well after our bedtimes during this period, and we hardly saw our father at all. My younger brother had been returned to the boarding nursery at the suggestion of Principal Gao, so that my mother would have "more time to devote to the Great Leap Forward." Liang-yue and I were left home alone night after night. On our own we worked out a system to get the essential shopping, cooking, and housework done. My brother was responsible for buying food and other necessities, picking up the grain ration every Saturday, and buying vegetables from the local farmers' market every afternoon after school. I remained at home, washing, sweeping, and cleaning while he went shopping. When he returned, I would rinse the vegetables he had bought and stir-fry them. That, plus steamed rice or Kaoliang, would be our dinner. After washing the dinner dishes, my brother and I would sit down to do our homework, if we had been assigned any that day by our harried teachers. My brother and I got along well, and I was secretly very pleased with myself that I was able to cook and keep house, or so I imagined.

But my days as a cook were over when Chairman Mao ordered everyone to "eat out of the same big pot." Across the country, in city and countryside, communal cafeterias were being established. Mao had defined Communism as "public cafeterias with free meals," Mother said. Private cooking was no longer allowed. Henceforth we were to take our evening meal in the school cafeteria with the other teachers and their children.

The food in the cafeteria, I discovered, was the same simple fare I had been serving at home. I didn't think it tasted any better, either, though I didn't dare share this opinion with anyone else. Still, my brother and I went willingly to the cafeteria each night, for there we could have dinner with our father and mother and feel like a family again. The end of home-cooked meals also made the following month's quota of scrap iron easy to gather. My brother and I simply handed in our family's two woks and small collection of cast-iron kitchen utensils to our teacher. They promptly disappeared into the large metal stew constantly simmering in the smelter.

At the time my mother had led us to believe that she was happy at the prospect of being freed from kitchen duty. "I approve of Chairman Mao's directive," she had told us enthusiastically. "No more waiting in long lines to buy wilted cabbage, no more cooking, no more dishes." Years later, my mother was to tell me that this had been nothing more than a brave front. "Step by step we were being drawn away from our families and into a regimented, collective life," she recalled. "Everything was to be held in common. I didn't like being ordered to put my youngest son in a boarding nursery. He was such a good little boy that the janitor's wife was willing to watch him for free. I didn't like being ordered to eat in the school cafeteria. There were even rumors that we would all be moved into dormitories, segregated by sex. The old Nationalist propaganda, that the Communists would take our children from us, and that women would be shared, seemed on the verge of coming true. I was very frightened."

We took our meals in the school cafeteria for several months. We cheered when Principal Gao announced to us that, according to the *People's Daily*, China had produced more wheat than the United States in 1958. He encouraged us to eat all we wanted, saying that the New

China had such a superabundance of food that there was no place to store it.

Then, in the dead of winter, the cafeteria suddenly closed its doors. Principal Gao described the problem as a temporary setback. Food shipments from the countryside were merely delayed. He told us that we would be issued enough grain coupons to tide us over until the cafeteria was back in operation. But the cooks whispered that in all of Shenyang there was little food, and when we went to pick up our grain ration, we found that it had been reduced. Principal Gao had not told us this.

The cafeteria never reopened, and the winter of 1959 was hard. Still, we counted ourselves among the fortunate. With my parents' salaries and my mother's savings, we had enough money to buy grain— and a used wok—on the black market, even though the cost of food was inflating by the week.

Beset as we were by the turmoil of the Great Leap Forward, Mother had not been happy to learn that she was again pregnant. My first inkling of her condition came when I heard her declare to my father that she "wanted to have the baby *nadiao*," or "taken out." I couldn't hear exactly what Father said in reply, but his voice was low and soothing. For weeks I worried about the fate of my sibling and was greatly relieved when she began to show.

My youngest brother, Ying-yue, was born in December 1959, two months after I turned eleven. He was a breech birth, and, after a daylong effort to deliver him vaginally, Mother had to have an emergency cesarean. Perhaps because his arrival had cost her so dearly, she seemed to want little to do with him. Although she had breast-fed all her other children, she decided that Ying-yue was to be a bottle baby. She returned to teaching as soon as she was able, giving Ying-yue into the care of the janitor's wife, who doted on him. During the evenings and weekends, I took care of him and spoiled him even more.

Chinese girls are often pressed into service as nursemaids for their baby brothers. Many accept their assignments with resignation, some with resentment. Not I. I was thrilled to be Ying-yue's caregiver and threw myself wholeheartedly into the task. For the first time in my life, I had something all to myself. Ying-yue was the doll I had longed for as a child but never received.

The happiest times of my childhood, other than my special moments with Father, were those I spent with Ying-yue, my baby brother. I devoted myself to making him happy, telling him stories, and making him laugh. Ying-yue grew up into a happy little boy with an easy smile and the natural self-confidence that comes from being surrounded by people who love you. In this he reminded me of my father, who had the same ready smile and cheerful disposition.

2

Famine and Death

ONE SUNDAY in late June 1960, my father playfully rousted us out of bed as soon as it was light. "How would you like to go swimming at Crystal Lake?" he asked us as we all sat up stretching and rubbing our eyes. We were wide awake in a second, cheering and clapping our hands at the suggestion. We were in the midst of the first real heat wave of the season, just the weather for wide sandy beaches and limpid blue water.

My father knew Crystal Lake well. He had recently spent two weeks at a lakeside convalescent hospital after developing a serious case of inflammatory arthritis in both knees. While at the hospital he had received daily hot wax and heat lamp treatments for his knees, along with regular injections of cortisone. But he was convinced that what had mended his joints were his secret swims in the lake. It was forbidden for patients to go into the water, but swimming was my father's favorite sport and he went anyway, sneaking off the grounds whenever he could to a little cove nearby. He had been released only three weeks before, and his left knee was still a bit gimpy, but I knew he was eager to show us the lake.

"The university has organized an outing to Crystal Lake for all professors and their families," he continued. "Buses will leave from the university for the lake at nine A.M. If we hurry we can make them." We were out of bed by the time my father had finished speaking, pulling on our clothes and talking excitedly.

Mother's voice cut through our chatter. "You know we can't go anywhere today," she said sharply from the kitchen. "The winter clothes have to be washed and put away."

My father winked conspiratorially at us and then disappeared into the kitchen. "I'll wash the clothes for you," his cheerful voice rang out. "You go ahead and make breakfast. When I am done, then we will go to the lake."

Father quickly gathered up all our padded cotton jackets and pants, while Mother filled up the washtub with boiling water. Then he set to work. Getting the ingrained dirt of an entire winter out of the thick cotton quilting, using nothing but lye soap and a washboard, was an exhausting and time-consuming chore. His white shirt was soon soaked through with sweat. But he refused to heed my mother's entreaties to take time out for breakfast or even pause for a cup of water. He scrubbed away, all the while enthralling us with stories of Crystal Lake.

It was after ten when Father finally finished. We all helped him carry the wet clothes up to the roof, where he hung them up on bamboo drying racks. By the time we returned from the lake, our winter clothes would be dry and ready to fold away until the first chill wind of fall.

The university buses were long gone, so we had to take a city bus to the main Shenyang station and from there transfer to the Crystal Lake line. It was almost noon before we finally arrived at the lake. It didn't take long to find the large crowd from the university. They were crowded together on a short strip of beach by the water's edge, close to the lifeguard tower. My father went over and greeted his departmental colleagues and then led us in the other direction. "We don't want to sit with them," he told us as soon as we were out of earshot. "There are too many people and no shade. I'll take you to a pleasant spot I found here last month."

We all took off behind him, coming in a few minutes to his little cove, which was surrounded by tall pine trees. It was a lovely spot, with far fewer people. We found a patch of shade and spread out our rice-straw mat.

"I'm going back to get us some food," he told my mother. "I haven't eaten anything yet today, and I'm famished. Chi An and Liang-yue can come with me."

Liang-yue and I looked longingly at the cool, inviting water and then at each other. Ming-yue was already splashing in the shallows. "Can't we go for a short swim first?" Liang-yue begged. "Just to cool off?"

"I need your help—" Father started to say, then broke off when Liang-yue's disappointment registered with him. "I have an idea," he added impulsively, putting his arm around my brother's shoulder. "I'll give you a chance to show me what a good swimmer you are. I'll race you to the island." Set in the middle of the lake was a low island covered with pines. "We'll wait until we get back to buy lunch."

They changed into their swimming trunks, did some quick warm-up exercises, then headed for the water. "First one to the island is a hero!" my father shouted. Before they had taken more than a few strokes, my younger brother burst into tears. "Father, Father," Ming-yue cried out in a heartbroken voice. "Come back!"

Father reversed his course and came hobbling back up onto the beach, giving Ming-yue a hug. "I'll be back in a little while," he said. "Don't be afraid." Then he headed back out into the deep. They covered the first hundred yards quickly. Then Father turned around and waved to us. This sight filled me with apprehension, for it was as if Father were waving good-bye. I couldn't take my eyes off him as he and my brother swam ever farther into the lake, until their heads were no larger than dots.

My mother put baby Ying-yue down for his nap and took out her sewing, to all appearances unconcerned about the swimmers. The hot sun and the cool water soon drove all worries from my mind as well. Ming-yue and I ran and played along the beach for what seemed like a long time.

All at once my older brother was back. he looked around wildly, as if expecting to see someone.

"Where is Father?" he said in a shaky voice. His chest heaved as he tried to catch his breath.

"Where is Father?" I stupidly repeated his words, feeling suddenly sick to my stomach. How could I have forgotten Father's tiredness, his lame leg, the long swim?

Liang-yue ran over to Mother. "Father beat me to the island, and then we rested for a few minutes. Then we started back. I thought Father was right behind me, but when I reached the shallows I turned around and he wasn't there."

"Maybe . . . he's gone to buy food," my mother said in a strange, despairing tone of voice. Her hands had stopped moving and lay lifeless in her lap.

Liang-yue instantly ran down the beach to see if Father was at the canteen. The rest of us stood on the beach, huddled together around Mother like shipwreck victims. "He wouldn't go buy food in his bathing suit," Mother kept mumbling to herself, a dazed expression on her face.

Liang-yue came running back. "I couldn't find him, Mother!" he shouted. All of a sudden he burst into tears and flung himself down on the beach, beating the sand with his fists.

The sight galvanized my mother. In an instant she had kicked off her sandals and was running down the beach to the lifeguard tower. I grabbed Ying-yue, and we all took off after her.

"My children's father hasn't come back," she yelled up at the lifeguard. "He was swimming back from the island."

The lifeguard looked out across the lake for a long second, then climbed down from the tower. "How long has it been?" he asked quietly.

"About thirty minutes," she replied.

"Then it's too late," he said, shaking his head. "Your husband has already drowned. We will have to wait until we can drag the lake and recover the body."

A look of rage darkened my mother's face. "You will look for him now!" she screamed. "Go and get the head lifeguard! Go!"

The two lifeguards, carrying the light raft they used for rescues, followed my mother to the cove. They found my father quickly, laid him facedown on the beach, and attempted to revive him.

They kept up their efforts for what seemed a long time, stopping occasionally to listen for a heartbeat. "It's no use," the head lifeguard said finally to Mother, his eyes averted. "He's gone."

The next few days went by in a gray blur. A sad procession of well-intentioned friends and relatives came to offer their condolences but only made us feel our loss more keenly. Mother, in particular, fell into a deep depression and took to spending more and more time in bed. Had Father's parents, whom my mother had not seen since she moved to Shenyang, not come to stay with us, I don't know how we would have gotten through those days. My grandmother cooked and kept house, while my grandfather handled all the arrangements for the cremation, traditional burials having been forbidden by Communist Party decree. On the appointed day we went to the municipal crematorium and were handed a small wooden box that was all that remained of our father. We buried Father's ashes in a small cemetery not far from where we lived.

That sad day marked not the end but the beginning of our mourning. The heavy gloom that the death of our father had cast over us only deepened as the weeks went by, until it immobilized us all in a thick, still fog of grief. We didn't even feel like a family anymore, for, as I now discovered, it had been our father's love and good cheer that bound us together. The central pillar of our household had been struck down, leaving one unhappy woman and four miserable children to grieve separately in the ruins, unable or unwilling to offer one another comfort.

Liang-yue talked to Ming-yue and me endlessly about the circumstances of Father's death, for which he blamed himself. These self-recriminations always ended with all of us sobbing, and after the first few times my younger brother and I began to avoid him. Thereafter he went around the house talking to himself, until I began to wonder if he might be losing his mind.

My younger brother spoke very little but burst into tears at the merest mention of our father. Although he never talked about them, he was apparently troubled by nightmares, for I often heard him cry out at night. He would sit bolt upright in bed and shout "Father, Father! Come back!" The words were those he had used at the beach, uttered in the same desperate tone of voice.

I had no time for either Liang-yue's self-reproach or Ming-yue's night terrors; I was too busy taking refuge in fantasy. I refused to believe that my father had died. He was just away on a long trip, I told myself, and one day soon he would return to be with us again. I am not sure how deeply I believed this pleasant fiction, but it did enable me to get through the difficult weeks after my father's death. At least, after my grandparents left, I was the one who kept the household afloat, shopping for food, cooking simple meals, and washing clothes. I did these things not for my mother or brothers but for my absent father. How joyous would be his homecoming, I imagined. How he would praise me when he returned!

A highly elaborate version of my daytime fantasy soon found its way into my nighttime imaginings. Every night I would have the same dream about his return: He would be standing there with a big smile on his face, his arms full of presents. There would be a happy family reunion. Then Father would take me into his lap and brush my hair, as he used to. "Why were you gone for so long?" I would ask him. He would just smile without answering.

I always woke up happy from the dream, for it was so vivid that it left me convinced that Father had actually returned to us. I would run to my parents' room, only to find my mother sleeping alone. As the weeks went by the reality of Father's death gradually impressed itself on my consciousness. I realized that Father wasn't coming back, not ever. After that the joy of the dream vanished as soon as I was full awake, and I would shed bitter tears of loss. Still, I continued to have the dream for months afterward.

Father's death was hardest on Mother. She had always told us that she had a *kuming* (bitter fate) and was predestined to suffer privation and unhappiness throughout her days. Until she went to Shenyang to live with my father, she had expected nothing from life and had gotten pretty much what she expected. Father had changed all that, giving her security and well-being.

He had even protected her from the pressures of the Great Leap Forward—from the irrational fears sown by this man-made whirlwind and the all-too-real famine it had reaped. Through the bleak winter of 1959 and into the following spring, he told us almost daily that better days were coming and that we had nothing to fear as long as we pulled together. The worse conditions became, the more cheerful was his outlook. Like my mother, all of us had come to live in a sanctuary of his construction, secure within steadfast walls of love, surveying the world from windows of pure optimism. No one had needed such a refuge more than my mother.

Mother sank into what I later recognized as a prolonged and severe depression. Always on the quite side, strict and unsmiling except when Father was present, she took to her bed, sleeping twelve to fourteen hours at a stretch, staring fixedly into space during the brief periods she was awake. She got up only to relieve herself and then returned immediately to bed. Her weight dropped dramatically, since she ate almost nothing. She showed no interest in me or my brothers, not even in baby Ying-yue, who desperately needed her love and attention.

I had discovered the drawer in her wardrobe where she kept her cash, and I took money from it regularly to buy food. She often observed these withdrawals from her bed a few feet away, but she never said a word to me, even though before her illness she had counted every penny. She didn't even grieve normally, for I never saw her with red eyes or heard her cry over Father's death. Weeks passed.

In the beginning I didn't care that Mother, lost in her present darkness, had abandoned us. I was too busy keeping house for Father, who I was convinced would soon be back. It was only after I admitted his death to myself and accepted that he would never return that my thoughts turned to Mother. She had to get back on her feet, I realized. I was only eleven years old, about to begin fifth grade. I had taken care of everyone as best I knew how, but I could not keep it up for much longer. I was worn down by the responsibilities of running a household and more than ready to go back being an ordinary girl. I needed Mother to get well.

The problem was that I had no idea what to do. She was so silent and withdrawn that my efforts to cheer her up got nowhere. She usually lay in bed with her face to the wall. She responded to my questions with grunts or monosyllables at best.

It was by accident rather than design that I finally got her attention. We were out of food, and I needed ten yuan to pick up our next month's ration of Kaoliang. My mother's drawer contained only a one-yuan note and some change. "I don't have enough money to pay for our grain ration," I told Mother. "I've used up almost all the money you kept in your drawer."

She rolled over in bed to face me and then sat up. I saw a flush of anger slowly mount to her cheeks. "You wasteful child," she grumbled finally. "We need that money to survive, especially now that your father is . . . no longer with us." Her voice was quiet and halting at first, but then picked up speed and volume as she continued to reprimand me. "Don't you know that we are in the middle of a famine? How could you possibly have used up all that money so quickly?" She continued reproaching me in this fashion for several minutes, working herself up into a pretty good heat. I could have cried for joy. Never had a scolding felt so good.

The next morning Mother got out of bed and dressed herself. She was going to the university, she told us, to find out why her first pension check had not yet arrived. As Father's surviving spouse, she should continue to receive 80 percent of his monthly salary. "I am afraid that I cannot authorize a pension for you," the Party secretary of the university told her. "We authorized the outing to Crystal Lake as a collective university activity. But your husband willfully refused to participate. He did not travel on the buses we had arranged. Once there, instead of joining his unit, he went down the beach and sat apart from us. If he had drowned while participating in a collective activity, you would be entitled to a pension. But since you were engaged in an individual activity, the university naturally has no responsibility—"

When Mother started to protest, Secretary Zhang put up his hands. "There are those who say that you should receive nothing from the university," he said. "I disagree. I think this is too harsh, too lacking in human sentiment. Although your late husband occasionally engaged in petit bourgeois behavior, he was absolutely loyal to the Party, and he was a fine teacher. I have therefore authorized that you be paid a sum of money equal to one year of his salary, discounted to 80 percent, of course." If she protested his decision, he warned my mother, he would see to it that she got nothing.

My mother was not in a position to bargain. The stakes were too high. We had used the last of our savings. The earthenware jars in which we stored our grain ration stood empty. Mother accepted his offer, asking only that the money be paid immediately. She complained bitterly when she returned home about how "the university officials were taking advantage of a poor widow." I scarcely heard what she was saying. I was too busy basking in her reborn vigor. I didn't care if she ever smiled again; anger was a sign of life as well.

Secretary Zhang did do one other thing for our family. He arranged for Liang-yue to become an apprentice at a machine tool factory affiliated with the university. Apprentices normally had to have a junior high school education and be at least fifteen years old, but this requirement was waived for my brother, who was only thirteen and a half. Liang-yue, who had wanted to follow in Father's footsteps and become an engineer, cried when he learned that he was being taken out of school. The family needed the twenty-four yuan a month he would bring home, Mother told him, settling the matter once and for all.

Three months after my brother started working there, the factory was absorbed into the air force. To upgrade the work force, all apprentices were assigned to a nearby technical high school. After completing the regular three-year course of study, they would return to the factory as fully qualified technicians. My brother was elated at the prospect of returning to school. Then, midway through his first year, with the famine worsening daily, the school closed its doors. "Good prospects never last," Mother consoled Liang-yue, who took the news badly. "*Hao jing bu jiu.*" But when the students were ordered down to the countryside to help with the crops, she refused to let him go. "There is no food in the villages. The peasants are eating the bark of trees."

Father died at the height of the famine, and the two events are inextricably linked in my memory—the terrible void left by his sudden death blending imperceptibly into the pain of an empty belly and the fear of starvation. My mother carefully husbanded the settlement she had received from the university, and for a time my brothers and I continued to eat better than our neighbors. But the price of black-market rice skyrocketed as food become scarcer; well before the end of 1960 my mother's cash drawer was once again empty.

My diet before the famine had almost no variety. My stomach could not deal with coarse grains like Kaoliang or field corn, so I had rice (steamed, boiled, or fried) or wheat (noodles, cakes, or rolls) for every meal. The only side dish Mother served us was boiled cabbage, the cheapest vegetable on the market. It made little difference to me when the monthly food ration for meat was eliminated in late 1959, since Mother hardly ever bought pork, chicken, or fish anyway, ration coupons or no ration coupons. The end of the cooking oil ration in early 1960 was a blow, though, because it meant that my rice could no longer be fried, only boiled into a congee or steamed. And I missed the cabbage that, along with all other vegetables, vanished from the public markets at about the same time. All that was left was our grain ration, and even that was rapidly being reduced.

The low point came at the beginning of 1960, when my mother

found that her ration had been cut to a mere ten *jin*, or 13⅓ pounds. The children's ration that my brothers and I received was pegged to our ages. I received about half of the adult ration, Liang-yue a little more, Ming-yue and Ying-yue a little less. The only concession made to our tender years was that our ration was issued entirely in rice, which was more nutritious and easier to digest than the coarse grains that my mother received.

My brothers and I had a little less than seven pounds of raw rice each to get us through a month. This worked out to about nine ounces of cooked rice every day, or one large bowl of rice apiece—a ration too small to sustain life. Soon we had hollow cheeks, our ribs were showing, and we had lost our youthful stamina. We no longer ran and skipped our way to school but plodded along, putting one foot slowly and deliberately in front of the other, walking like the very old.

Mother, who had her own haunting memories of childhood hunger, frequently told us that we all were going to starve to death. "Our grain ration is less than enough to keep us alive," she would say. "With this little to eat, people starve to death fairly quickly. We won't last until the spring."

Despite this running commentary of doom, however, she seemed determined to pull us through. She carefully rationed our food and put us on a strict schedule for mealtimes. Breakfast was served precisely at 6:30 A.M., lunch at 11:30 A.M., and dinner at 5:30 P.M. However much we begged, Mother would not let us eat one minute sooner. She made sure that we were in bed by 6:30 each night and would not let us get up until breakfast. "The more you rest and the less you move, the less hungry you will be," she told us. Even so, I was often awakened in the middle of the night by the gnawing hunger in my belly. When I slept, my dreams were often of food, so that I woke up ravenous. The small bowl of rice I had three times a day took only a second to devour and did little to quell my increasingly insistent appetite.

The schools remained open, and my brothers and I continued to attend class. Mother would not permit us to stay home, as many other children were doing. I had always been a good student, but now I found it impossible to concentrate on what the teacher was saying. The only topic that held any interest for me was food, but at school we were forbidden to discuss the food shortage. When the teacher began her instruction each morning I tried to listen, but her words soon receded before the angry demands of my empty stomach. I would then take refuge for a time in pleasant daydreams of my father, but my hunger had a longer memory than my mind. It grew in size until it filled my whole being.

My inattention to my lessons scarcely mattered, of course. The teachers were on the same limited rations as the rest of us and no longer had the energy to be strict. They, too, were just going through the motions. My teacher did not stand in front of the blackboard anymore but remained seated at her desk, which made it even harder to follow what she was saying. Children who yawned in class no longer got a reprimand, and those who fell asleep were gently shaken awake. "Do you need to go home and rest?" the teacher would ask in a solicitous voice. In the afternoon, when everyone's energy was at low ebb, she would have us put our heads on our desks and close our eyes. She did the same. We dozed away entire afternoons in this fashion, roused at the end of the school day by the closing bell.

One day in the bleakest midwinter, a school assembly was held. Principal Gao, thinner now and less effervescent than he had been, stood up and denounced the Soviet Union. "Our onetime 'elder brother' has betrayed us," he told us. "Khrushchev the Revisionist has summoned home all the Soviet engineers and technicians who were in our country helping with socialist construction. He has torn up all the agreements calling for scientific and technical cooperation. He has called in all the loans that the Soviet Union has made to China."

I paid little attention to what Principal Gao was saying until he brought up the subject of food. "Chairman Mao has said that we must pay back our debts to the Soviet Union," he went on. "China must not be a debtor nation. This is a matter of national pride. We must scrimp and save, scrimp and save, until the loans are repaid. That is why we have no fruit, vegetables, or grain. They are being sold to raise money. The reckless behavior of the Soviet Union is responsible for our food shortage."

This was a revelation to me, although not in the way that Principal Gao intended. For the first time I realized that food was in short supply not only in and around Shenyang but in other parts of China as well. This was confirmed a few weeks later, when our family received a special issue of ten pounds of wheat flour from the state grain store. The government had put the flour in locally made sacks to disguise its origin, but the employees at the state store whispered that it was from Canada. It shocked me that the Party, still touting enormous increases in grain production during the Great Leap Forward, would import flour from a foreign country—and a hated capitalist one at that. Liang-yue and I concluded that there was no grain to be had in all of China. The rumors we had heard of a massive famine throughout the length and breadth of China must be correct.

I was later to realize that Mao's crash programs were to blame. The Chairman had imagined that forcing his countrymen to eat together from the same big pot and work together in the same big fields would lead them to put the collective good above narrow self-interest. But canny peasants would have none of his pipe dreams. The old allegiances to self, family, and kin continued to reign supreme. To be sure, the peasants eagerly filed into the cafeterias morning, noon, and night to eat their fill of the free food. But when it came time to march to the fields, they dragged their feet. Knowing that they would eat whether they worked or not, they labored as little as possible, preferring to spend their time sleeping off their heavy meals.

Food production was further hurt by the emphasis on making "steel." The leaders of the new communes pulled out all the stops in their efforts to meet the quotas demanded by their Party superiors. At the height of the campaign, it was estimated that more than a hundred million able-bodied men were at work at the smelters, keeping them supplied with scrap iron and fired up with fuel. The 1958 harvest was a poor one, not because of poor weather conditions, as Mao later claimed, but because so much of the harvest was left to rot in the fields. The harvest in 1959 was even worse.

As the famine continued, many people in Shenyang began suffering from edema. It did not leave us untouched. With the exception of the baby, all of us swelled up and turned a whitish yellow, like pale turnips. We had so much fluid under our skin that if we cut ourselves, we no longer bled. Instead of blood, little beads of faintly pink liquid would ooze out. A scab never formed, and even the smallest scrape took a long time to heal.

As we grew weaker from malnutrition, we came down with various other illnesses as well. We were all anemic, and both Mother and Liang-yue came down with hepatitis B. The doctors could do little more than extend my mother's medical leave: There was no medicine to be had. "If you could buy some placenta powder . . . ," one sympathetic doctor whispered to her.

There was a thriving black market in human placentas, which Chinese pharmacists baked dry and ground up into a powder for use as a food supplement. Placenta powder, as it was called, was known to be a rich source of iron and protein and a good remedy for anemia and edema. The problem was that, by the spring of 1961, a single ounce sold for upwards of ten yuan. Most women had stopped menstruating as soon as the famine hit, and few babies were being born.

Many of our neighbors had sold their furniture to buy food and medicine, but we didn't have any to sell. Immediately after my father's death, his university had reclaimed the lacquered mahogany furniture that had been lent to us, leaving us with an empty apartment. We scrounged a dozen crates of different sizes, which we used as tables and chairs. Most of these were so rickety that they were in constant danger of collapsing. "If only your father hadn't died, we wouldn't be in this predicament," Mother moaned.

Still, she knew she had to come up with some money somehow. Liang-yue especially, whose hepatitis seemed to be worsening, needed to eat better to get well. The weather had now turned warm, and Mother resolved to sell most of our winter clothing in order to buy food. Our padded cotton jackets and pants brought some twenty yuan on the black market, enough to buy an ounce of placenta powder and several pounds of flour. The temporary improvement in our diet reduced the swelling from the edema, and my brother made a quick recovery.

Once this extra food was gone, my mother announced that the time had come to make "leaf pancakes." The street were we lived was lined on both sides with majestic poplars. It had been a wet, warm spring, and they were covered with a thick mantle of green leaves. My mother sent Liang-yue shinnying up the nearest tree, basket in hand. Following her instructions, he picked only the tenderest, youngest leaves. These we soaked in water overnight to get rid of the tannic acid. Then we dipped the wet leaves in flour front and back and browned them one by one in the wok without oil. The result was a big, irregular-shaped pancake with a leaf in the middle.

The smell of these leaf pancakes frying made my mouth water, but they didn't taste nearly as good as they looked. Despite the soaking, the poplar leaves retained an acid bite that made my salivary glands scream in protest. The worst part was the constipation they brought on. A day after Mother added them to our diet, we stopped having bowel movements. For a week after that, we felt increasingly bloated and crampy. Finally, Mother told us that we would have to dig the hard little balls of feces out with our fingers. My brothers and I were too hungry to mind very much, though; we continued to devour the pancakes without protest.

Our neighbors, being city folk, hadn't known that poplar leaves could be eaten. When we began picking baskets of leaves, they laughed at us. But word of our leaf pancakes spread rapidly. Soon dozens of people were climbing the trees every day, stripping entire branches clean. Even green twigs were broken off. In the end not a touch of green life remained on any of the trees. It looked as if winter had set in again.

Conditions must have been desperate in the countryside, for the streets of Shenyang were full of hungry beggars. There were patched and tattered scarecrows with hollow cheeks and lifeless eyes who resembled living skeletons. There were children with pipestem limbs and swollen stomachs crying piteously for food. There were young men so crazed with hunger that they would snatch a leaf pancake out of your hands if you ventured too close.

Those who suffered from edema were the worst to behold. Many had travelled long distances on their "turnip feet" and had huge blisters on their feet and ankles. I remember one peasant who had a blister on the bottom of his right foot so large that it extended the length of his sole, from his heel all the way to his toes. He walked with a bad limp. Still, he was better off than many others, the soles of whose feet were so flayed and festering they could no longer walk at all. They had to crawl on their hands and knees to do their begging.

Beggars aside, I had little idea at the time just how bad things really were in the countryside. I tended to dismiss as exaggerations stories of villages decimated by starvation, and hamlets in which every living soul died. It was only years later, in nursing school, that I learned from rural classmates of the horrors they had experienced. One told how, at the every onset of the famine, her village's communal pigsty was closed for lack of fodder. What sorghum husks and crushed corncobs they had on hand were boiled into a kind of mush and eaten by people. The pigs were moved instead to the communal outhouse, where they were fed on human excrement. "Everyone was ordered to take their 'big convenience' in the outhouse so that the pigs would have enough to eat," she told me. "But I used to sneak off to go in the fields instead. I couldn't stand three or four pigs nosing me with their snouts as I squatted, each trying to be the first to get at my droppings." The villagers soon turned the tables on the hungry pigs, which were slaughtered and eaten before their shanks grew any leaner.

Another friend recalled to me how deeply the famine had cut into the population of her native village. Forced to work but lacking the strength to do so, some peasants collapsed in the communal fields and died. Others sought to flee to the cities but managed to cover no more than a mile or two before exhausting their strength and their lives. Those who remained, weak from hunger and swollen to enormous size from malnutrition, often died in their beds, leaving bloated children wailing for food by their dead bodies. She had been lucky, my classmate said. She and her father had survived by scouring the hills each day for leaves and seeds of all kinds and descriptions. "Once my father and I spent a week stripping the bark from a large elm tree," she told me. "We peeled off the thin layer of live cells from the inside of the bark, dried it, and then ground it into a powder. For several weeks we lived on tree-bark porridge." When I asked about the rest of her family, she looked away. "My mother died first, then my baby brother, and then my two younger sisters," she said softly. "In my family only my father and I survived."

The Shenyang provincial Party newspaper had even reported cases of cannibalism in the countryside, which I had trouble believing until another classmate told me that it had happened in her own hamlet. A peasant woman, unable to stand the incessant crying for food of her two-year-old daughter, and perhaps thinking to end her suffering, had strangled her. She had given the girl's body to her husband, asking him to bury it. Instead, out of his mind with hunger, he had put the body into the cooking pot with what little food they had foraged. He had forced his wife to eat a bowl of the resulting stew. His wife, in a fit of remorse, had reported her husband's crime to the authorities. The fact that she voluntarily came forward to confess her guilt made no difference. Although there was no law against cannibalism in the criminal code of the People's Republic, the Ministry of Public Security treated such cases, which were all too common, with the utmost severity. Both husband and wife were arrested and summarily executed.

Had Chairman Mao admitted that China faced a serious food shortage, I later realized, and asked for emergency assistance from international agencies, millions of lives could have been saved. Yet rather than reveal China's problems—and his own incompetence as leader—he tried to cover up the famine, in effect condemning many of his countrymen to a slow and agonizing death. Mao was not only inept, he was cruelly indifferent to the sufferings of my people.

The death toll in this, perhaps the worst famine in China's long history, was enormous. According to figures later published by the State Statistical Bureau, the population of China declined from 672 million in 1959 to 658 million in 1961, but the actual number of deaths was more than twice as high. Millions of children were still-born or died within a year or two after birth, and their names were never entered on the census lists. Millions more perished in 1962 and into 1963, weakened by years of progressive malnutrition. In 1963 the median age of those dying was only 9.7 years old, down from 17.6 years old before the Great Leap Forward. To put it another way, more than half of those who died in China that year were children under ten.

Altogether, I have learned, more than 30 million people, the vast majority of them peasants, died as a direct result of the Great Leap Forward. The highest respectable estimate comes from Chen Yizhi, who served from 1982 to 1989 as a member of then Party Secretary Zhao Zhiyang's brain trust. After visiting most of China's provinces and collecting local estimates of the number of casualties in each, he put the total number of dead at between 43 and 46 million. This would make it, by far, the worst famine in human history.

Things began looking up for us in the spring of 1962. The janitor who lived below us found a small plot of ground on the university grounds for us to plant a vegetable garden. As soon as the weather turned warm and the danger of a late frost was past, we hoed the soil and planted corn, sweet potatoes, and tomatoes. We spent nearly every day that summer at the university, watering the growing plants and keeping an eye out for thieves. The sweet potatoes did particularly well, and by the end of the summer we were carrying basketfuls home every week. For us the famine was over.

Later, after coming to the United States, I discovered that most people were unaware of this catastrophe. Some American China watchers, I was incredulous to learn, had even gone so far as to deny that a famine had taken place in China at all. I could not decide whether this was willful ignorance or merely indifference. But whichever it was, it was mirrored by the willful ignorance and indifference with which many of the same experts were later to greet reports of abuses in the one-child policy.

By the fall of 1962, Mother had regained her health sufficiently to go back to work. She was still laid low by the occasional migraine headache, and she would ever after suffer from high blood pressure, but she had recovered from the hepatitis, anemia, and edema that for a time had kept her bedridden. She was taken off medical leave and returned to teaching full-time.

My older brother and I worried more about her mental state, since in many respects she remained a prisoner of her past. She was angry at her parents for orphaning her as a child, angry at her husband for dying, and angry at her husband's relatives, especially his parents, for not helping to raise us.

Though Mother was not a happy person, we were reassured by the orderliness and regularity she now imposed on herself. She set her alarm clock for 5:00 each morning and rose promptly when it went off. She rousted us out of bed at 6 A.M. to eat breakfast. She walked out the door at 6:30 A.M. sharp so that she would arrive at school at 6:50 A.M., ten minutes before the opening bell. She would return, we knew, at exactly 5:30 P.M. Her bedtime was 9:00 P.M., ours an hour earlier.

Mother's obsessive desire for order also extended to my brothers and me. Between us, we were responsible for virtually every household task. My primary duties were to take care of Ying-yue and cook the evening meal. Mother's instructions were extremely detailed; she would specify exactly how much cabbage was to be purchased, at what price, and how it was to be cooked.

Mother controlled the purse strings, like the rest of our lives, even more tightly than before. Her salary was forty-seven yuan a month, and she literally kept track of every penny. I went through my entire childhood without seeing a single movie. Even though student tickets, which were sold through the schools, cost only a dime, this

was too much for my mother. "It's hard to imagine," she was fond
of saying, "why people would pay good money to watch shadows
dance on a screen. You waste an afternoon and have nothing to show
for it."

I suppose it would have been easy for me to resent my mother
for regimenting our lives down to the last cent, but somehow the
thought never entered my mind. When I was young I simply accepted Mother the way she was, neither blaming nor pitying her. As
I grew older I recognized that her bitterness over Father's death had
deepened her already profound insecurity. It was only by locking
herself—and all of us—into a rigid budget of time and money that
she could cope with the outrages that her unhappy fate had inflicted
on her. Even after I realized that her passion for order was obsessive,
I was strangely reassured by it. At least she could function.

When Liang-yue's technical high school reopened in February 1963,
he was allowed to reenroll, even though two years earlier he had
refused the order to go "down to the countryside." We found out
that many other students have gone AWOL at the same time, and
even those who had boarded the convoy of trucks bound for the
countryside had not stayed long. Two months after they arrived the
commander of the state farm to which they had been sent announced
that all food supplies were exhausted. Liang-yue's classmates had deserted en masse, slipping back into Shenyang clandestinely. Like Liang-
yue, they had lived at home through the worst of the famine.

Once back in class, Liang-yue was again eligible to draw his apprentice's salary. Payday fell on the first of the month, and Liang-
yue would arrive home from work waving his twenty-four yuan. "This
is for you, Mother," he would say after he had everyone's attention,
handing her the money with a flourish.

Mother's eyes would be glowing. It was the nearest I ever saw
her come to a smile. "You are a good son, Liang-yue," she would
say. "When the rest of you get older and get a job like Liang-yue,

things will be better for all of us. We will have better things to eat and wear."

Listening to Mother praise Liang-yue month after month, I began to suffer from what the Chinese call *hong-yen bing*, the "red-eyed disease" of jealousy. I didn't so much covet the coins that Liang-yue always seemed to have jingling in his pocket. What I really envied was the expression of joy that lit up Mother's face each time he handed her his pay, and the words of praise she then lavished on him. No matter how much I did around the apartment, no matter how many chores I performed, I had never once won a compliment from Mother. I knew that I needed to make money, and lots of it, to make Mother's face light up like that.

3

Choosing a Nursing Career

Wɪᴛʜ ᴀʟʟ ᴛʜᴇ ᴘʀᴇssᴜʀᴇs of my childhood, I grew up quickly. I had no time for games or gossiping with the girls, and truth to tell I didn't even miss such things. I had no close friends at school, not because I was unpopular but because all the other girls seemed so immature to me. There was a vast distance between us, measured not in years but in outlook.

By my early teens I had thought long and hard about my goals in life. Most of my classmates were planning to enter the work force on graduation from junior high school, when they would be assigned by the state to some factory or clerical job. I was intent on winning admission to a three-year professional school after junior high, so that I could go on to be a nurse or a teacher like my mother. Those selected to attend such schools received generous state scholarships, so I imagined I could help support my mother and younger brothers while I was still in school. After graduation I would receive a good job assignment at good pay and could help even more.

In order to be considered for admission to a professional school, I had to do well in junior high and, equally important, be a member in good standing of the Communist Youth League. Equal weight was given to grades and to family background for purposes of matriculation. Getting good grades was no problem for me, since I had always found schoolwork easy. I was blessed with a retentive memory, had a head for figures, and buckled down and did my homework every night. Joining the Communist Youth League proved to be more difficult, however.

From the time I was a small child, I had known that the world was divided into Reds and Blacks. The Reds were members of good classes—workers, poor peasants, revolutionary officers, and the like—and were the favored of the revolution. The Blacks were bad classes, undesirables like capitalists, landlords, rich peasants, bad elements, and people with links to the Kuomintang, or Nationalist Party. These class designations dated from the time of the revolution, when the family background of every single person in China had been investigated. A man's class status affected not only his own future but that of his children, who inherited their father's class. Only the sons and daughters of Reds could join the Communist Youth League, attend elite schools, receive a higher education, and look forward to promising careers in the government and Party. The children of Blacks were kept under surveillance, given only a junior high school education, and assigned to menial work.

I had always thought of myself as a Red, since my father had been assigned in 1950 to the class of "student," which was considered to be a good one. My mother's class status was more questionable. She had been declared to be a "smallholder" in 1950, on account of the small plots of land that her grandmother had rented out to others. A "smallholder" fell somewhere between a middle peasant and a rich peasant and was neither Red nor Black. In the relatively relaxed atmosphere of the late fifties and early sixties, mother's questionable class affiliation had not proved to be a handicap. She had been able to become a teacher, a highly respected profession, despite her "smallholder" status. We children had not experienced any problems either on account of her. My brothers and I joined the Young Pioneers in elementary school with no questions asked. We listed our class as "student," after that of our father, and that was good enough.

I was in ninth grade when, having reached the minimum age, I first applied to join the Communist Youth League branch at my school. As always I wrote on the form that my class was "student." To my surprise my application was immediately rejected. The secretary of our local branch explained to me, in a not unfriendly fashion, that "student" was merely an interim designation assigned to those, like my father, who were in school at the time of the revolution. It was not a real class.

In order for my application to be considered, he went on, my father's family history would have to be investigated. If I was really a member of the Red classes, the league would welcome me. Otherwise, he hinted darkly, I would have to "draw a clear line" between my father's family and myself before I could be admitted to the organization.

Both of my grandparents had died in the famine. I wrote the only two surviving members of my father's immediate family, his two brothers, explaining that I wanted to join the Communist Youth League and needed to know their class status. My father's older brother wrote back that he was *cheng-pin*, or "poor urban lumpenproletariat," which meant something along the lines of a day-laborer. My heart swelled with pride. You couldn't get much "Redder" than a day laborer. That same day I filled out a new application form for the league, writing *cheng-pin* in bold characters in the class-status box, and submitted it to the admissions committee.

Two weeks later a letter came from my father's younger brother, who still lived in my family's ancestral village. "Dear Niece," he wrote:

> *I received your letter asking about our family's class status. I am afraid that what I have to say will make you unhappy. Our family was once very wealthy. My grandfather—your great-grandfather—once owned 120 mou of land [about 20 acres], and lived in the biggest house in the village. However, during the years of the Japanese*

invasion all was lost. We had to abandon our house and our land and flee to Beijing. After the war my older brother remained in that city, but my parents and I decided to return here to our village. Our house had been destroyed and our land had been taken over by our former tenant farmers, one of whom had become the village head. Our tenant farmers, who thought we had all been killed, were unhappy to see us. Led by the new village head, they refused to pay rent. We decided to sell them the land they were farming for a token amount, keeping only a few mou to farm ourselves. This was in 1945. Still, during the land reform six years later my parents and I were hauled out and attacked as landlords. This was unfair, for I was only a boy when the Japanese came and we fled. I believe that our family should really be classified as "bankrupt landlord," but the local Party branch refuses to consider changing our class status. To my shame I remain classed as a "landlord." If my deceased brother were still alive he, too, would be classed as a "landlord." And you are his daughter.

Your uncle.

I was sick at heart to learn that my father's family had once been landed gentry, a class I had been taught to hate as inhuman exploiters of the peasantry. Yet I did not worry overmuch about my own prospects for joining the Communist Youth League. I was sure that the league, in its wisdom, would consider me to be a "bankrupt landlord" rather than a member of the depised "landlord" class. After all, my uncle himself had written that we had been wrongly classified. "Bankrupt landlord" was not nearly as revolutionary as "poor urban lumpenproletariat." Like "smallholder," it fell into a gray zone somewhere between Red and Black, but it was probably still good enough to get me into the league. In a burst of innocence and candor I filled out the application form for the league a third time, putting "bankrupt landlord" as my class status. I attached my uncle's letter to the form and handed it in, feeling optimistic about my chances.

The branch secretary of the league called me into his office the following day. He glared at me sternly as I walked in and offered no greeting. All trace of his friendly attitude of two weeks before had disappeared.

"What is your class status?" he asked me sharply.

"My uncle . . . ," I began uncertainly.

"Your uncle's class status is clearly landlord!" he barked. "And so is yours. Why did you falsely put down that it was 'bankrupt land-lord'?"

"But my uncle's letter—" I managed to utter before bursting into tears.

The branch secretary interrupted me impatiently. "Your uncle's letter proves only that he refuses to accept the judgment of the masses!" he said. "If the poor and lower-middle peasants of his village have declared him to be a landlord, then a landlord he is! You should not follow his errors by falsely claiming to be a 'bankrupt landlord.' " He waved my application in the air.

"We cannot accept your application to join the Communist Youth League," he continued, speaking more formally now. "If you still wish to join, you must write a history of your family and an auto-biography of yourself. When you finish, submit it to your homeroom teacher. You must convince us that you have drawn a clear line be-tween yourself and the rest of the members of your landlord family. Then we may reconsider."

Drawing "a clear line" meant criticizing the past mistakes of your family, and cutting yourself off from any future contact with them. I wrote in my autobiography that I knew nothing of my father's fam-ily history except that they had been landlords. That my grandpar-ents had wrongly exploited their tenant farmers, I was certain, but with my father dead I could not know the details of their crimes. Nor did I wish to associate with the surviving members of the family, now that I knew were class enemies. I finished my autobiogra-phy and turned it in to my homeroom teacher, sure that the league would realize that I had long since drawn a clear line between myself and my father's family. In fact, we never had any contact at all.

Perhaps in years past my protests of ignorance would have been accepted, my class background overlooked, and an exception made to allow me to join the league. But this was 1964, the year that Chairman Mao, in an attempt to recapture the authority he had lost after the Great Leap Forward, advanced the slogan: "Never Forget Class Struggle." Mao's essay on this theme had been printed in all the newspapers and read at a school assembly a few weeks before.

Questions of Red versus Black, which had not been important since the early fifties, quickly came to dominate our lives and thinking. Following Mao, our teachers taught us that we were to be "cruel and ruthless" toward class enemies. Constant vigilance was required to forestall the plots of the reactionaries to overthrow the Chinese Communist Party and deliver China back into the hands of the Kuomintang and the American imperialists. As evidence, they whispered to us that in 1962, at the height of the famine, Chiang Kaishek had sent thousands of Nationalist agents to the mainland to organize a rebellion.

In this atmosphere of paranoia, my claim that I was ignorant of the offenses of my ancestors aroused great skepticism in my homeroom teacher. "You must be honest and open," he told me a week later, as he handed my first attempt at an autobiography back to me. "We need a full and frank answer to the question of how your father's family exploited the poor peasants. If you want to join the Communist Youth League, don't try to hide anything."

I again protested that I knew nothing, but to no avail. "Be honest and open," he repeated. "Leave nothing out. Then we will know that you are sincere in wanting to draw a clear line between yourself and your relatives." He dismissed me with a wave.

I knew that, with my bad class background, my hope of going on to a professional school hinged on being allowed to join the Communist Youth League. Over the next half year I rewrote my autobiography over and over again, each time stretching the truth a little further. By my fifth attempt, my grandfather was extorting rapacious rents from his tenants and beating them when they could not make their payments. I did not even consider the effect that such fictions might have on my uncles. Still my homeroom teacher wasn't satisfied.

Once it became generally known among my teachers that I was the granddaughter of a landlord, I found myself treated like a pariah. In class I was never called on to answer questions and was reprimanded for the slightest infraction of the rules. Though I was studying harder than ever before, my marks dropped as my essays and exams were graded more strictly. Teachers who had once been friendly now ignored me.

Only my homeroom teacher, who was officially responsible for supervising my political development, would still talk to me outside class. Like all individuals with a "problematic past," I was required to report my thoughts to my political supervisor at least once a week. He encouraged me to solicit his advice even more frequently than this in order to "speed up [my] mental rehabilitation." I overcame my feeling of awkwardness and sought him out, sometimes walking with him to school in the morning, or talking with him at the end of the school day before going home. "How is your understanding today?" he would invariably greet me. "A little bit better, I think," I would respond modestly. If my plans were to have any chance of succeeding, he had to think well of me.

Although I was blackballed by my teachers, I was still on good terms with my classmates, who as yet had no inkling that I was of landlord stock. My teachers had agreed not to publicly announce my class status until the league made a final decision about my application. I was grateful for their discretion. If my class status had been publicly announced, I would have been shunned by my fellow students. They would have had no choice.

Out of my homeroom class of fifty-two students, five had already been ostracized as class enemies. Two were the sons of former Nationalist officials, two were the daughters of capitalists, and one was the daughter of a rightist. I had been close to this last classmate, whose father had been declared a rightist during the Hundred Flowers Campaign in 1957, when Chairman Mao encouraged the people to speak out ("let a hundred flowers bloom"), then had many who did arrested. She was a good student who, like myself, had ambitions to continue her education. Those hopes had been dashed six months earlier, when the class struggle heated up. She and the four others had been called up to the front of the class and forced to recount to us the "crimes against the people" that their fathers had committed. "Draw a clear line between yourself and these class enemies," our homeroom teacher had warned us in conclusion. After that day I dared not speak to my friend, though sometimes I would chance a quick smile when I caught her looking in my direction.

Sometimes this class prejudice was carried to even more extreme levels. In June 1964, a doctor came to our school to inoculate us against meningitis, which often reached epidemic proportions during China's humid summers. My teacher singled out the five "class enemies" and told them to wait in the classroom. He took those of us with clean class backgrounds, a group in which he still included me, to the cafeteria. There we were inoculated with the meningitis vaccine.

Later, when I was walking home from school with him, I asked him why the five had not been inoculated against meningitis. He looked at me askance, as if the answer were self-evident. "These people come from bad class backgrounds, so they are not allowed to enjoy the privileges of the working class."

"What happens if they get sick?" I asked.

"That is their problem," he said brusquely, dismissing my objection. "As class enemies who have exploited the masses, they deserve to get sick."

Without thinking, I asked again: "But what if they get sick and then communicate their disease to us Reds? After all, we sit right next to them in class."

"Your understanding of the class struggle is not good," my teacher said, his clipped tone signaling an end to our conversation. "Your thought still needs much improvement."

Everyone in junior high school—class enemies excepted—was required to join the *minbing*, the people's militia. The militia practiced on the school's athletic field, its members learning how to march in formation, perform the manual of arms with a wooden rifle, and throw "hand grenades" made of pig iron. This time my homeroom teacher decided that I should not be allowed to participate. Who knows what a landlord's granddaughter might do, he intimated to me, if she were taught how to use a gun and throw a grenade. Fortunately, my fellow students didn't know the real reason I had been excluded. Everyone assumed that it was on account of my small size, since I was a head shorter than most of the girls in my class. I stood on the sidelines as my friends presented arms and practiced throwing hand grenades, again feeling the pain of exclusion.

Yet it was probably a good thing that I was kept out of the drills. The shudder of paranoia that had rippled through China led to the most innocent of accidents being given bizarre misinterpretations. One day during our physical education class we were practicing the discus throw. My friend, the rightist, lost her grip on the discus, just narrowly missing a member of the Communist Youth League.

My friend was instantly accused of trying to harm the sons and daughters of the proletariat. The poor girl was dragged sobbing in front of the entire student body in the assembly hall, where the physical education instructor, my homeroom teacher, the principal, and the secretary of the Communist Youth League branch took turns trying to wring a confession out of her. She initially tried to protest her innocence but was soon in such a state that her only response to their repeated accusations was to sob all the louder. Only when the league secretary tried to get her to implicate her father did she respond coherently.

"My father had nothing to do with it," she said in a firm voice that carried to the ends of the hall. "If you won't believe it was an accident, if you must blame someone, blame me."

"She admits her guilt!" the secretary exulted. "This is a resumption of the class struggle. This spawn of a rightist must be dealt with severely." My friend disappeared from school after that class struggle session. I later heard that she had been sentenced to two years of reeducation at a labor camp, working long hours in the fields by day and studying the works of Chairman Mao in the evening.

After witnessing this incident I stopped admiring my classmates in the militia. What if I accidentally hit someone with a three-pound slug of pig iron during grenade-throwing practice?

The class struggle continued to intensify as the months passed. I continued to write and rewrite my autobiography, but each new submission was quickly rejected by my homeroom teacher. These successive rebuffs left me more and more dejected, until I lived in a constant state of self-loathing. Why was I unable to reform my thoughts sufficiently to draw a clear line between myself and the class enemies in my father's family?

It was only years later that I grasped the truth. It had not mattered to my teacher how much I criticized my father's family and/or abased myself in my autobiography. Given the heated atmosphere of the time, it would have been politically dangerous to recommend that the granddaughter of a landlord should be allowed to join an organization reserved for the Red classes. He had decided not to take the risk.

I never was allowed to join the Communist Youth League, although I still managed to squeak into a technical college on the strength of my near-perfect scores on the entrance exam. (Fortunately my class status was not yet disqualifying.) Two years later, during the Cultural Revolution, the general secretary of the Communist Youth League, Hu Yaobang, was accused of being a revisionist. Shortly thereafter the league itself was abolished. I was secretly pleased.

My dream in elementary school had been to become a teacher like my mother. When I was growing up, I never heard anyone call my mother by her given name. She was known even to her closest friends as Teacher Chen. Secure in their high niche in society, teachers carried themselves with assurance, lectured with authority, and answered questions with an air of confidence. I would be Teacher Yang.

At the same time, I was also my father's daughter, for I had inherited his nurturing spirit. After I entered junior high school, this side of my character was increasingly attracted to the medical profession.

With my nebulous class background, becoming a doctor was out of the question, but nursing school was a possibility. I had always enjoyed helping people in need. Shepherding my little brother through the scrapes, bruises, and colds of early childhood gave me great satisfaction. I had willingly cared for my mother during her months of depression following Father's death. And she remained in poor health, a consideration that weighed heavily on my mind. If I were a nurse, I reasoned, I would be better able to take care of my mother when she was older. The more I thought about it, the more the idea of becoming a nurse appealed to me. In ninth grade, when it was time for me to indicate my choice of schools, I picked nursing school over normal school. Despite my later experiences with the one-child policy, it was a choice I have never regretted.

I was admitted to the Shenyang School of Nursing in the fall of 1965. The school of nursing was part of a larger state-run institution called the Shenyang Medical College, which included schools of medicine, dentistry, and pharmacology. The nursing, dental, and pharmacological schools were the equivalent of technical high schools, admitting junior high school graduates like myself to a three-year course of study. The medical school had slightly higher requirements for matriculation. Admission was limited to high school graduates, and the course of study was a year longer—three years of classroom instruction were followed by a one-year internship. Of the college's fifteen hundred students, about a thousand were medical students, four hundred were nurse trainees, and the remaining hundred or so were evenly divided between dentistry and pharmacology. The heart of the college was a large hospital, where the teaching staff served as residents and the students received practical training. Graduates were licensed to practice in their fields, receiving their work assignments from the state.

Like all college and university students in China, I attended school on a full scholarship. Tuition and dormitory space were free, and I received a stipend of fifteen yuan a month to cover food and miscellaneous expenses. I was determined to give as much of this as possible to my mother, so I ruthlessly cut corners. To avoid spending money on toothpaste, I brushed my teeth with salt I took from the school cafeteria. I went without store-bought shampoo, using hard, hospital-issue soap instead to lather my hair. My main expense was the cost of meals, for while the food in the cafeteria was cheap, it was not free. I always chose the least expensive dishes. My meals consisted of either steamed rice or wheat rolls, along with a side order of vegetable soup, which was usually winter melon or turnip. Such dishes cost only a few cents each. By making every penny count, I found that I could get by on about four yuan a month. The remainder of my stipend, eleven yuan a month, I gave to my mother.

Though I ate off the bottom of the menu, as we Chinese say, the food was plentiful and nutritious, at least compared to what I had been eating at home. One consequence of my improved diet was that I finally reached puberty. Two months after I started school I had my first menses. Shortly after that I realized that my pants no longer reached the tops of my shoes. By the time my growth spurt ended a year later, I was five feet four inches tall, which, although average height for a Chinese girl, was about half a head taller than I ever expected to be. After years of being the smallest in my class I finally caught up with my schoolmates. I even passed a few.

After I moved away my mother seemed a bit less pressured by life. Her oldest son was attending an industrial high school, from which he would soon graduate. Her only daughter was attending nursing school and was no longer eating at home. My mother's long years of "eating bitterness" seemed to be drawing to a close, and her smiles came easier now. I took great pleasure in handing her my eleven yuan each month, though I did not make a public demonstration out of it as my older brother always did. I would wait until no one was looking and then slip the money into her hand. The look of appreciation that crossed her face was reward enough.

The first-year curriculum of the nursing school was devoted to theoretical courses in biology, chemistry, biochemistry, human anatomy, and the like. We were just about to take our year-end exams when the Cultural Revolution broke out. "Stop classes, foment revolution" (Tingke nao geming), Chairman Mao told the students of China, and that's exactly what we did. Our final examinations were canceled by the now-cowed college administration, and we spent our days holding political rallies and street marches.

Our second year was supposed to be spent in the laboratory, learning how to use microscopes, dissect dead animals, and perform various tests on blood, urine, and tissue samples. Instead we organized ourselves into militant Red Guard factions that contested each other for control of the campus. It wasn't until April 1968 that we returned to regular classes. During our final six months in school we virtually lived at the hospital, where we received classroom instruction in various procedures followed by hands-on training with actual patients. Even so, a number of practical courses had to be eliminated and others radically shortened. We graduated in October 1968, having completed only half of the normal course of instruction. Some medical procedures I learned only after graduation, by trial and error. People suffered from my ignorance.

One of our abbreviated third-year courses was Obstetrics and Gynecology. In it we learned such things as how to administer a pregnancy test, perform a pelvic examination, and deliver a baby, as well as how to treat the most common female disorders. A doctor would first cover the material on, say, pelvic examinations, in class and then supervise us as we practiced on patients. I thoroughly enjoyed this part of the course, which involved helping women with their problems. When I first witnessed the birth of a baby it struck me as nothing less than a miracle. Then it was my turn to assist a mother in labor. I laughed with pleasure when the tiny, wrinkled baby girl I soon held in my hands filled her lungs and announced her existence to the world.

Birth control was an important part of our curriculum. Chairman Mao had originally disapproved of "birth planning," as it is called in China, which he viewed as tantamount to genocide. Following his lead, the People's Daily in the early fifties had condemned birth control as "a way of slaughtering the Chinese people without drawing blood. . . . [The people] are the most precious of all categories of capital." So strongly did Mao feel on the subject that when the then president of Beijing University, Professor Ma Yinchu, publicly advocated population control, the Chairman had him declared a rightist in 1957. After the famine Mao changed his mind about birth control (though not about Professor Ma, whom he resented for disagreeing with him), and the policy on having children gradually became stricter. We spent many weeks studying the various means of contraception— birth control pills, IUDs, and sterilization—and their proper use and possible side effects. We learned how to insert an IUD and assisted a surgeon in performing a tubal ligation. We also learned how to perform vasectomies, at least in theory. We had no volunteers on whom to actually practice that procedure, however. Chinese men are notoriously reluctant to submit to the operation, which they complain leaves them emasculated and unable to lift heavy loads.

The last unit of the "birth planning" portion of the course, which we completed just before we graduated in June 1968, concerned abortion. We were taught to perform a suction abortion, which, upon graduation, we would be authorized to perform up to the end of the fourth month of pregnancy. Beyond that stage, abortions could be performed only by doctors, since the procedures used required the surgical removal of the fetus. Our instruction in this area was brief, lasting only a week, but I will never forget it. The first three days were devoted to classroom instruction, the fourth day to observation, and the fifth to practice. To pass this part of the course we had to perform a suction abortion under a doctor's supervision, in preparation for the abortions we would be expected to perform on our own after we graduated.

The patient assigned to me was a big, easygoing peasant woman with coarse, bony hands that bespoke a lifetime of hard work. From the information written in her file, I knew that she was pregnant with her third child. At the time, couples were urged to have no more than two children, but it was not yet forbidden to have a third, or even a fourth for that matter. Most peasants did, yet she had come in voluntarily.

Clipboard in hand, I sat down across from her to record the rest of her reproductive history before the procedure. "How many children have you had?" I began.

"I already have two boys," she answered. "They're really a handful. They hardly listen to anything I say. Their father has to whack them at least once a day to keep them in line. I want a girl to help me around the house, not another boy. I don't want another boy—"

"Two children," I recorded on the form and moved on to the next question. "Why do you want an abortion?" I asked, breaking into her monologue.

"I don't want another boy," she repeated stoutly, as if she had not heard me. "I want a girl to help me around the house, not another boy."

I put my hand up to interrupt the torrent of words and then tried again. "Yes, I know you don't want another boy. But why do you want an abortion?"

"I already told you," she replied good-naturedly. "This baby is going to be a boy. I want a girl to help me around the house."

"But how can you possibly know the sex of the child you are carrying?" I asked, puzzled.

"My husband told me that this baby is going to be a boy. He checked the *Sheng Nan Yu Nü de Yuce Biao*."

"The what?" I exclaimed. She had rattled off the string of words so quickly I hadn't caught their meaning.

"The Prediction Chart for Birthing Boys and Bearing Girls," she repeated, scarcely slowing down. "You haven't heard of it? If you know when the baby is due, and the sign under which the mother and father were born, the chart will tell you whether it's a girl or a boy. My husband checked. The baby I am carrying is a boy."

Up to this point in my life I had had almost no contact with people from the countryside. I knew that many peasants were illiterate and superstitious and guessed that the woman sitting in front of me was probably both. She truly believed that this "chart," or whatever it was, had predicted the sex of her fetus. I would soon disabuse her of that notion, I decided. "There is no scientific way to know the sex of your fetus," I began. "We can't know whether it's a girl or a boy. It is not possible."

"The Prediction Chart says this baby is going to be a boy," she said stubbornly. "I don't want another boy."

I knew from the unyielding note in her voice that she would not lightly abandon her faith in the "chart" or the purpose that had brought her here today. There was nothing to be done. I sighed inwardly and turned back to the form. What should I give on the form as the reason for the abortion? I could hardly put down "Patient believes fetus to be of the wrong sex." Then I would have to explain the Prediction Chart for Birthing Boys and Bearing Girls. I was tempted to write "Peasant superstition," but that too would require a lengthy explanation. I tapped my pencil on the clipboard. Finally I wrote: "In line with national policy, patient does not wish third child."

"How long have you been pregnant?" I asked, my pen poised over the last blank on the form.

"About three months," she answered.

But when she gave me the date of her last period, I calculated that she was well into her fourth month, or very close to the outer limit for a suction abortion.

The peasant woman had been prepped and was lying on the table. I held the vaginal "gun," as we called it, a metal cylinder with a pistol grip that held the suction tube. "The uterus will contract as soon as you make contact with the cervix," my supervisor said. "So hold the gun steady. Once you are inside the uterus, you have to be very careful. If you put it in too deep or use it too vigorously you will rupture the uterus. If you do not put it in deep enough, you will leave part of the fetus in place. Then there will be hemorrhaging."

I inserted the metal cyclinder into the vagina and felt a slight spasm as it penetrated the cervix. Then I began to move the gun around in small circular motions as I had been taught. "It's like peeling an apple from the inside," the doctor said. "You have to be very careful."

"See if we have got everything," the doctor ordered after I finished.

Following his directions, I took the collection bottle and poured its contents into a shallow pan. Then I used water to rinse off the blood and smaller particles that clouded the bottom of the pan.

"Now look closely," the doctor said. "It is important that we have got all the stuff out."

I looked into the pan to find that the "stuff" consisted of the remains of what had been, a few minutes before, a thirteen-week-old fetus. I could make out the remains of arms and legs and trunk and skull. I tried to piece them back together in my mind, to see if there were any missing parts.

Most of the pieces were so battered and bloody they were not recognizably human. Then my eyes locked upon a perfect little hand, less than half a centimeter long. I started at four tiny fingers and a tiny opposed thumb, complete with tiny translucent fingernails.

And I knew what I had done.

4

"Stop Classes, Foment Revolution"

Gradually, almost imperceptibly, politics became more intense after I started nursing school. Chairman Mao was making his comeback after the debacle of the Great Leap Forward, and his writings and pronouncements soon came to dominate our lives. A class in politics, which consisted mainly of Mao's essays, was added to our already rigorous curriculum. School assemblies were held to promulgate the Chairman's latest teaching on this or that subject. This crude but effective indoctrination had two consequences: Our reverence for Mao soon reached the dimensions of a cult, and we came to obey his "instructions" unquestioningly.

Most of Mao's instructions during these days were only marginally concerned with politics. On one occasion he denounced grass and flowers as useless bourgeois affectations, calling for their replacement by useful crops like cotton and cabbage. Our school had no lawn to attack, but we redeemed ourselves by uprooting every struggling weed we could find. We next turned our attention to the school's flower beds, where in place of vain blossoms we grew good Chinese bok choy.

On another occasion Mao called on us to "aid agriculture." This time the school authorities took the lead, making arrangements for us to spend two weeks every semester working in a rural commune a three-hour walk from Shenyang. Thirty or so of us were assigned to each of the twenty-three villages that made up the commune. During the spring break we weeded the newly planted fields, which were mostly corn and yellow beans. During the fall we helped with the harvest. We were slow and clumsy by rural standards, and neither the quantity nor quality of our work impressed the locals. "Work harder, little city pups," they shouted good-naturedly at us from across the fields, using the Chinese word for a newborn animal: "Work faster, *xiao zaizi.*"

Hard work or no, I looked forward to these stints in the countryside. Because we worked, ate, and bunked together, we quickly developed the easy camaraderie of kids at a summer camp. We had little contact with the locals. We were assigned work each morning by the village head but otherwise were left pretty much to ourselves. Three of the older girls volunteered to cook meals for the entire group, which we usually ate in the open air, weather permitting. For sleeping quarters the villagers gave us two sheds normally occupied by buffalo, complete with a generous gift of fresh straw. The boys, who outnumbered us two to one, took the larger manger, while we girls crowded together in the smaller, in the straw bedding. We always marched back from "aiding agriculture" cheerful and fit. The only drawback was that these working vacations left us behind in our lessons, and we had to study all the harder to make up for lost time.

The Cultural Revolution began in earnest in June 1966, just as we were preparing for our final examinations. Mao had wrested control of the *People's Daily* away from his opponents at the end of May, and overnight transformed it into his personal mouthpiece. Slogans exalting Mao were splashed in bold red type across the top of the first page: CHAIRMAN MAO IS THE RED SUN IN OUR HEARTS! ESTABLISH

CHAIRMAN MAO'S ABSOLUTE AUTHORITY! WE WILL DESTROY WHOEVER OPPOSES CHAIRMAN MAO! Under the slogans was a daily box of quotations from Mao. The rest of the page was covered with long editorials exhorting the masses to join with Chairman Mao in launching a Great Proletarian Cultural Revolution. The goal of this new revolution was to "establish Chairman Mao's absolute rule" and to "sweep away all ox devils and snake demons," which is what Mao now called class enemies. Sometimes, instead of slogans, quotations, and editorials, Mao's beaming portrait took up the entire front page.

Our final examinations were postponed indefinitely, although we still went to class every day to study the latest *People's Daily* editorial. Afterward we turned our attention to *The Quotations of Chairman Mao*, a red-plastic-covered pocketbook that contained passages from Mao's writings. Everyone was issued a copy of this "Precious Red Book" in mid-June, and it immediately became our sole textbook. We carried it wherever we went and competed in reciting and memorizing the quotations it contained. A work team was stationed in our school and began conducting covert investigations of the administration and faculty. Members of the team visited our classes to lead us in the study of Mao's word and to encourage us to denounce our teachers as "reactionary bourgeois intellectuals."

The *People's Daily* editorials grew increasingly inflammatory in tone, and singled out the educational establishment as especially corrupt and reactionary. "Smash the examination system!" the *People's Daily* cried. "Denounce the bourgeois intellectuals who masquerade as teachers." For all my instinctive veneration of Chairman Mao, and my deep-seated desire to follow him and carry out his commandments, I found his attack on education profoundly unsettling. If my own teachers were class enemies, then traitors and spies must be everywhere and I could no longer trust anyone in authority.

The next day I walked into the school's central quadrangle to find a large group of my fellow students clustered around a poster. At first I thought that there had been another public execution by the security forces. Whenever this happened the Shenyang Municipal

Department of Public Security posted printed announcements in schools and public places for their deterrent effect. As I walked closer I saw that this poster was different. It was larger than those used by the Department of Public Security, and its characters were not printed but handwritten.

I began to read it and to my shock discovered that it was a denunciation of my physical education instructor, Professor Wang. "Isolate and attack the capitalist poisonous weed, Wang Zaojun," the poster began.

> *His crimes are too numerous to mention. Several years ago this bourgeois intellectual divorced his middle-aged wife and married a young college student who was a former student of his. He told his students that he didn't want children, he just wanted sex. Another crime of this dog's head is that he is fond of dancing by himself in his apartment, using a chair as his partner. Proof positive that he is in thrall to the wasteful attitudes of the capitalist class comes from his dress and grooming. He dresses up like a woman, wearing tight pants and colorful shirts, and grows his hair longer than is proper for a man. These attitudes come from his parents, who were Indonesian Overseas Chinese. Wang claims that he came back to the motherland in 1950 to make a contribution to the revolution. In truth he came back to amuse himself with women. Proof of this lies not only in his divorce and remarriage, but also in his lewd behavior during his physical education classes. While instructing women he frequently brushes their busts and derrieres, pretending that these pawings are accidents. These are the actions of a capitalist poisonous weed. Wang Zaojun must face the people and admit his mistakes. If he does not surrender, then he must be annihilated.*

The poster was signed by several other teachers in the physical education department, who had been encouraged by the work team to make clear their disapproval of their colleague. Having been in one of Wang's classes, I knew that the charge of indecent behavior, at least, was genuine. A shapely friend of mine from the same class had complained to me more than once about his loose hands, but she had not dared object openly to his fondlings for fear that he would lower her grades or order her to do, say, a hundred sit-ups. Wang's manner also set him apart from the other teachers. Despite fifteen years in China, he still spoke Chinese with an accent and seemed foreign in his habits. Still, I had been taught to address teachers with respect. To see such scandalous accusations made in public took my breath away. The violence of the large, black characters in the poster totally unnerved me.

The next day a dozen other attack posters joined the first. Although (as we later discovered) they were written by members of the work team, the names that appeared at the bottom belonged to nurses, janitors, cooks, secretaries, and maintenance men who worked at the hopsital and school. The targets of this orchestrated proletarian wrath were doctors, who were criticized for a variety of offenses. One poster scolded a Doctor Chen, who "comes to school wearing long-sleeved shirts and carrying a parasol even when it is hot outside. This is the behavior of a pampered member of the capitalist class. The proletariat does not fear the sun's rays."

Other posters made more serious charges, the gravest of which involved the mistreatment of patients by doctors with bad class backgrounds. A typical poster, which attacked another teacher of mine, read:

Dr. Bai is the son of a capitalist exploiter of the proletariat. Because of his bad class background he treats peasants as if they were dumb animals. Once when a woman from the countryside came in with a four-inch gash on her foot from a sickle, he poured pure alcohol directly on the wound. Her screams of pain could be heard throughout the hospital. While Dr. Bai treats the wounds of the poor and lower-middle peasant classes without anesthetic, he is careful not to cause pain or discomfort to members of his own Black class, who are treated with consideration and respect.

I read such posters aghast at the behavior of these doctors toward their patients. That a doctor would deliberately inflict pain on someone who had come to him or her for help was to me a barbarity almost beyond belief. Chairman Mao's explanation for these cold-blooded acts was the only one that made sense to me: These were reactionary bourgeois intellectuals working to sabotage the revolution from within by brutalizing poor and lower-middle peasants. As I thought of Chairman Mao's concern for the proletariat, tears welled up in my eyes. Were it not for him we would never have known of these atrocities against the Red classes, despite the fact that they were occurring beneath our noses. I repledged my loyalty to Mao and vowed to carry out his Cultural Revolution until all the enemies of Communism had been unmasked and defeated.

Encouraged by the work team, student activists took these doctors and the physical education instructor into custody. Locked up in what was called a cowshed (actually one of the classrooms), they were taken out only for periodic "interrogations" that often degenerated into beatings. Two weeks later, after they had confessed to a wide variety of crimes going far beyond those listed in the original posters, they were dragged out in front of a schoolwide assembly and publicly criticized. The "struggle objects,'" as they were now called, hung their heads abjectly as the activists read their crimes out loud one by one. The massed students roared with anger at each new revelation. Overcoming my instinctive dislike of militancy, I joined in with the rest of the students. "Smash Doctor Bai's dog's head!" I shouted with the best of them. "Annihilate Doctor Jiang if he does not surrender!" I had convinced myself that no punishment was too severe for these enemies of the revolution.

On August 1, Chairman Mao turned his already heated rhetoric up a notch further. A month earlier, with his tacit backing, a group of Beijing university students had formed a new organization they called the "Red Guards of Chaiman Mao." Now Mao wrote them an open letter, promising his "ardent and passionate support" of their new venture. When we college students read Mao's letter in the August 1 edition of the *People's Daily*, we were electrified. The school's phalanx of activists immediately declared themselves to be the Shenyang Medical College Red Guards. From somewhere they acquired olive-drab army uniforms and broad leather belts with brass buckles, and to their upper sleeves they pinned the distinctive Red Guard insignia: a red felt armband with *Hong Wei Bing* (red guard) written in bold gold characters. Then they set about recruiting others into their organization. Given Mao's endorsement, everyone was eager to join.

Once again I found myself excluded. Following the practice in Beijing, the leaders of the Red Guards divided students into Reds, Blacks, and Grays. Those whose parents were Reds were welcomed into the Red Guards. Blacks, from bad class backgrounds, were the villains of the political drama now unfolding. I fell into the third category of Grays because, although my personal history, going back to my father, was clear, my family background was bad *(chushen bu hao)*. The Grays were people whose class status was neither Red nor Black, such as the sons and daughters of clerks, shop managers, and middle peasants. While Grays were not allowed to join the Red Guards, neither were we marked for persecution. Our part in the Cultural Revolution was left ambiguous.

As one group of students after another was inducted into the Shenyang Medical College Red Guards, I grew increasingly anxious to prove that I, too, was worthy. Soon more than half the members of the student body were striding around campus in faded army uniforms with red armbands pinned proudly to their sleeves. Eager to fit in, I borrowed an army uniform from a retired serviceman, which my mother cut down to my size. Although I felt the lack of an

armband keenly, and the old soldier couldn't bring himself to part
with the leather belt that went with the uniform, it was still better
than going around in civilian clothes.

Thus accoutered, I went to see the leader of our college's Red
Guards, a nineteen-year-old medical student named Yao. Though not
exactly handsome, Yao had a fresh look about him. He had regular
features, very fair skin, and black glossy hair carefully parted on the
left. (Before the Cultural Revolution it was said, the part had been
on the right). His most outstanding feature was his voice. It was the
mellow and resonant baritone of a natural public speaker, capable of
carrying to the corners of a large hall. "How can I help with the
Cultural Revolution?" I asked him.

Yao reviewed my file and then assigned me to work as an auxil-
iary of the Red Guard troop in my nursing class. "The leader of that
troop is very militant," Yao told me in that mesmerizing voice of his.
"Follow his lead in everything. That way you will be able to overcome the handicap of your background and become a true Red Guard
of Chairman Mao."

After the Red Guards were organized, Chairman Mao unleashed
them on society at large. On August 18, 1966, Marshal Lin Biao,
who was soon to become Mao's second in command, made a speech
calling on the Red Guards to "destroy the four olds." These he vaguely
defined as "old ideas, old culture, old customs, and old habits." As
always, we followed Mao's instructions with a fanatical literalness.
My troop, led by its militant leader, charged off campus determined
to destroy anything that could be connected with the past or with
the West. We spent many days ransacking the homes of neighboring
"five Black types" families, cutting up traditional Chinese gowns and
Western suits, smashing carved god images and antique vases, and
tearing up photographs and scroll paintings. Books received special
treatment: We carried them back to the campus and burned them in
huge bonfires on the athletic field.

We also pillaged our own college library, throwing thousands of literary works—everything from kung fu tales to Dickens novels—onto the flames. Some of the more zealous among us wanted to burn all books in foreign languages, including those on medical science. Cooler heads prevailed, with the argument that such reference works were necessary to provide proper medical care to the revolutionary classes.

When we went on off-campus raids our leader made sure we carried bamboo poles and several pairs of scissors. The poles were useful for knocking flowerpots—"useless bourgeois affectations"—off window ledges, as well as for beating those who resisted our efforts to destroy any "four olds" in their possession. The thick leather belts with heavy brass buckles worn by many Red Guards were also used for this purpose. The scissors came in handy when we encountered men or women on the street who were dressed in a fashion we had come to recognize as bourgeois. Men in narrow Western trousers had their pant legs slit; women in colorful skirts had them cut to tatters. Women pedestrians with long or permed hair were stopped and given what we called a yin-yang haircut: All the hair on one side of their head was cut off; the other side was left uncut. Shaving them after the traditional Chinese symbol of a dark side (*yin*) and a bright side (*yang*) meant that they were demons rather than people. On one occasion we stormed the Street of the Tailors, where several dozen tailors had their shops, and cut up all the "decadent" Western suits on display. We also cut up almost all of their woolen yardage, sparing only that in the plainest of colors. The shopkeepers did not dare protest, but simply stood behind their counters wringing their hands as we destroyed their livelihood. They knew that Chairman Mao was behind us.

The uncertainty of my status weighed increasingly heavily upon me. In the back of my mind lurked the fear that, if I did not somehow succeed in joining the Red Guards, I might suddenly be declared a Black at any time. I became more and more anxious to demonstrate my loyalty to Mao in some unmistakable way, short of engaging in acts of violence I found repugnant.

Yao, the Red Guard leader, stopped by our group frequently to chat with me—not that our conversations were ever very personal. Yao seemed more comfortable giving speeches than making small talk, even when I was the only one in the audience. But I sensed his interest in me, and this emboldened me to ask for a favor. I was hoping for a transfer to the Red Guard headquarters, where I would no longer have to go on house raids or harass passersby. "Could I not contribute better to our common work," I said demurely, "if I worked at headquarters with you? That way I could be on the front lines of the Cultural Revolution." Yao cleared his throat awkwardly, for once at a loss for words. "I . . . er . . . think we do need some help in the propaganda office," he said. "I will introduce you to the person in charge."

I reported for work in the propaganda department of the Red Guard headquarters the following day. Our main publication was a weekly newsletter, about four pages long, which was called the *Shenyang Medical College Red Guard Headquarters Newsletter*. But we also put out handbills on almost a daily basis. When I joined the propaganda office it had a staff of four. There was an air of zealotry about the office, and we kept extremely long hours. Having grown up in a one-party dictatorship that exercised tight control over the press, we all understood instinctively the power of the printed word. We were all determined to wield it with absolute and unswerving loyalty to Mao, not always an easy task given his sometimes vague and contradictory pronouncements. Each sentence had to advance the cause of Mao's kingdom. Because I could write fast and well, I was assigned to draft the handbills, which were less politically sensitive than the editorials which appeared in our newsletter. My efforts would then be reviewed by our editor and typeset. I often worked from early morning until after midnight, writing handbills by day and delivering them by night. I kept up this schedule for weeks at a time, energized by the importance of my mission. At sixteen, I was sure that I had come of age and was engaged in a great enterprise that would change the face of China.

The high point of our day was the 10:00 A.M. arrival of the latest edition of the *People's Daily*. Together we would eagerly scan the front page. First we would recite the boxed quotes from Chairman Mao at the top of the page, committing them to memory. Then we would devour the latest editorial, to see what new revelation the Chairman had vouchsafed us that day. Finally, we would discuss what the latest editorial revealed about the thoughts of Chairman Mao. Our deliberations over the meaning of the editorial would sometimes continue for hours, as we weighed conflicting interpretations of this phrase or parsed that sentence.

We were all eager to study Chairman Mao's "great revolutionary line" so that we could serve him better, but our endless discussions of his latest words were not sparked solely by our fervor. We had to be very careful about what we wrote in our own editorials. In the highly charged atmosphere of the time, the slightest ideological deviation from Chairman Mao's line was grounds for criticism. Often I would go out into the city to copy the big character posters of other Red Guard groups, whose best material we would reproduce word for word in our own publications. Our editor felt it was safer that way. Every group did this. All the newsletters published in Shenyang contained identical paragraphs, as editors sought safety in plagiarism. Even newsletters from places as distant from one another as Shanghai and Harbin often bore a strong family resemblance, with barely disguised rewrites of essential points. We also had to make doubly sure that no errors crept into the drafting or typesetting of articles.

Once, in a hurry to finish a handbill urging all Red Guards to "protect Chairman Mao," I handed the completed draft to our editor without first checking it myself. I did not realize that I had mistakenly written the word *depose* instead of *protect* at one point in the text, so that it now read "depose Chairman Mao." When my editor pointed

out the offending phrase to me I burst into tears. He quickly handed
me the page and turned away, telling me to make another copy. Had
the editor and I not been on good terms he could easily have had me
arrested for advocating the overthrow of Chairman Mao. This was a
capital crime, especially for a Gray like me. Against this charge I
could have mounted no credible defense. For the first time, fear tempered my enthusiasm and slowed my writing. My calligraphy, which
had always flowed easily, became halting and stilted as I carefully
printed out the text for the handbills.

I often volunteered to deliver the printed handbills to the two
universities that lay north of our campus. Not realizing that my
mother's apartment lay on the way, everyone was impressed by my
dedication and unselfishness. I relished these midnight visits, for otherwise I rarely saw my family. We students were encouraged to devote ourselves to revolution round the clock.

My mother did not share my enthusiasm for the Cultural Revolution, and we often ended up arguing. She found the chaotic atmosphere Mao had created frightening and the "revolutionary actions"
of his Red Guards threatening. As a teacher, she had already been
verbally abused by young activists at her school, even though they
were little more than children. In her opinion there was enough uncertainty in life already without deliberately setting out to cause more.
I disagreed, parroting Chairman Mao's line that the old ways had to
be throughly demolished before a new proletarian society could rise
from the ruins. I sensed that Mother did not entirely trust Mao's
motives, while I regarded them as a selfless attempt to better the lot
of the Chinese people.

One evening in mid-September our editor came bursting into the
propaganda office with a startling announcement. "Tomorrow morning we are going to attack the biggest bouregois reactionary authority
of them all!" he shouted. "Fang Kai, the president of the college, is
to be publicly denounced!"

We greeted his news with stunned silence. I knew that Fang Kai,
like all senior college officials, had been locked up in a cowshed and

secretly interrogated for several weeks. But I had assumed that the investigation would prove his innocence. President Fang was a veteran of the Long March, and his exploits with the Eighth Route Army were legendary. Not only did he have impeccable revolutionary credentials, he was very popular with the students. Unlike other high officials, President Fang never put on airs but stopped and chatted with students and staff during his walking tours of the campus. Besides, in addition to serving as the president of the university, he was a senior member of the Shenyang Municipal Party Committee. I could tell from the faces of my coworkers that they were as dismayed as I by this turn of events.

Before I could recover from my shock, my editor ordered me to compose an announcement of the upcoming denunciation meeting. I rushed to comply, but it was still after 1:00 A.M. before the last stack of handbills was copied. Each of us grabbed piles of handbills and set off in different directions. I rode north as fast as I could pedal but stopped when I reached my mother's apartment half an hour later, badly in need of a cup of hot tea to dispel the fog of weariness that had enveloped me. When my mother saw how tired I was, she begged me to stay the night and continue my errand in the morning. I shook my head. "Tomorrow morning we are going to attack the biggest bourgeois reactionary authority of them all," I said, echoing the words of my editor. "Fang Kai, the president of the college, is to be publicly denounced."

My mother was aghast. She, too, knew of Fang Kai's long years with the Eighth Route Army. In a low, urgent voice she began to plead with me: "I am very frightened for you. Please think carefully about what you are doing. If you must participate in this denunciation meeting, don't stand in the front ranks. Think before you open your mouth. Don't shout slogans too loudly. Don't be too militant. Don't allow yourself to be manipulated like a wooden puppet. The day may come when you will regret the things you have said and done."

"We must follow Mao's Great Proletarian Cultural Revolution," I interrupted loudly. "We must smash whoever opposes Chairman Mao!" After two months of working in the propaganda office, speaking in slogans came naturally to me.

"It is my past experience in political campaigns that makes me cautious," she continued softly, ignoring my outburst. "You were just a child during the Hundred Flowers Campaign. Let me remind you what happened. Chairman Mao called on the people to criticize the Party for its shortcomings. People were cautious at first, but then grew bolder as the encouragement to speak out continued. Suddenly, when the criticism had reached a crescendo, the ax fell. Those who had found fault with the Party were declared to be rightists and sent to prison. Mao, you see, was just 'enticing the snake out of its hole to behead it.'"

My mother's attack on Chairman Mao hit me like a bombshell. I opened my mouth, but for a second no sound came out. "I obey Chairman Mao!" I was finally able to whsiper. Then I turned on my heels and strode out of the apartment. As I rode on to the universities to deliver my handbills my mother's traitorous words kept ringing in my ears. They made a mockery of everything I believed in. As a follower of Chairman Mao, I knew where my loyalties belonged. "Father is dear, Mother is dear, but neither is as dear as Chairman Mao," we had been taught to sing in lower-middle school. Those words had never rung truer to me than right now. I knew that I should report what my mother had said to my Red Guard leader. By doing so I would be drawing the clear line between myself and my family that had been demanded of me. I would be rewarded for such a dramatic demonstration of my loyalty to Mao. Yet how could I report my own mother, even if it meant being allowed to join the Red Guards?

I continued to wrestle with this dilemma as I dropped off the handbills and then pedaled slowly back to the medical college. By the time I returned to my dormitory at 3:00 A.M., I had come to a decision. There was only one thing to do. I would atone for my mother's disloyalty by personally rededicating myself to Chairman Mao. The following day at the denunciation meeting I would display a revolutionary spirit second to none.

I woke up after only a few hours' sleep, eager for the day to begin. As I had hoped, I was one of the first to arrive at the assembly hall. I purposely took a seat in the front row, immediately in front of the stage, where I could be seen and heard. Fang Kai was the first member of the Municipal Party committee to be attacked, and everyone was curious about the kinds of crimes he would confess.

"Red Guard Fighters," Yao began at precisely 9 o'clock. "We in Shenyang have vowed on a rock to protect and defend Chairman Mao's revolutionary line. His instructions we have followed as closely as lips are to teeth. We have soundly and pitilessly hammered the reactionary bourgeois authorities, the reactionary intellectuals, and the capitalist bloodsuckers and parasites at our schools." His mesmerizing voice swelled to reach the ends of the hall, filled with energy and conviction for the revolutionary struggle he was engaged in. "We have done rightly!" he shouted. "We have done splendidly!"

The crowd was caught up in Yao's enthusiasm and bounded to its feet to give a wild cheer. "Long live Chairman Mao!" I found myself screaming. Others joined in, until that howled expression of loyalty filled the hall. Yao stood proudly erect, his face flushed with excitement, pleased at the frenzy he had generated.

"Now we have to take our struggle one step further," he continued after we had quieted down again. "Chairman Mao has warned us about those in power who are following the capitalist road. For years, these capitalist-roaders have secretly worked to undermine the revolution from within the Party. They have protected the reactionary scholars and other class enemies from the wrath of the proletariat." The thought of these turncoats evoked a rumble of disgust from the crowd.

"We must unmask and destroy these traitors!" Yao's voice was once more rising to a crescendo. "We must carry through the Great Proletarian Cultural Revolution to the bitter end. We all know that the president of our college, Fang Kai, was a reactionary bourgeois authority. But his crimes were far worse than you have imagined. Fang Kai is a senior member of the Shenyang Party committee. Fang Kai will admit to you this morning that he was a capitalist-roader!" The hall erupted with hysterical cries of outrage.

At this moment Fang Kai was pushed out onto the stage by two husky students. His clothes were dirty and torn, probably from being manhandled during interrogations, but his face was unmarked. As soon as he appeared, several of us in the front row started taunting him. "We are going to beat you down into the dust, Fang Kai! We are going to crush your spine so that you shall never rise again! *Da dao Fang Kai!*" we began to chant. "Beat down Fang Kai!" Instantly the entire hall was with us: "Beat down Fang Kai!"

Fang Kai tried to lift his head to look at us, but the two students grabbed his arms and twisted them, elbows locked, back and upward behind his body. Fang was being "jet-planed." He had no choice but to lower his head and bend his knees and back, in order to take some of the pressure off his arms. He looked like a swimmer on the starting block waiting for the gun to sound. The pain of holding this unnatural position would soon grow excruciating. But if Fang tried to relax, the students would give his arms a vicious jerk, threatening to wrench them out of their sockets.

One by one, with great feeling and deliberateness, Yao read the charges against Fan Kai from a document he held in his hand. The president was accused of everything from creating a viper's nest of class enemies—that is, the college faculty, more than 70 percent of whom were landlords, rich peasants, counterrevolutionaries, bad elements, and rightists—to wasting a large sum of money constructing a garden complete with a fish pond.

After each revelation of Fang's past misdeeds we in the audience would revile him anew. Yao would then turn to Fang Kai and ask rhetorically, "Is this charge true?" Fang would say not a word in response, but one of the guards would grab his hair and force his head up and down in a puppetlike imitation of a nod. Fang's face remained expressionless throughout, showing not the slightest sign of guilt or remorse. His stoic attitude made me angry. He should have been crying and begging forgiveness from the masses for his terrible crimes.

It took Yao the better part of two hours to get through the list of charges, which seemed endless. Finally the Red Guard leader turned to President Fang and said, "Is everything that has been written correct?" After the guard had once again forced Fang to nod, they released his arms. It was Fang's turn to speak.

Fang Kai slowly, stiffly straightened his back and stood upright. Then he brought his arms around to the front and flexed them. You could almost hear his joints creak. He looked straight at the audience, his face still expressionless. "Students," he began slowly. "You know me. For many years I have served as the president of the Shenyang Medical College. Throughout this time, my heart has been *wenxin wukui* (warmly devoted to my work), and I have done nothing that I regret. From the time I joined the Communist Party in 1936, I have always been extremely loyal to the Party—"

This was as far as he got. We all realized at once that Fang Kai was denying his crimes, and pandemonium broke out. "False testimony!" the person sitting next to me cried. "Clever lies!" someone else seconded. "*Si wu zhang shen zhi di!*" screamed a third. "When you die you will be carrion for the vultures!" I leapt to my feet and shook my fists in anger. "You cannot resist the will of the masses!" I shrieked. "Admit your crimes, capitalist-roader!" Hatred welled up inside me. I wanted to punch Fang Kai's expressionless face in.

I jumped up on the stage and struck Fang Kai full in the mouth. It was the only blow I delivered. A dozen people had followed me up onto the stage and now surrounded Fang, punching and kicking him from all directions. Fang was knocked off his feet in seconds, but the blows continued to fall as he lay writhing on the floor. From behind this mob, I caught a glimpse of his face. It was a white mask of pain. Still, I did not once hear him cry out.

While the beating was still continuing, Yao came over to congratulate me. "You are a true Red Guard," he said with a smile. "Your performance today was outstanding. You showed the others how to deal with diehard capitalist-roaders who oppose the Cultural Revolution. I am going to recommend that you be allowed to join the Red Guard Rebels."

Yao turned away to call off the attack on Fang Kai, who by now had been pounded senseless. I watched from distance as several Red Guards carried Fang's limp body offstage. But I was too elated by my own triumph to give any thought to Fang's pain and suffering. My time as a Gray was drawing to a close. I was finally going to be admitted to the class ranks as an equal!

By that evening my initial euphoria had evaporated, and I lay awake in bed mulling over what I had done. Never before in my life had I struck anyone in anger. I had not thought that I was capable of such hatred and violence. Fang Kai's taut, white face came back to me. I tentatively extended my right fist in the darkness, and felt again the shock of the blow I had delivered to his mouth. *It could easily be me on the receiving end of such blows*, I reflected. *I am nothing but a lowly Gray, and I attacked a Party leader*. My audacity took my breath away. *What if my mother was right?* I thought. *What if all of us who attacked Fang Kai would one day be declared rightists?!*

No! I told myself sternly. *My loyalty to Mao would soon be publicly acknowledged. And as for Fang, he had merely pretended to be a revolutionary hero and a loyal follower of Mao. The charges against him proved that he long ago abandoned the Communists. Fang's Party membership was a lie, a disguise adopted to hide his true colors. The man I had attacked was not a leader of the Party but a loathsome member of the blackest of the Black: an unrepentant capitalist-roader. We Red Guards had done the right thing in scourging him.* I rolled over and closed my eyes in preparation for sleep, but the mystery of Fang's motives kept tugging at my consciousness. *What could have led Fang Kai to this pass? How could anyone turn away from Chairman Mao, our Red Sun, whose words brought warmth into our hearts and light into our minds? Fang's soul must be dead*, I concluded just before I dropped into a dreamless sleep.

Yao was as good as his word. I and two other non–Red Guards who had joined in the attack on Fang Kai were inducted into the Shenyang Medical College Red Guards a few days later in that same hall. The ceremony was attended by the entire Red Guard contingent, which now numbered some seven hundred. In a rousing speech, Yao praised our "revolutionary actions" against Fang to the repeated cheers of those present. Then he had us raise our right fists high in the air as we clasped the "precious red book" to our bosoms with our left hands, and he led us in a formal pledge of allegiance to Chairman Mao.

"We swear that we will protect Chairman Mao's revolutionary road," we chanted after Yao, the volume of our three combined voices scarcely matching that of his. "We will struggle to the bitter end with the 'cow demons and the snake demons,' with the reactionary bourgeois authorities, and with those in power who have taken the capitalist road. We will carry the Great Proletarian Cultural Revolution through to the bitter end. Chairman Mao is our strength and our power! We can mount to heaven and plunge into the earth because our great leader Chairman Mao is our booster!" Finally, Yao pinned the armband I had for so long coveted, the one with "Red Guard Rebels" written in bold gold characters across it, to my upper sleeve. It was the proudest moment of my young life.

Relations between different Red Guard units in Shenyang, which up to this point had been relatively cordial, began to deteriorate. An organization that called itself "Red Shenyang," based at the Shenyang Institute of Science and Technology, began to accuse us in their publications of having betrayed Chairman Mao's revolutionary line. We quickly discovered that they were mostly the sons and daughters of provincial- and municipal-level officials, and so responded in our own newsletter by labeling them "loyalists who want to protect the capitalist-roaders in power."

The confrontation escalated when Red Shenyang began to recruit members on our campus, competing with us for the support of the uncommitted. Yao doubled the staff of the propaganda department and ordered us to publish our newsletter twice a week—and fill it with editorial broadsides at Red Shenyang. I put in, if anything, even more hours at work than I had before, but my energy and enthusiasm were inexhaustible. I had finally been accepted, without reservation or qualification, into Chairman Mao's shock troops. In late September the head of the propaganda department (I suspect at Yao's suggestion) made me his administrative assistant. This promotion meant that during the department head's frequent absences I was effectively in charge, editing text for handbills and signing vouchers for purchases and travel. It was the first real authority I had ever enjoyed, and I relished the opportunity it provided to better serve Chairman Mao.

As the propaganda war intensified, so did our efforts to outdo each other in showing reverence to Chairman Mao. We avidly scanned the *People's Daily* and other publications for new ways of proving our superior loyalty. When it was reported that some Beijing Red Guards prayed to Mao three times a day, we promptly did likewise, "asking for guidance from Chairman Mao in the morning, harmonizing our actions with His teachings at noon, and reporting everything to Him at night." Yao ordered that a huge poster of Chairman Mao be hung in the entryway to the cafeteria. Before each meal we abased ourselves before this image of Mao, praising his wisdom and invoking his aid.

These devotions followed a ritual as fixed as a military drill. It was forbidden to worship Mao in groups smaller than six—anything that smacked of individualism was frowned on—so that those first to arrive would wait outside the double doors of the cafeteria until the necessary quorum had assembled. Yao often arrived shortly before or after I did, whether by habit or coincidence I was never quite able to figure out. Those present would then form themselves into a little platoon, with the senior Red Guard commanding. Our right hands would clasp the little red book to our chests, our left hands would be swinging military style, and we would march into the lobby. We would halt in front of the poster, then make a right turn to face it.

Our opening invocation was "Long live our Great Leader Chairman Mao!" which we would repeat three times. Then, while we stood at attention, our leader would offer up the opening prayer. "Dear Chairman Mao," he would intone. "Thou art the brightest, the greatest, most wonderful leader in the history of the world. Chairman Mao, thou hast started the Great Proletarian Cultural Revolution with thine own hands. Chairman Mao, thou wert the spark that ignited this great conflagration. Chairman Mao, thou art the one who gave us such a magnificent opportunity to improve our proletarian spirit and to become true revolutionaries."

Next all of us would join together to recite a kind of Maoist creed. "Chairman Mao, Chairman Mao," we would chant in a singsong. "Whatever road thou wouldst we travel, we shall follow. However strong the gale, however fierce the waves, never shall we falter, never shall we retreat. We shall follow thee closely and carry thy Great Proletarian Cultural Revolution through to the final victory. Chairman Mao, place thy trust in us. We shall always carry out thine orders."

At this point we would usually insert a brief salutation to Lin Biao, a military commander whom Mao had anointed as his second-in-command. We were careful in our choice of phrases, since we did not want to appear to be placing Lin Biao on the same plane as Chairman Mao. "Assistant Commander Lin, may you stay healthy forever," was the usual formula we would use. Then we would end as we had begun, with "Long live our Great Leader Chairman Mao!" repeated three times. Our morning devotions over, we marched into the cafeteria proper and sat down to breakfast.

The "Chairman Mao loyalty dance" also became popular, especially after we discovered that our rivals were doing it three times a week. Yao instantly decreed that we would do it every day, in full public view in the central square of our college. Raising our hands above our heads, we moved them in little circles, as if we were washing imaginary windows. Our feet danced a shuffling two-step—forward, sideways, and back, and again. All the while we sang, in a kind of a sustained howl, "Chairman Mao, *oooh*, Chairman Mao. Chairman Mao, *oooh*, Chairman Mao." We moved slowly and deliberately, taking our exercise with the utmost seriousness. We looked very much like *t'ai chi ch'uan* practitioners, except that Chinese shadowboxers all move to their own drummers, while we performed this ridiculous song and dance in unison. Several minutes of such choreographed folly were usually required to satisfy Yao that we had sufficiently demonstrated our devotion.

Throughout October and November, we were holding denunciation meetings two or three times a week. Despite daily grillings, we still had not succeeded in extracting a confession from Fang Kai. At the same time, we had arrested so many other school officials that the cowsheds were full of presumed offenders. One day after breakfast, as Yao walked me over to headquarters, he said to me in a conspiratorial voice: "Would you like to help with the denunciation meetings?"

I gulped. I had vowed not to repeat my attack on Fang Kai, who was being regularly pummeled by others.

"I'm not asking you to strike anyone," Yao added quickly, sensing my unease. "But I need a couple of trustworthy comrades to lead the audience in shouting slogans. You always sit in the front row. You are a senior member of the propaganda department. You will know what to say. And the others will follow your lead." After I agreed to help, Yao told me that he had already recruited one other person to shout slogans. We should talk privately with each other, he said, in order to work out some formula for taking turns. It was important that our exclamations appear spontaneous, not staged.

I was very conscientious about my new assignment. Well before a meeting began, I would be in my customary seat in the front row. As Yao announced the crimes of the accused, I would become increasingly agitated, seconding any cries of anger I heard from the rows behind me. This was not playacting, for at this time I still felt deeply the righteousness of the cause that engaged us. When Yao had finished, I would jump up and begin shouting slogans, confident that the rest of the audience would join in—as they invariably did. Yao's second agent would take the lead every second or third go-round, often enough so that I appeared to be an activist, not a plant.

To help me keep my head during heated moments, I made it a point always to write down beforehand the slogans I intended to shout. This was not difficult to do. In the first place, the person denounced was always guilty, so the outcome of the meeting was never in doubt. Second, the repertoire of appropriate slogans was not particularly large. The main thing was to get the name of the official being denounced right, and to choose slogans that matched his or her crimes. There were also certain established formulas, appropriate for any and all crimes, such as "Protect Chairman Mao, attack Fang Kai!"

One evening Yao was winding up his standard denunciation of Fang Kai's crimes, which I had by then virtually memorized. I looked down at my crib sheet one final time and discovered to my horror that I had written: "Attack Chairman Mao, defend Fang Kai." Once again I had written the exact opposite of my meaning! Had I mistakenly shouted out such sentiments, I would likely have been attacked on the spot. I quickly folded up the crib sheet and put it away. When it came time to shout, the words would scarcely come out of my mouth, and I saw Yao looking at me quizzically. After the meeting I received another shock: The sheet was not in my pocket where I had put it!

Late that night there was a knock on the door of my dormitory room. I opened the door, and Yao and two of his lieutenants strode in without so much as a nod. Men usually did not come into a woman's dormitory rooms, out of a sense of propriety. Yao dismissed my startled roommate with a curt "Wait outside." Then he thrust a piece of paper into my hands, as if he were eager to be rid of it. It was my crib sheet! My hands began to tremble and my mouth went dry. "How could you have written such a thing about our beloved Chairman Mao?" he burst out after a few seconds, obviously unable to contain himself any longer. "Do you want to be declared a counterrevolutionary-in-action?"

It was as if he had slapped me. I could feel tears beginning to well up. A counterrevolutionary-in-action was someone who was actively working to overthrow the Communist Party, the most serious crime imaginable. An eight-year-old girl at my mother's school had been declared a counterrevolutionary-in-action after she had said she felt sorry for President Liu Shaoqi, who was then being attacked as "China's Khrushchev" and the leading opponent of Mao. As she was only a child, she had not been sent to prison but rather thrown into the cowshed with the other Blacks and capitalist-roaders. Her parents, under pressure to prove that they had not put their daughter up to this counterevolutionary act, had denounced her at a school assembly. "We publicly disown you as our daughter," the father and mother had both screamed, slapping her repeatedly across the face for good measure. This little girl, once a favorite student of my mother's, now bore little resemblance to her former self. There was a strange light in her eyes, my mother reported, and she spent her days in a corner of the cowshed crooning to herself. Her parents, in a fit of remorse, had once sneaked in to visit her, but she showed no sign of recognition. If the Red Guards could do this to an eight-year-old, what would they do to me?

"I was in a hurry," I finally stammered. "I had no idea I had written this until I got to the meeting. When I realized what I had written, I was mortified. When I shouted the slogan, I shouted it correctly. This was just an innocent mistake. I would never say such a thing about our beloved leader Chairman Mao. I love Chairman Mao with all my heart!"

"Even if it *was* just a mistake, as *you* say," Yao responded, "there must be some explanation. Such thoughts must have crossed your mind at one time or another or you would not have written them."

"No!" I cried out. "I swear I have never had such thoughts. I love Chairman Mao with all my heart." I sat down helplessly on my bed and broke into loud sobs.

At the sight of my distress, Yao seemed to soften a little. "I accept your explanation," he said abruptly. "Write a self-criticism and give it to me tomorrow."

Once again I had only narrowly escaped disaster. That I was a member of the Red Guards had made no difference. If Fang Kai, a long-trusted Party leader, could be denounced as a "hidden enemy of Communism," where did that leave me, a lowly Gray? It would be a small matter for Yao to send me to the cowshed. In the atmosphere of paranoia created by the Cultural Revolution, no one would dare question his decision. The thought made the breath catch in my throat. I worked until the wee hours of the morning rewriting and polishing my self-criticism. I also rehearsed the pleas for forgiveness I intended to make personally to Yao.

When I visited Yao's office the following day he refused to see me. I had to leave my self-criticism with his secretary. A few days later I found myself transferred out of the propaganda department back to an ordinary Red Guard unit. Obviously I could no longer be trusted. Yao started avoiding me on campus and never spoke to me again.

5

Exiting the Red Guards

*F*OR SOME TIME I had been troubled by indigestion. I returned to the diet of my childhood—rice and boiled cabbage—but found even this soft, bland food hard to digest. Nothing agreed with me anymore. My nausea became a permanent state.

I thought at first my problems stemmed from the long hours I was putting in at the propaganda department. Then came my transfer to a regular Red Guard unit and slack days and nights of light guard duty in the cowshed, punctuated only by an occasional raid. My nausea only got worse. The sad-eyed prisoners I guarded shrank back when we Red Guards walked into the room, and my own stomach twisted in response. I found excuses to absent myself when the arrogant young interrogators began their work.

It's not overwork at all but a bad case of nerves. The thought came to me one afternoon late in November as I stood guard duty. *I must have an ulcer.* Fear and zealotry not only surrounded me on all sides, it had begun to wreak havoc in my guts. The fear of the captives I guarded had become mine, their confinement my own. *After all, I had almost been one of them*, I thought. *One more miscue, one more wrongly spoken phrase, and I will be.* At the end of my shift I went to see my unit commander. I told him I was ill and would like to go home and rest for a few days. He grudgingly granted me permission.

"Ah, you've come back, child," my mother greeted me, a rare smile on her careworn face. This was instantly replaced by a worried frown as I told her of my recurrent stomach trouble. "And we have no steamed rice for you," she said to herself, as if in reproach. "Only coarse Kaoliang cakes."

"Don't worry about me," I said easily. "Now that I am home my nervous stomach will disappear." To prove my point I picked up a leftover Kaoliang cake and took a hearty bite out of it with an air of confidence I did not feel. "I'll be fine."

I woke up in the wee hours of the morning in agony. A huge boulder, hard and heavy, occupied the spot where my stomach had been. I had just enough time to stagger to the bathroom before the boulder shattered into spasms of retching. My stomach quickly emptied, but the heaving continued long after the last trickle of bile, leaving me jacknifed on the floor.

I felt my mother's cool hands in the darkness, brushing my damp hair back from my forehead. "Get up, Liang-yue," I heard her call out to my older brother. "Chi An is burning up with fever. We must take her to the hospital."

It took a few seconds for the meaning of her words to penetrate the fog of pain and fever that enveloped me. "I'll be all right," I protested weakly, but Mother was already helping me down the stairs and onto the bicycle. She and my brother walked the bike to the hospital between them, one hand on the handlebars and the other around me.

The pressure of the admitting room doctor's probing fingers on my stomach caused me to cry out. He straightened up from his examination and turned to my mother. "Your daughter has a fever of 103.5 degrees and a tenderness in her lower abdomen. The pain associated with appendicitis is usually a little more to the right but, if you want my guess, that's what this is. The chief surgeon will probably want to operate in the morning."

But by morning my temperature was down slightly, and the sharp cramping in my abdomen had subsided to a constant throbbing. The chief surgeon, a Doctor Ouyang, was a small man with a round, kindly face and a formal manner. He was puzzled at the sudden disappearance of my "appendicitis." "I think we will keep you here under observation for several days, Nurse Yang," he said politely. "That is, if you are in agreement."

I quickly nodded. I had been seeking a refuge from the violence and chaos of the outside world. *A hospital will do just as well as home*, I thought, looking around with pleasure at the small, orderly confines of the eight-bed surgical ward to which I had been assigned. Little did I know that, instead of being an oasis of healing and peace, the hospital, much like the world outside its walls, was a seething bedlam of political discord.

There were six other patients in the ward. A garrulous bunch, they all introduced themselves in short order. Only the woman in the bed next to mine lay still and silent, her eyes closed, her neck a thick mass of bandages. A robust-looking man dressed in blue peasant garb sat dozing in a chair next to her bed.

"Her name is Ah Fei," offered a patient with her ankle in a cast. "She was operated on yesterday. The man next to her is her husband, Ah Lung. Doctor Ouyang, the chief surgeon, found a huge cancerous mass where her thyroid gland should have been. He cut out as much as he could, but it had already spread to other parts of her body."

"It's really a pity," another wardmate clucked sympathetically. "I heard Doctor Ouyang tell her husband, Ah Lung, that she does not have long to live. And she with four children, the youngest only eight months old!"

A nurse popped her head in through the doorway. "It is time to ask our Great Leader Chairman Mao for instructions," she barked. "Everyone assemble at the nurses' station." She was gone as quickly as she had appeared.

Her announcement caught me by surprise. "Even here we have to ask for—" I caught myself in midsentence, clapping my hand quickly to my mouth. *Of course we must ask our Great Leader Chairman Mao for instructions here in the hospital*, I silently chastised myself. *Just last week the* People's Daily *said that we must do it every day, even when sick in bed!*

I got out of bed and gingerly stood up. Behind me I heard Ah Lung pleading with his semiconscious wife. "Please . . . wake up, Ah Fei," he said slowly. "We have to ask . . . our Great Leader Chairman Mao . . . for instructions." His speech was clumsy and disjointed, even allowing for his thick peasant brogue. Ah Fei moaned something indistinct in reply.

My instinct to help compelled me to turn around. Together Ah Lung and I helped his wife off the bed and onto the floor, half carrying, half dragging her to the doorway. The hallway was crowded with the lame, the halt, and the wounded, all moving in slow motion toward the nurses' station. It looked like a stream of refugees from a bomb blast. *This is madness*, a voice kept saying over and over again in my head as the three of us hobbled down the hall to the station.

"It's time to begin," a tall young man in doctor's garb shouted impatiently at the last of the stragglers. Then he ordered the ragged crowd of patients who surrounded him: "Line up in ranks."

"Surely that's not necessary, Doctor Lu," interjected the man I knew as the chief surgeon. "These people are ill."

"Then they can ask Chairman Mao to heal them," snapped Doctor Lu. "We must have order. Or don't you agree, Doctor Ouyang?"

The chief surgeon glared briefly at his younger colleague. Then he abruptly launched into the opening chant of the ritual. "Long Live our Great Leader Chairman Mao," he shouted. The young doctor instantly joined in, his loud baritone drowning out the chief surgeon's weak tenor. The rest of us followed in feeble chorus.

There was a power struggle under way in the department, I understood instantly. These two men—the chief surgeon, Doctor Ouyang, and the ambitious young physician, Doctor Lu—were the principal antagonists, each trying to outdo the other in "Redness."

Their joint leadership of the ritual was a fig leaf masking an intense rivalry.

Fixing their eyes reverently on the Chairman's poster, both doctors took turns praising Mao and quoting verbatim from his works. This duel went on for several minutes. The strain of standing at rigid attention—anything less would be to show disrespect to Mao—began to tell on the patients. First one and then a second of our number crumpled to the ground. They lay where they fell, for neither the other doctors nor the nursing staff dared interrupt the ritual to tend to them.

I turned my head slightly to see how Ah Fei was faring and caught my breath. A crimson stain had appeared in the very center of her bulky neck bandage and grew visibly larger as I watched. The forced march down the hallway had reopened her incision. All at once her eyes rolled and she slumped, unconscious, against her husband. Without thinking Ah Lung picked her up in his arms, staggering a little under the weight of her limp body, and started back to the ward. From the look of outraged righteousness that appeared on Doctor Lu's face, I knew that Ah Lung would soon come to regret his premature exit.

Back in the ward after "asking for instructions," everyone seemed subdued. Ah Fei was still unconscious, her bandage now completely blood soaked. When the nurse came by on her rounds, a distraught Ah Lung begged her to call Doctor Lu. "Call him yourself," she retorted coldly. "Doctor Lu has washed his hands of your case. He has left orders that your wife is not to receive any further treatment. She is to be discharged as soon as she regains consciousness."

"Please help her!" Ah Lung cried out, his thick voice breaking in desperation. He fell to his knees in front of the nurse and began banging his head against the floor with loud thuds in an exaggerated kowtow. The nurse hesitated.

"I come from the nursing school," I said to her quietly. "Isn't there something we can do for this poor woman? She's suffering greatly."

She pursed her lips together in indecision and then, after a long second, gave an almost imperceptible nod. Together we removed Ah Fei's neck bandage, replacing it with a compress to help stop the bleeding. On her own authority, she administered a blood transfusion to Ah Fei, who gradually regained consciousness.

As we cared for Ah Fei, I asked the nurse the reason for the bad blood between Doctors Ouyang and Lu. It was as I suspected. Two Red Guard groups, the "Rebels" and the "Loyalists," were locked in a bitter struggle for control of the hospital. Almost all the doctors and most of the nurses had joined one of the two groups, some for their own protection. Those few doctors who tried to remain above the political struggle were accused of emphasizing expertise over "Redness." Many of the nurses were gentle, nurturing souls, by their very nature repulsed by violence. "Were it not for us nurses," she whispered to me, "many patients would have died from neglect."

We had no sooner finished than Doctor Lu's cruel voice echoed down the hallway. "Who ordered the blood transfusion for the woman with cancer?" he was shouting. "You are wasting resources. Why give her the precious blood of the proletariat? She'll be dead in a month!"

I stole an embarrassed glance at Ah Fei and her husband. They were looking helplessly at one another, tears coursing down their cheeks. "What is going to happen to my children?" I heard her say softly. "The poor orphans."

These words pierced my heart. I, too, had been orphaned in a way. I had lost my father to the lake, and my mother to her own private agony for a year afterward. "How old are your children?" I asked.

"My oldest boy is only eight," Ah Fei said. "My two girls are five and three. And my baby boy is only eight months old." This admission brought on a fresh gush of tears.

"Your children will be all right," I said, anxious to console her. "Heaven has eyes. You are a good person. Heaven blesses the good and punishes the wicked."

These were favorite proverbs of the janitor's wife who had helped raise us. She had repeated them in every adversity, firmly believing that a good person, whatever suffering he or she had to endure, would be rewarded in the end. I wasn't at all sure I believed in something called heaven, and I was certain that it wasn't just. My father had been the kindest, most wonderful person I had known, yet he had been taken from us when we were small children. Where was heaven then? What was just about leaving four children without a father? Still, I repeated her sayings to the young peasant woman, and she seemed to take some comfort from them.

We were soon rousted out of bed again to "ask for instructions." Doctor Lu began to shout short slogans: "Swear to protect Chairman Mao's revolutionary line! Defeat the capitalist-roaders!" Faster and faster he went, until even I, a practiced sloganmonger, had trouble keeping up.

Ah Fei didn't even try. From the first she stood leaning against Ah Lung's chest, apparently on the verge of fainting. Ah Lung nervously tried to make up for her silence, shouting the slogans with forced enthusiasm. But as Doctor Lu speeded up, he fell behind, until he was still stumbling through the last slogan when we were already on the next. Out of synch and confused, he fell silent.

Without warning, Doctor Lu rounded on him. "You refuse to shout slogans!" he yelled. "Are you trying to protect the landlords and capitalist-roaders?"

Ah Lung looked as if he had been poleaxed. His hands fluttered near his heart in a silent plea for mercy.

"Tie him up," Doctor Lu snapped. Several of his radical followers grabbed Ah Lung's arms and twisted them behind his back, binding them with bandage strips. "Why did you refuse to shout the slogans?" Lu bellowed to his now trussed victim. "What do you have to say for yourself now? Admit your guilt or we will beat you."

Ah Lung made no effort to answer his tormenter's questions. In his terror, he had probably not even heard them.

"The peasant refuses to admit his guilt!" Lu snarled to his followers. "Teach him a lesson!" The pack fell on Ah Lung with a vengeance, and he began grunting and moaning in pain.

The voice of Ah Lung's wife could be heard over the fray. She was kneeling in front of Lu, clasping her hands in a gesture of supplication. "Don't beat him to death!" she implored. "My children's father is a simpleton. He can't talk very well. He didn't mean to stop shouting slogans."

As she continued to speak the air seemed to go out of Ah Lung's assailants. Fewer and fewer blows were struck.

"You know I am dying of cancer," she went on, weeping freely. "Please don't beat my children's father to death. My children are still small. They need their father. I beg you not to make them orphans."

Lu's followers unclenched their fists and began backing away in embarrassment from Ah Lung's huddled form.

Ignoring her pleas, Lu tried to rekindle the hatred in his followers. "We must never forget that we are revolutionaries!" he shouted. "We must not be afraid of chaos and killing!" But the eyes of Lu's followers remained downcast, their hands motionless at their sides. "The peasant must go to the cowshed until he confesses his crimes," Lu said finally, admitting defeat. He gave a quick bow in the direction of Chairman Mao's poster, pronouncing the ritual complete.

Unable to offer a single word in his own defense, Ah Lung was beaten senseless that afternoon. In the interminable "interrogations" that followed, he proved equally unskilled at making a satisfactory "confession." Lu's questions to Ah Lung were delivered using boots, fists, and belt buckles. Ah Lung answered in silence and blood.

Difficult though her husband's ordeal was, it was Ah Fei who suffered more. Anyone caught attending this "consort of a suspected counterrevolutionary," Lu raged to the nurses, would have to answer to him. On his orders Ah Fei's pain medication was stopped, her neck bandage was left unchanged, and her bedpan went unemptied. Ah Fei seemed scarcely to notice, for Ah Lung's arrest had broken her spirit. She lay motionless under the worn blanket that was her cover, her face a frozen mask of pain. All the while her cancer continued its relentless march through her body.

I was no less terrified of this cruel zealot than the nurses. Perhaps more so, for I realized on how slender a thread hung my political respectability. But the sight of Ah Fei lying silent and neglected was more than I could bear. So it was that when Lu and his informers weren't around I slipped out of bed and, fighting my pain and weakness, did what I could for her. By the second day, Ah Fei's eyes no longer stared vacantly into space but followed me as I worked. It took her two more days to smile, but the following morning I received my first simple thank-you. By the end of the week she was talking constantly, as if somewhere deep inside her a dam had burst. Her words rushed out in a torrent, picking up her spirits along the way and depositing them in my heart as I listened.

Ah Fei chuckled as she told me of the big-hearted but slow-witted man who ten years ago became her husband. A smile played across Ah Fei's face as she recalled her children to me. The prospect of leaving them motherless filled her with anguish, yet she did not rage against her fate, she simply remembered, long and well, the times of their lives.

Each day Ah Fei grew frailer, until her clothes hung on her skeletal frame and she could not speak above a whisper. Yet, paradoxically, her memory grew more acute, until it seemed to me that she was able to number the very hairs of her children's heads. She also spoke of the future, anticipating marriages and grandchildren that she would not live to see. Toward the end, when the pain from her rapidly spreading cancer kept her awake late into the night, she would talk for hours, until, exhausted, she finally fell into a numb and dreamless sleep.

As I listened to Ah Fei, my eyes often filled with tears. Without really knowing what I was saying, I would mumble a few words about the end of suffering and a just heaven, words as much for my own consolation as for hers.

Doctor Lu belatedly realized that Ah Fei was near her end and released her still-mute husband from the cowshed. I scarcely recognized Ah Lung, his face bruised and misshapen from the many beatings he had received. Ah Fei herself was spared the sight, for she had already fallen into a coma. She died at daybreak, leaving her husband weeping soundlessly beside her fleshless frame. Ah Fei, at least, was beyond the reach of their tormentors.

This entire episode had a great effect on me. Before when people had been persecuted, I could never be sure that they were not guilty of the charges against them. But I was absolutely certain that Ah Lung was innocent—unless being a slow-witted, unlettered peasant was now a crime. For all my years of schooling I, too, had once come close to garbling a slogan. I was even more appalled by Ah Fei's victimization. Depriving a dying woman of pain medication because she was the "consort of a suspected counterrevolutionary" seemed to me the work of inhuman monsters rather than human beings.

At first, believing that Chairman Mao would never countenance such cruelty, I angrily blamed Lu alone. Lu was desperate to win his power struggle with the "Loyalists." . . . Lu was crazed by ambition. . . . Lu was obsessed with being the Reddest of the Red. . . . But as Ah Fei lay dying, doubts about Mao himself crept into my mind. In showing no mercy to "class enemies," wasn't Lu simply following in Mao's footsteps? Had not Mao himself condemned humanitarian considerations as "bourgeois hypocrisy?" Who was it who had said, "Mercy to the enemy is cruelty to the people?" Who with a single word could end all this pointless brutality?

By the time I left the hospital the ardor I had once felt for the Cultural Revolution had been replaced by the chill of fear. No one was safe in the atmosphere of paranoia that now prevailed. With my checkered background and my repeated slipups, I was already under suspicion. It was not possible simply to resign from the Red Guards. Once you had been admitted to their ranks, you could never leave. Any attempt to opt out of the system would send me straight to the cowshed. The only safe course was to take my mother's advice: "Don't say too much. Don't stand on the front lines. Calmly reflect on what is happening. Always remember the victims of the Hundred Flowers Campaign in 1957. They spoke out against the Party and were later declared to be rightists. Don't let this happen to you." This would be my watchword. No more would I be a wooden puppet, brainlessly following orders. I would fade into the background, doing only enough to avoid arousing suspicion. My militance was a thing of the past.

———

"Your fever is down and your nausea seems to have subsided," Doctor Ouyang told me a week after I had been admitted with "appendicitis." "I think it is time you ate some solid food."

That was fine by me. Days of watery broth had left me painfully lightheaded. No feast ever tasted better than the bland dishes of winter-melon soup and rice congee that arrived that noontime.

Yet my nausea returned even before the tray had been taken away. It grew steadily worse, until by midafternoon I was convulsed by a fit of violent retching. Every last grain of rice I had eaten came back up. A high fever followed, and I drifted in and out of consciousness for a day or two.

I awoke to find Doctor Ouyang in conversation with a woman I did not know. "The X ray shows that Nurse Yang has an intestinal blockage," she was saying. "This segment would appear to be narrower than a pencil in diameter. It is also infected, hence the fever. I recommend trying to clear it with oil. If that doesn't work, you can operate."

The treatment prescribed was simple though unpleasant. Once a day peanut oil was poured into my stomach. It was four days before I could keep the oil down, but lubricated by the oil, the blockage gradually broke up.

I was discharged with the admonition that I must never again eat coarse grains like cornmeal, millet, and Kaoliang—especially Kaoliang, which was extremely high in fiber. "If you eat it," Doctor Ouyang told me, "you will surely get another intestinal blockage. The next time it could kill you."

I went from the hospital directly home, where I repeated to Mother the doctor's parting warning. "Nothing but meat, rice, and vegetables is ever going to pass your lips again," she declared at once. "I am in charge of your diet from this day forward." For my first meal she served me a bowl of steamed rice, a small plate of finely chopped vegetables and—wonder of wonders—a whole yellow fish about eight inches long cooked in peanut oil and soy sauce, with garlic and green scallions on top. I was touched by my mother's extravagance.

My embarrassment grew as Mother continued to serve me expensive meals of steamed rice, vegetables, and even meat day after day—while she and my brothers made do with tough Kaoliang cakes or chewy cornmeal muffins. I ate as little as possible of what was set before me. Thinking that my stomach was acting up again, Mother did not scold me for this. I did not tell her that the real reason I left food in my bowl was on account of my guilt.

In January 1967, while I was recuperating at home, the *People's Daily* reported that the Red Guard Rebels had seized power from the capitalist-roaders in Shanghai. Mao applauded this "January storm" and called on his followers everywhere to do likewise. The cry "Seize power!" (*duo-quan*) echoed throughout China. In Shenyang officials at all levels were exposed and targeted. Loyalist organizations came under fierce attack and disappeared virtually overnight. Yao marched on the stronghold of Red Shenyang, and its defenders fled in panic. Lu ordered Doctor Ouyang and other leaders of the hospital Loyalists arrested, and they joined the unfortunate Ah Lung in the cowshed.

Victorious over the Loyalists, endorsed by Chairman Mao, the Shenyang Medical School Rebels, like Rebels everywhere in China, attracted swarms of new members. The membership rolls doubled, then doubled again. For a time Yao and Lu commanded the huge new organization jointly, but the two men soon had a falling out. The Rebels fractured into two competing groups: the Red Guard Rebel General Headquarters, still headed by Yao, and the newly formed Red Guard Rebel Army, headed by Doctor Lu, which drew most of its support from the hospital and the rest from off campus.

I kept up my membership in the Rebel General Headquarters, reporting to the head of my old unit as soon as I was released from the hospital. He did not press me to return to regular guard duty, accepting that I needed time to recuperate from my illness. Later, on his own authority, he gave me a kind of extended medical leave, for which I was extremely grateful. I reported infrequently after that, for I found my visits dispiriting, and not just because the number of prisoners in the cowshed had doubled: My attitude toward the Cultural Revolution itself had changed.

I saw Commander Yao, as he now styled himself, only once on these visits. He was dressed in a new army uniform, tailored to fit, and there was in his bearing an arrogance I had not seen before. A cluster of fawning subordinates practically fought for the privilege of opening a door for him. I was thoroughly disgusted by the whole scene.

"What happened to the egalitarianism of the early days?" I protested to a friend of mine from the propaganda department. "All the leaders are out for themselves now," she responded, giving her head an unhappy shake. "Once the Loyalists were defeated, all the central committee members of the Rebel General Headquarters engaged in a mad scramble for cars, offices, and staff. Now they strut around in new uniforms and address each other using impressive titles they've made up themselves. They still talk about making a Cultural Revolution, but their real loves are eating, drinking, and spending money."

She also talked matter-of-factly about the affairs that a number of leaders, mostly medical students, were carrying on with the nursing students. "Of course, last year such things would have been unthinkable," she said. "Many couples are openly dating, and quite a few are even living together. People say that some nursing students have become pregnant and have been aborted by their medical student boyfriends." In fact, during the next two years, many illegitimate babies were born throughout China from the promiscuity of that time, but none to the women of the Shenyang Nursing School.

The war of words between the Rebel General Headquarters and the Rebel Army continued to escalate. Allegations flew back and forth with dizzying speed, each one more serious than the last. Fights broke out between opposing groups of General Headquarters and Army partisans armed with homemade clubs and spears. Both sides secretly began assembling small arsenals of handguns and rifles, obtained from sympathetic army and police officials.

Open warfare between General Headquarters and Army partisans broke out after Yao's girlfriend, Yali, was killed by a sniper's bullet. After a few pitched battles, with heavy casualties, both sides settled down into a war of attrition. The campus was effectively divided into two sectors, with a broad no-man's-land in between. Snipers were a constant menace, and people quickly learned which paths between buildings were safe to use, and to stay away from windows during the day. Most of the real fighting took place under the protective cover of darkness. Over the next year, at least twenty students from the Shenyang Medical School were killed, and a hundred or more were wounded. Many, many more people died in the city at large.

Sickened by the pointless violence, I reached a turning point. It was time to abandon all pretense of continued involvement with the Rebel General Headquarters. I took off the army uniform—with its Red Guard Rebel armband I had once been so proud to wear—for the last time and hung it in the wardrobe. I vowed that I would not set foot on campus again until the killing had stopped and order had been restored.

I spent the rest of 1967 and early 1968 at home taking care of Ying-yue, who had grown into an energetic seven-year-old. He was fascinated by my uniform, especially its gilt-lettered armband. "I want to be a Red Guard like you and my older brothers," he said at least a dozen times a day. He begged me to sew the armband on his sleeve. This I refused to do. Instead I wound strips of old cloth tightly together until they made a large ball, about the size of a softball, and then stitched the felt armband over it as a cover. It gave me a perverse pleasure to watch Ying-yue playing with his new ball. "You may only play with it inside the apartment," I cautioned him. "You must never take it outside." I was sure that others would not find my little act of rebellion against the Red Guards amusing.

Although I did not realize it at the time, my act encompassed the Great Helmsman himself. I had sold my youth, patriotism, and idealism to Mao in exchange for a vague promise of power and a cheap felt armband. It was his sponsorship that had imbued the armband with magical power, so that it became a sacred and untouchable symbol of authority, used to persecute, maim, and even kill with impunity. It was only fitting that I had taken this armband and turned it into a plaything for children. It should never have been anything else.

In reflecting on the first two years of the Cultural Revolution, Mao must have been pleased by how many of his Jovian shafts had struck home. The teenage Red Guards he had incited to anarchy in mid-1966 had destroyed his enemies outside the Party, inflicting a blow on the "five Blacks" and other "bad elements" from which they would never recover. The Rebels of early 1967 had attacked his enemies within the Party, torturing and imprisoning tens of thousands of so-called capitalist-roaders. Of Mao's arch-rivals, President Liu Shaoqi was now dead and Deng Xiaoping was in Rebel custody. Even the fighting between various Rebel factions later that year had served to advance his aims, thoroughly pulverizing all authority except his own. Now the moment had come to reassert control on his own terms. The army, which up to this point had been kept out of the factional strife, was ordered to intervene in force. Rebel factions were disarmed, and open warfare ceased.

To replace long-defunct party organizations and local governments, Mao invented a new instrument of power: Revolutionary Committees were established at all levels of government, from the provincial down to the county. Dominated by the military, they also included "revolutionary officials" and Rebel leaders. The committees cut their teeth on a nationwide campaign to "clean up the class ranks," which spread terror throughout the population. No one was exempt. Former Rebels found themselves in jail alongside despised capitalist-roaders and "loutish common criminals." Those who had once loved Chairman Mao now feared him.

———

The universities were pacified by Mao Zedong Thought Propaganda Teams. The team that took control of my school consisted of thirty soldiers and was commanded by a retired army lieutenant who had risen through the ranks. Lieutenant Liu was from the countryside and had a pleasant, folksy manner. But he was very small-minded, uninterested in anyone's opinion but his own. We quickly came to detest his lectures, which were filled with the simplest kind of Maoist cant. Everything was Chairman Mao this, Chairman Mao that. For some reason known only to Lieutenant Liu, he decided on the day of his arrival that the "true" Revolutionary Rebels had been the Rebel Army, not the General Headquarters. This was a stroke of good fortune for Doctor Lu, who was allowed to continue in nominal command of the Rebels, into which the General Headquarters was now merged. For Yao, on the other hand, it foretold disaster. As soon as the "cleaning up the class ranks" campaign got under way, the one-time commander of the General Headquarters was arrested and sent to prison. Not that either Yao's fate or Lu's good fortune mattered to me. I was relieved that peace had returned to the campus and anxious to get on with my studies.

As soon as the situation calmed down, all the nursing school students got together and drafted a petition to the new authorities asking that classes be resumed. Though divided on every question but this, all my classmates signed the petition. Classes began again in April 1968. We spent the next six months studying eighteen hours a day, trying to make up for all the time we had lost in the classroom. We graduated on October 20, 1968.

6

Sent Down
to the Countryside

ONCE WE GRADUATED, my classmates and I anxiously awaited news of our job assignments. We all hoped to be sent to hospitals in or near Shenyang, where life was more comfortable than in the more distant towns. Not that our preferences mattered: Our entire future would be decided by a handful of junior officials in the provincial employment bureau who fitted people into openings like identical coins into so many slots. A "good fate" was everything.

On the day our assignments were to be announced, we were called to a meeting with Lieutenant Liu, the head of the Mao Zedong Thought Propaganda Team that now governed our school. While we waited impatiently to find out where we were going, he launched into a speech that, with all its stilted jargon, could have been lifted directly from the pages of the *People's Daily*. "The poor and lower-middle peasant classes have much to teach educated youth such as yourselves," Lieutenant Liu was saying. "This is why our Great Leader

Chairman Mao has called upon educated youth like yourselves to go down to the countryside."

My friends and I exchanged puzzled glances. From the sound of things, we were not going to be posted to Shenyang city—or any other major city in the province, for that matter. Were we about to be assigned to hospitals in county seats or even sent all the way down to commune medical clinics? No one dared ask, but we were by now anxiously hanging on his every word.

"In order for you to learn from the poor and lower-middle peasant classes and participate in rural socialist construction, we have arranged for all of you to be sent down to the Shanhaiguan region," Liu said finally, his face wreathed in smiles.

Shanhaiguan? A low, uneasy murmur arose from my classmates. The Shanhaiguan region was 250 miles to the southwest of Shenyang, a full day's journey by train. Except for a narrow strip of coastal plain, it was a rugged and sparsely populated region.

"Once you reach the Shanhaiguan region, you will be divided into small groups, and sent down to the villages in the interior," Liu went on, his smile never wavering for an instant. "You will not be working as nurses, for that would be putting you above the poor and lower-middle peasant classes. You will share the life of the peasants themselves, living, working, and eating with them that you might better reform your thoughts. Make good use of your new life in the villages. Our Great Leader Chairman Mao believes that the poor and lower-middle peasant classes have much to teach you. You will be building China's great socialist future."

Liu continued to prattle on about how much he had learned from the peasants during the course of his career with the People's Liberation Army, but I was no longer listening. *If Chairman Mao wants me to spend the rest of my life in a village, I will live about one week*. Not that I was afraid of the brutish grind of manual labor or even of the primitive living conditions. It was the skimpy and coarse diet of the countryside that terrified me. The staple food of villagers everywhere in the Chinese Far North was Kaoliang. Sending me to a village was tantamount to a death sentence.

"You will leave for Shanhaiguan by train in two weeks," I heard Liu saying, as if from a great distance.

I hurried over to Lieutenant Liu's office early the following morning, only to find a small cluster of my fellow students already milling around in the hallway outside. All had come to beg Lieutenant Liu to exempt us from the order expelling our graduating class to the countryside.

It was midmorning when my turn came. "As a loyal Red Guard, I would like to respond enthusiastically to our Great Leader Chairman Mao's call," I began. "Unfortunately I have a medical problem which makes it . . . uh . . . inconvenient . . . for me to go down to the villages." I went on to tell Lieutenant Liu the details of my recent hospitalization—what a high fever I had run, how many weeks I had been required to remain in bed, how the doctors had finally diagnosed a partial blockage of the small intestine, how careful I now had to be with my diet. While I was speaking, Liu smiled and nodded continually, which instead of putting me at my ease had the perverse effect of making me even more nervous than I already was. "The doctors have ordered me never to eat Kaoliang again," I stammered in conclusion. "If I do, it could kill me. And in the villages other grains are sometimes, uh . . . difficult . . . to obtain."

"You haven't even been to the Shanhaiguan region yet," Liu responded. "Already you are imagining all kinds of problems. Let me tell you a little secret." At this point he leaned forward over his desk in a conspiratorial manner. "People here in Shenyang don't understand that the Kaoliang in the villages is a better quality than what we get here. Country Kaoliang is easier to chew, more nutritious, and easier to digest. I have a suggestion for you. Why don't you go and try it first and see if it doesn't agree with you. I'll bet that after a few meals, your problem will disappear."

After a few meals of Kaoliang, I'll be dead! flashed through my mind. But I held my tongue. Instead, choosing my words carefully, I said after a moment, "The doctors don't think so, Lieutenant Liu. The doctors say that the fiber in Kaoliang blocks my bowels and makes me deathly ill. Each time I have eaten Kaoliang—even in small amounts—I have had to be hospitalized. I don't want to be a burden on the peasants."

"The poor and lower-middle peasant classes will take good care of you," he responded, waving off my objections. "Should you fall ill, they will take better care of you than your own father and mother. You must place your trust in the revolutionary classes in the countryside. If you don't trust in the poor and lower-middle peasant classes, how can your thoughts be reformed?" Above his vapid smile, Liu's eyes had narrowed and he was watching me closely. Not trusting in the poor and lower-middle peasants was a serious accusation, serious enough in these days to get you tagged a Black. Liu had upped the stakes considerably.

"I trust the poor and lower-middle peasants with all my heart and will," I countered, speaking with what I hoped was convincing sincerity. "I realize I need to be reeducated. I would like to participate in rural socialist construction. But a steady diet of Kaoliang is sure to cause me problems. I will get a high fever and throw up. I will not be able to work in the fields. I don't want to be a burden to the revolutionary peasant classes."

"Do you imagine that you will be eating Kaoliang every day?" Liu queried impatiently. "Under the leadership of Chairman Mao, the communes have greatly expanded food production. Why, the peasants eat better than we do!"

My incredulity at this absurd claim must have been apparent, for Lieutenant Liu quickly shifted gears: "Many of our local Red Guards are being sent to the barren steppes of Inner Mongolia. Others are going to the *Beidahuang*—the Great Northern Wilderness—in the far northeast of Manchuria. You should consider yourself fortunate to be able to stay in China proper."

I did not consider myself fortunate at all, but I refrained from saying so. "I have examined your file from the Red Guard Rebel personnel office," Liu went on, speaking slowly and distinctly. The smile never left his face, but his voice now carried a rasping undertone of threat. "I know that you stayed home for most of the last year. You claim that this was for reasons of poor health. Others have accused you of *tuoli geming luxian*, 'leaving the revolutionary line.' These witnesses say that you early on joined the *siaoyao pai*, those who were content to sit out the glorious revolutionary struggle on the sidelines."

"But I *was* ill!" I protested.

"In my opinion," Liu countered, the note of menace in his voice growing more pronounced, "the only illness you suffer from is the condition of *jiaoqi bing*. You think like the spoiled daughter of a wealthy family, a *xiaojie*. You imagine that you are better than other people and demand special treatment from the People's Government. The best cure for this illness is to spend time in the countryside with the peasants. I promise you that you will be permanently cured of the *jiaoqi bing*." He paused and fixed me with a cold smile. "Should you refuse to be sent down to the countryside, it will prove that you have indeed left the revolutionary line. I would have to treat such a refusal with the utmost seriousness."

Now that I had been openly threatened, I had no choice but to agree with Lieutenant Liu on all counts. Perhaps I *was* just spoiled by city life, I told him. I would answer Chairman Mao's call to go down to the countryside. I would do my best to learn from the poor and lower-middle peasant classes. Liu was still smiling when I left his office a short time later. From my vantage point it was the grimace of death itself.

The next two weeks passed swiftly. Every day more college and middle-school students in Shenyang were summarily "graduated" and ordered to decamp to faraway destinations. A mass exodus of urban youth was under way. With the government in the hands of newly established Revolutionary Committees, Mao had no further use for the Red Guards, who had swept the old administration from power. He wanted these potential troublemakers out of the way.

For all of the high-flown rhetoric about participating in rural socialist construction, my classmates and I instantly understood that we were being sent to the countryside as punishment. Why else would Mao talk about the need for us to be "reeducated" by the peasants through "hard labor"? Why else would we be told that this rural internment was for life, without hope of parole back to the cities? Why else would the most radical Red Guard factions be sent to particularly grim and inhospitable places? I had to admit that Lieutenant Liu was right on one count, though: Compared to the bleakness of Inner Mongolia or the frozen tundra of the Great Northern Wilderness, rural Shanhaiguan was not so terribly uninviting—except for someone who could not digest Kaoliang.

All too soon it was December 28, the date of our departure. I was up early that day, nervously repacking my duffel bag one more time. "I have something else for you to pack," Mother said, coming into my room carrying two small burlap sacks. I knew without looking inside them what they contained. "Here is 20 *jin* of rice," Mother said with studied carelessness. "Maybe you can mix it with your Kaoliang to make it easier to digest."

"Oh, Mother," I said softly. I was unable to meet her gaze for fear of bursting into tears. I swallowed hard, determined not to increase her pain by revealing my own. "You know that we sent-down youth must all follow Chairman Mao's instruction to share the life of the peasants. And they will all be eating Kaoliang. How can I mix rice with mine? I would be criticized."

"Please take it," she urged. "You might have occasion to need it."

I looked up and saw that Mother's eyes were glistening with unshed tears. I nodded brusquely. "All right," I said, "I'll take it."

"I'll send you more when I can," Mother said, watching me happily as I tried to stuff the two sacks into my already overfull bag.

The Shenyang train station was festively decorated to celebrate our departure. A military band, provided by the local army commander, played one stirring march after another. Lieutenant Liu and Doctor Lu gave short, rousing speeches about the glorious experience that awaited us in the countryside. Throughout this forced gaiety, the mood of my classmates remained somber. Their heartbroken parents hovered about, anxiously whispering last-minute instructions about what to eat and wear to their departing offspring. My mother said nothing—what could she say?—but she gripped my hand so tightly it hurt.

After one final speech by a member of the Shenyang Revolutionary Committee, the band launched into the Red Army March. At last we were all aboard. I craned my head out of the window hoping for one final glimpse of my mother. I spotted her on the edge of the crowd, wringing her hands and looking far older than her thirty-seven years. The tears she had held back for so long were streaming down her face. I, too, began to cry, though from sadness or joy I could not say. For the first time in my life, I felt certain that she loved me.

We arrived in Jinzhou City on the morning of December 29 and were herded directly from the train to a waiting column of army trucks. We spent the next three hours bumping over an uneven dirt road that ran ever deeper into the low but rugged hills. From the small opening in the back, we were able to see only where we had been, not where we were going.

When the truck jerked to a halt, we found ourselves in front of the Jin County Government Labor Department. After the fanfare with which we had been sent off, my friends and I had expected to be greeted with banners and bands. Instead our welcoming committee consisted of one elderly man who looked to be well past retirement age. Whispers of disappointment could be heard.

"Welcome to Jin County," the man said after we had quieted down. "I know that you are tired from your long trip, so I am not going to make any speeches. I am the head of the county labor department, which is responsible for assigning you work. Jin County is a poor county, and most of our production teams [villages] are very small, consisting of only ten to twenty families. None can afford to take more than four of you educated youth. Since there are eighty-two of you, we have had to split you up between twenty-one production teams in Lilong Commune. You will spend the night here. Tomorrow morning I will give you your production team assignments. Afterward you will leave for Lilong Commune."

With that we were dismissed. But as the rest of my classmates hurried off to the dormitory the department head had arranged, something made me follow him into his office. Perhaps it was his thoughtfulness in arranging for us to rest here overnight, which we appreciated far more than ceremonial speeches or red paper flowers. Or perhaps it was that when he smiled, he reminded me a little of my father. Whatever it was, I decided to tell him my story.

I went quickly over my hospitalization, my intestinal blockage, my dietary restrictions, ending with my unsuccessful efforts to be excused from this assignment on medical grounds. "I am not a spoiled young lady who thinks herself better than other people," I said with some heat. "I really do have a serious problem. If I am forced to eat Kaoliang at every meal it will kill me."

When I finished speaking, the department head stared at me so long that I began to fidget nervously in my seat. "Nurse Yang," he said finally. "I believe that you have been brought here today to me by heaven. You see, I have exactly the same problem. The first time I ate Kaoliang I became violently ill. The Red Army soldiers in my work team, peasants themselves, laughed at my reaction, calling me a city boy. I was ashamed of what I saw as my weakness, and swore that I would overcome it. You know what happened? I ruined my health in the effort. Why do you think I am so emaciated? Kaoliang ruined my gut. I can't eat anything besides rice congee and broth. Nothing else will stay down. Nurse Yang, there is no shame in being unable to tolerate Kaoliang. You are simply unsuited for rural life.

"Operator," he said, speaking now into the phone. "Get me the provincial department of education." For the next few minutes he went back and forth with some functionary. "She is unsuited for rural life!" the department head finally bellowed into the receiver. "Can you hear me? We cannot use her here in Jin County! She will be a burden to the poor and lower-middle peasants! She must be given permission to go back to the city!" He slammed down the phone and turned to me.

"I am afraid that, because of your illness, we are going to have to send you back to Shenyang City," he said, a smile lighting up his gaunt face and making him look years younger. "The provincial department of education has agreed that this is the only suitable course of action." He wrote out a travel order as I watched, including the fact that he had consulted with the provincial department of education, and then stamped it with the official seal of his department. The next morning I said good-bye to my classmates as they boarded the trucks for Lilong Commune. That same afternoon, I was on a train back to Shenyang.

My mother, who had despaired of ever seeing me again, couldn't believe her eyes when I turned up on her doorstep. I quickly filled her in on my encounter with the head of the Jin County labor department.

Mother said, "You ran into a *guiren*, a saintly person."

The first thing Mother did was call Lieutenant Liu, informing him that I had been *ordered* to return to Shenyang and asking that my urban residency be restored. Liu was sitting in our living room less than an hour later, studying my travel order intently. For once he wasn't smiling. He could not defy the department of education and send me back down to the countryside, but neither was he in a mood to welcome me back. "Whatever the opinion of this county official," he said, waving the travel order disdainfully in the air, "I am still convinced that you left the revolutionary line. And I am not convinced that your allergy to Kaoliang is anything more than an aversion to hard work. If you stay on in Shenyang, it will be as a *hei bukou*, an 'illegal resident.' Perhaps one day soon you will beg me to go back to the countryside."

After he left I started crying. "The other girls got paid when they arrived in Jin County," I told my mother. "I didn't because I didn't officially register as a sent-down youth. I even had to borrow money from my friends to buy my train ticket back. How am I going to repay them? Now I won't be assigned work because I am not officially registered in Shenyang. I won't even receive a rice ration. How can we afford to buy grain on the black market? How will we live? I will be nothing but a burden to you. What a useless girl I am—what a bad daughter! Maybe I should go back to the countryside."

My mother wouldn't hear of it, of course. The next day she went to the Shenyang City office in charge of the program for sent-down youth and complained to the official in charge. The provincial department of education had approved her daughter's transfer back to Shenyang, she told him, and yet his subordinate, Lieutenant Liu, was blocking her reregistration.

This visit had dramatic results. Within the week, my household registration had been restored and I was drawing a grain ration. Though I was not assigned work immediately, the Shenyang Medical College reinstituted my scholarship. I stayed home for the next six months, going to the school once a month to pick up my scholarship money. Twice on these visits I saw Lieutenant Liu, but both times he walked the other way as soon as he caught sight of me. He had eaten a fly, as we Chinese say, and did not want to be reminded of it.

After six months at home, I finally received my first posting. I was overjoyed to learn that I had been assigned to the Shenyang Tuberculosis Sanitarium, which was only thirty minutes by bus from my mother's apartment. I was to work there for the next eleven years.

As for my classmates, most of them spent several years in the countryside before they were able to beg, bribe, or steal their way back from Shanhaiguan. The last ones didn't show up in Shenyang City until the late 1970s, a decade after they had been sent down.

Shortly after I began working at the Shenyang Tuberculosis Sanitarium, the campaign to learn from the poor and lower-middle peasant classes was greatly expanded to include professionals of all kinds.

Every government organization was told to rotate its cadres down to the countryside for short stays. The head of our sanitarium, a committed doctor and a practical man, quickly divided our professional staff into three teams. Each team consisted of twelve or so individuals—a team head, three or four doctors, four or five nurses, and three or four other technical staff members. Each, he decided, would spend two months out of every six in the countryside. Nominally we would be in the villages to live with the peasants and be "reeducated" by them. In actual fact we would be traveling from village to village and providing much-needed medical care. The sanitarium head gave us three assignments: to diagnose cases of tuberculosis using portable X-ray machines, to inoculate children against this disease, and to treat the common ailments of the peasantry. A couple of years later, after the birth control program had begun in earnest, he added a fourth: to perform sterilizations and IUD insertions on peasant women.

I was to spend a total of three years in the villages over the next decade, although in circumstances far better than those I would have faced as a sent-down youth. My medical team worked out of county hospitals in whose cafeterias steamed rice was often available. When we went down into the villages, as we did frequently, I took a supply of rice with me and cooked my own meals. Everyone on my team was aware of my medical problem and, being doctors and nurses themselves, were mostly sympathetic. Not even our most radical team member, a former Red Guard Rebel still infatuated with Mao, insisted that I eat Kaoliang along with everyone else. By carefully watching my diet, I had no further problems with intestinal blockages and only occasional discomfort.

Our "reeducation" at the hands of the peasantry took the form of "speaking bitterness." This was a ritual in which poor, elderly peasants took turns reminiscing about the hardships of life before liberation. Whenever we arrived in a new village, the local Party chief would call a "speak bitterness" meeting. Then for several hours we would hear depressing tales of rapacious landlords, starving children, and, above all, Japanese cruelty.

After a while the stories we heard in these sessions took on a numbing familiarity, although there were occasional surprises. I still remember one peasant woman, her face lined with the toil of years, who told us of the terrible famine that had once descended on their village. Relief grain was promised but never came. She and her husband had divided their last few ears of Kaoliang between their two teenage daughters, going hungry themselves. A few days later, in a desperate quest for food, her husband had hobbled off in the direction of Shenyang city, but the strength had already left his legs. His body was discovered only a few miles from the village. She had forced herself to go out every day, staggering over the barren fields in a futile hunt for enough bark and leaves and grass to keep her girls alive. First one and then the other had gasped and died in her arms. It was a tale of suffering and loss so heartwrenching that I had to close my eyes against the horror of it.

"My only solace in my old age is my son," the woman said at the end. "Thanks to old heaven he also lived through those difficult years. He was taken away in 1958 to mine coal for Chairman Mao's backyard furnaces and didn't return until the worst of the famine was over." All along I had assumed she was talking about some preliberation calamity, but it was 1960–62 she was talking about. Her family had fallen victim to the Great Leap Forward famine!

Once we had been force-fed our mandatory dose of "reeducation," we got down to the real business of our visit: providing medical care to the villagers. We treated every malady imaginable, from scabies and intestinal worms to farming injuries and tuberculosis.

I threw myself willingly into this work, trying not to complain about the hardships we faced, such as sleeping on the hard surface of a brick *kang* or going a week between baths. My mother and father had been born and raised and come of age in similar circumstances. Some of my colleagues from the sanitarium saw the peasants as crude, unlettered bumpkins and treated them as such. I regarded them as the country cousins, aunts, and uncles I had never met and felt a sense of kinship.

To me, a refugee from a poisonous urban politics in which playacting and deception were the order of the day, the peasants seemed utterly guileless. Certainly no patients could have been more grateful for the treatment they received. "You are really a good *guniang*, a good girl," they would say after I had lanced a boil or stitched and bandaged a cut. "We will never forget you in this life."

The health of many older villagers had been broken by long years of hard labor, poor diet, and chronic infections. Their wounds took longer to heal, their infections stubbornly resisted medication, and their tuberculosis-ravaged lungs were often beyond repair. Our stay in a given village rarely lasted more than a few days, and it was professionally frustrating to have to leave such patients before they began showing signs of improvement. I enjoyed treating the young because they responded better. Young adults could usually be counted on for a speedy recovery from most ailments. Children, for the most part ruddy-cheeked and resilient, made some remarkable turn-arounds.

One day as dusk was approaching, I arrived in a tiny hamlet, little more than a dozen thatched huts of mudbrick perched on the side of a hill. I was working alone, my team having split up to better cover this area of small, widely scattered mountain villages. No sooner had I set foot in the village than a young man appeared in the door-way of one of the huts and started calling out to me. "Miss Doctor, Miss Doctor," he said, anxiously beckoning me to come in. "It's our little daughter, Ah Lan."

There on the family *kang* lay a three-year-old girl. Her mother hovered over her, her face filled with concern. I could tell at a glance that the little girl was deathly ill. Her breathing was shallow and uneven, and her lips were tinged with blue. I felt her brow, and the heat of her fever radiated an urgent warning against my hand.

As I quickly unpacked my medical kit, her father explained to me that Ah Lan had come down with a cold the week before. "We are simple peasants," he said, "We thought if we let her rest for a day or two she would get better. She has always been a strong, healthy little girl. Three days ago she started coughing, a deep, rattling cough. And then yesterday the high fever came. We had planned to take her to the commune clinic today, but we were afraid—" His voice broke in midsentence, but I knew what he was trying to say: Ah Lan wouldn't survive the journey.

I checked Ah Lan's ragged breath with my stethoscope. Everywhere I listened, I heard the hiss and crackle of bubbles as she tried to draw air into her congested lungs. The pneumonia was deep in her lungs and spreading. Another few hours and she would be dead.

I straightened up and looked at the parents. "Pneumonia. Both lungs," I told them. "Ah Lan is very ill." I reached down and smoothed the child's damp hair away from her forehead. She opened her eyes at the touch and looked at me helplessly. "But there are some things we can try."

I did a quick skin test to rule out an allergic reaction. Then I injected her with a potent combination of penicillin and ampicillin. I attached an intravenous glucose drip to her arm to keep her hydrated and gave her another injection to bring down her fever. Finally, to help cool her down, I gave her a sponge bath. Having done all I could, I sat down on the *kang* beside her to keep watch.

We spent the night in darkness. The village had no electricity, and oil was too precious to waste in lamps. I no longer had to use my stethoscope to hear Ah Lan's distress. The sound of her labored breathing filled the pitch-black interior of the hut.

The graylight of predawn revealed the mother's gaze locked on the white, pinched face of her little girl. The child seemed to be breathing on sheer willpower, breathing to please her mother. I looked away. I had done all I could.

As I was sponging Ah Lan off later that morning, she broke out in a light sweat, a sign that her fever was finally breaking. Her temperature dropped rapidly after that, until it was soon back to normal. Her heart was beating normally and a touch of color had returned to her face. Even the bubbly sound in her lungs was less noticeable. I gave her another antibiotic shot. Soon she fell into a deep and peaceful sleep. "I think she is going to be all right," I said to her mother.

Ah Lan bounced back from her illness with the swiftness that only children can manage. By the end of the week, the only sign of her recent illness was a certain lack of stamina. To ward off a relapse,

I continued to give her daily injections of antibiotics. Each time I appeared in the doorway of the hut her mother would call out: "Here comes the *guniang* who saved your life, Ah Lan. You must never forget her."

In April 1972, a few days before my medical team was to leave for its regular two-month stint in the countryside, the head of our sanitarium called a meeting. "Last July the State Council, under the direction of Premier Zhou Enlai, called for strengthening birth control work," he began. "They decreed that the control of births is essential for socialist revolution and socialist construction. Lowering the birthrate is in accord with the fundamental interests of the masses. New regulations have recently been promulgated that will affect our work in the communes.

"In the past we have given priority to diagnosing tuberculosis and curing the common ailments of the peasantry," he continued. "Now the Liaoning provincial department of health has given us a new assignment: birth control. The watchword of the new campaign is 'late, spaced, and few.' 'Late' refers to late marriage. 'Spaced' means that children are to be born at least four years apart. 'Few' means no more than two children. You will help in this campaign by sterilizing and inserting IUDs in rural women as directed by local birth control officials."

We arrived in the countryside to find everyone caught up in a birth control "high tide." Officials of the Women's Federation, an arm of the Communist Party, were barraging local women with the new message: "One is not too few, two will perfectly do, and three are too many for you." Young mothers were informed at mass meetings that large families were now prohibited. Directives were posted in village squares outlining the rewards for accepting birth control—and the penalties for rejecting it. "The struggle for birth control is an important aspect of the class struggle," the posters proclaimed. "Those who oppose it are class enemies." Holdouts were paid house calls and told that they could no longer simply let nature take its course: If their first child had been born within the last four years, they *must* have an IUD implanted; if they already had two or more children, they *must* be sterilized.

The Women's Federation officials were relentless. They kept detailed notebooks on the fertility histories, monthly cycles, and means of contraception (if any) of all the young women under their control. From this information they prepared lists of names—those to be sterilized under the new regulations, those to be fitted with IUDs, those to be X-rayed to see if previously fitted IUDs remained in place. And they served as escorts—one might almost call them guards—for the women on their lists, bringing them one by one to the commune clinics. Often they came into the operating room to witness the procedure. No slipups were tolerated.

Gone were our days as itinerant doctors, traveling from village to village, treating peasants for every ailment under the sun. Now we rarely left the commune medical clinic, where we performed an endless series of sterilizations and IUD insertions. We no longer used our portable X-ray machine to diagnose cases of tuberculosis but only to search out missing IUDs. The device itself, manufactured of steel, showed up in the middle of a fuzzy gray uterus as a crisp white butterfly—if it was where it was supposed to be. Sometimes, over the course of a day, our technician would X-ray as many as a hundred women. Whenever an IUD turned up missing, we replaced it immediately.

During a birth control "high tide" we would perform as many as a dozen tubal ligations a day for eight or ten days running. Though I greatly preferred inserting IUDs, I was sometimes pressed into service as a surgical assistant. I found these marathon sessions physically and emotionally exhausting. We worked very fast—one four-inch incision in the lower abdomen, clamps to hold it open, the bladder flipped up out of the way, left and right fallopian tubes severed, the several layers of muscle and skin sutured back together, and then on to the woman on the next table. "This is like spaying sows or cows," the doctors used to joke coarsely after several days of morning-to-night sterilizations. "I bet we are almost as fast as veterinarians." Indeed, our "patients" might as well have been animals for all the care and consideration we showed them.

It seems incredible to me now, but in the beginning I actually believed that these young women were streaming in for sterilizations of their own free will. We saw them only briefly on the operating table and had no inkling of the sanctions used to get them there. The Women's Federation presented them to us as "volunteers" and insisted that their ever-present "escorts" were only along to provide comfort and assistance. Only gradually did I begin to question what I had been told.

No woman happily submits herself to the knife. But the women we saw, at least a great many of them, were suffering from much more than surgical anxiety. They came into the operating room shuffling their feet and wearing carefully concealed expressions. They laid themselves down on the operating table with a defeated air. Often, as the doctor made his first incision, big tears would form in the corners of their eyes and roll down their cheeks. The first few times this happened I thought that the woman was in pain, so I gave her an additional injection of the local anesthetic we were using. It made no difference. She cried all the same. The members of the Women's Federation who had accompanied the women to "provide comfort" made no effort to do so. Instead they stood aloof, silently observing the procedure from a few feet away. I had been taught not to question government policy, so I automatically pushed the question of coercion out of my mind. But I was occasionally confronted with it in a way I could not ignore.

Two days after I helped sterilize a village woman, her only son was struck down by meningitis and died. Her only other child, I was sad to learn, was a sickly ten-year-old girl, who had a goiter as big as a pomegranate bulging out of the side of her neck. The woman went out of her mind with grief. As soon as she had recovered from surgery enough to walk, she took up a vigil outside the clinic. With loud laments we could hear inside, she mourned her son who was no more. With equally loud curses, she damned us for denying her the ability to bear other sons.

The bereft mother saved her worst venom for the Women's Federation official who had arranged for her sterilization. She began lying in wait for her. When the official appeared, usually bringing yet another woman to be sterilized, she would spring out, cursing, into her path. "You forced me to be sterilized!" she shrieked one day. "You told me it was the law. I was willing to wear an IUD or to take pills. But you wouldn't agree. You told me I had no choice. If it weren't for you, I would be able to have another son in place of my little Ah Ben." A string of curses followed.

The Women's Federation official was a woman of about fifty, with an erect bearing and an air of authority. "I have no sympathy for you," she fired back without hesitation. "No sympathy at all." Women's Federal officials were known for having tongues as sharp as knives and this one could—and did—cut the woman to pieces with a few words. "Everybody knows your house is filthy!" she shouted. "That's why your son died. You practiced poor hygiene. You killed your son, not I! If you want to blame someone for not having a son, blame yourself! It's your fault, not mine!"

By the time the official finished, the woman was reduced to incoherent sobs and moans. Spoken at the time when the boy was not yet even cold in his grave, her callous words sent chills through me. *She has ice water for blood*, I thought, *and a stone for a heart*.

I couldn't tell the Women's Federation official what I was thinking. We Chinese believe that the liver is the seat of courage, and my liver was far too small—*danzi tai xiao*—to say anything publicly, either about the peasant woman's tragic situation or the official's heartlessness. That would be tantamount to criticizing the sterilization campaign itself. But I quietly resolved to try and do something to help.

I went to see the head of our medical team. "You know the woman we sterilized whose only son just died?" He nodded. "Why don't we try to reverse the operation?" I pleaded. "We can at least attempt to reconnect her Fallopian tubes. At least then she would have the hope of conceiving another son."

"That's none of our business!" he said brusquely. "*Shao guan xian shi!* Her problems have nothing to do with us. Our orders are to help the local authorities 'take the work of birth control firmly in hand.' We are here to perform sterilizations, not to reverse them!"

I dropped the matter. It was dangerous in China to be too sympathetic with the problems of others. If you were, it could lead to trouble with the authorities, especially if the problem was related to a government campaign. A few days later the woman disappeared from in front of the medical clinic. Everyone on the medical team was relieved not to have to listen to her shouted curses any longer. I wondered what had happened to her.

It wasn't until 1978 that the sanitarium finally stopped organizing these trips to the countryside. The political line had shifted with Mao's death, and it was no longer necessary for urban residents to be "re-educated" by the poor and lower-middle peasant classes. I did not miss our work in the villages, which over the years had increasingly focused on birth control. The sterilization campaigns were pretty unpleasant business, and I was glad to put them behind me. At the sanitarium I had nothing to do with birth planning, and I preferred it that way.

7

In Search of a "Marriage Object"

I GREW UP into a rather ordinary woman of medium height and slender build. I had Manchu blood on my mother's side, and had inherited the Manchu fair skin and brown hair. My friends considered me pretty, but to my way of thinking my nose was too short and flat. A Mongolian nose, my father used to call it jokingly.

As soon as I reached my twenty-fourth birthday in 1973, my mother decided that it was time to find me a husband. I was still a year away from the legal marriage age of twenty-five, but she calculated that it would take at least that long to find a suitable candidate. She was determined that I would marry well. "You are my only daughter," she told me more than once. "And you have been sickly. We must find a man who will take good care of you. Because you are a girl, our family's bad class background will not be too much of a handicap."

I knew what she meant. By Chinese custom a bride becomes a member of her husband's family. No girl from a Red family would willingly soil her pedigree by marrying into a Black family, or even into a Gray family like ours. Our family's nebulous class background had caused several girls to reject my older brother's suit. The girl Liang-yue eventually married came from a Black family of counter-revolutionaries. For her, marriage into a Gray family was a step up. It was different for me. If I could marry into a Red family, I could pass as Red myself.

Mother counted the attributes of my future husband on her fingers: "First, he must be well educated. Second, he must have a good job. Third, and even more important, he must have a friendly, outgoing personality and a good disposition. Fourth, he mustn't be too tall, too strong, or too quick to anger, lest he *qifu* you, treat you badly, or even beat you. Fifth, he must be in good health and from a good family. Sixth, he should be like your father in every way."

I couldn't have agreed more. I, too, wanted to marry someone with my father's loving disposition, who would be good to me and to our children. In fact, when I closed my eyes and imagined what my future husband would look like, it was my father's kindly face that floated into view.

Mother and I formed an alliance to seek out a suitable "marriage object" for me. Both of us quietly let it be known to our friends and colleagues that I was interested in meeting eligible young men. Since I had reasonably good "qualifications"—a good job, an excellent reputation, and a gentle, soft-spoken demeanor—there was no shortage of interested candidates. It also helped that I faced very little competition. There were many young women my age prettier or more coquettish than I, but most of them were grinding out their lives in pointless labor in the countryside. Men in their mid- to late twenties, on the other hand, who were now seeking brides in their early twenties, were old enough to have escaped being sent down to the countryside in large numbers. The demographics were very favorable.

Some candidates, such as factory workers with only elementary school educations, Mother and I would rule out sight unseen. More likely sounding prospects I would meet for a *xiang-qin*, a formal "premarital encounter." This was more than just a date, because each party went into it knowing that the other was interested in marriage. After my suitor and I had been properly introduced, we would spend a Sunday afternoon getting acquainted, taking a walk in South Lake Park. I am afraid that I wasn't very good company on these outings: I took my job too seriously. I was usually too busy grilling my suitor about his family and his aspirations for either of us to have much fun.

Meanwhile my mother would investigate my prospective suitor's background, using her network of former students as informants. My mother had been teaching in Shenyang since 1956, and it was a rare government office, Party organization, or factory that did not employ one or more of her students. Despite the attacks on teachers during the Cultural Revolution, they still commanded great respect from those they had once taught. Normally, if you wanted to ask a favor of someone in another unit, you went to see them, gift in hand. Such was the high regard in which they held their former teacher that graduates of my mother's fourth-grade class were more than happy to accommodate her for free.

Mother was always able to find former students among my latest suitor's coworkers. Visiting her onetime pupils, she would ask them what they knew about the potential "marriage object" and his family. Was he well liked? What were his prospects in the unit? Was he known for a quick temper? What was his family background? What was his class status? Had he or anyone in his family ever been in trouble during a political campaign?

Next she would go to the apartment where the young man lived and ask his neighbors what they thought about him and his family. Had he ever had any problems with the neighborhood committee or with the local police precinct? What kinds of friends did he hang out with? Sometimes, if she knew someone in his unit's personnel department, she was even able to take a peek at his personnel file. These files were strictly confidential, containing notes on such things as a person's attitude toward the Party, membership in Party organizations, and past brushes with the political authorities, if any. Naturally she didn't want me to get involved with anyone who was likely to be a target of a future political campaign.

Mother was particularly thorough in her inquiries about the Cultural Revolution. She didn't mind if someone had been a member of the *bao huang* faction, the "Loyalists," who tried to protect principals, teachers, and others in positions of authority. She herself had briefly been a member of the Loyalists. Neither did she mind if he was a problem intellectual, a member of the class that Mao disdainfully referred to as the "stinking ninth," since most people with any education had been so designated. But she was opposed to anyone who had been a member of the Revolutionary Rebels, for it was these "rebel barbarians," as she called them, who had persecuted her. Above all, she did not want me matched up with an activist, a former Rebel leader or the like, for it was activists who were responsible for much of the violence and hatred of the Cultural Revolution. Taking the lead in anything political was, as she told me many times, as dangerous as falling too far behind. She was looking for someone who had stayed pretty much in lockstep with the masses. Once she had talked to a young man's friends, neighbors, and co-workers, she would come to me and share the results of her sleuthing.

If our approach sounds businesslike and unromantic, that's because it was. Mother went about her investigations the same methodical way she managed our family food budget. Every penny of information about a potential candidate was valuable. Nothing was to be left in the hands of a capricious fate. What she offered me was a clearheaded evaluation of each "marriage object" from the standpoint of my own self-interest. Had she been aware of Western notions of romantic love, she would have scoffed at them as fanciful expectations that had nothing to do with the reality of married life. To Mother's way of thinking, marriage was a contractual arrangement for procreation, parenthood, and physical security, nothing more. "Love" was not only unnecessary, it was a positive hindrance in making a wise choice.

I shared her views. At least I did not expect to be "in love" with the person I married. It seemed to me that Westerners who married for love, blinded to the faults of the other person, often ended up separating. This was unthinkable in China, where divorce rates were extremely low. I hoped to marry a good man and establish a relationship of trust and mutual respect with him. If I were lucky, this relationship would gradually deepen into love as the years went by, as it had for my father and mother. If I were unlucky or careless in my choice, my future husband and I would end up despising each other. Would I rejoice in my choice of a husband or would I one day come to rue it? I sighed over the weighty consequences of the decision I would soon have to make. I welcomed my mother's advice, knowing that she wanted only heaven's best for me. After each prospective suitor had made his appearance on the scene, we would sit down and compare our impressions of his character, I from my walk, she from her interviews. We invariably agreed.

My first suitor was a handsome young worker named Bai. I had known Bai since 1969, when he had come to my school with Lieutenant Liu's Mao Zedong Thought Propaganda Team. He had kept in touch over the years, stopping by the sanitarium from time to time to chat. I had never given him any encouragement, even though I suspected that he was interested in more than just reminiscing about good times at the Shenyang Medical School. Now, when he stopped by again, I asked him what he liked to do on his days off. One thing led to another, and soon we had a date to visit the Shenyang Municipal Zoo.

I enjoyed our Sunday afternoon together. Bai was as humorously well spoken as ever. He laughed a lot, showing strong, white teeth, and was good company. He was a bright and clever man despite his limited book learning. But I ended the day wondering if Bai's pleasant personality made up for his lack of prospects. After the Propaganda Team had been disbanded, Bai had been reassigned back to his old factory job. He was just an ordinary worker, employed on a truck assembly line. It troubled me that Bai kept turning aside my questions about his future. All he wanted to talk about was the past, when for a time at the Shenyang Medical School he had been a person of substance, a person whose word carried weight. He must have reminded me three times in as many hours that he was responsible for my being in Shenyang. I was grateful to him for his help with my city residence permit, but it irked me that he kept bringing it up.

Meanwhile my mother had been making the rounds of her former students. She hadn't liked what she'd heard. Rumor had it that when Bai was a member of the Propaganda Team he had taken bribes from sent-down youth who had escaped back to the city and needed help obtaining residence permits. "I will just forget about him, then," I told my mother.

Next my supervisor at the sanitarium wanted to introduce me to a nephew of hers. I lost interest as soon as I found out that the young man in question was a soldier. She was amazed by my negative reaction, since at the time the reputation of the People's Liberation Army was flying high. She was convinced that he was the best catch in Shenyang.

But I had my reasons. I wanted children, and had heard that the birth control regulations were strictly enforced in the military. If I married a soldier, sooner or later he would be transferred away from Shenyang, and I would have to go with him, leaving my mother and brothers behind. Even if he continued to be stationed on one of the bases that ringed Shenyang, he would have to stand duty every third or fourth night. He would not be there to help me with the children. And there was always the possibility that he would be sent to a lonely frontier outpost along the border with the Soviet Union. If this happened I and the children would only see him once or twice a year. My mother was against the idea of a soldier, too. "Soldiers have guns and are trained to kill people," she said in her direct, no-nonsense fashion. "What if he gets angry at you?"

———

There were other suitors that year. Walks in the park with a technician, a policeman, and a junior official of the United Department were pleasant outings but led nowhere. Either there was a problem with their family background, or they had been activists during the Cultural Revolution, or they were dull-witted boors. Maybe I was being too picky or too proud, I told my mother.

"Don't force yourself into a marriage you are not happy with," she chided me. "Wait for a bridegroom worthy of the match."

After more than a dozen different "premarital encounters" and still without a fiancé, I began to weary of the whole enterprise. I began rejecting prospective suitors for the slightest flaw, sight unseen, rather than make one more round through South Lake Park, where every path, bench, and tree were now tiresomely familiar to me. Sensing my ennui, even my mother, who was quite anxious to see my future settled, slowed down her search. My next suitor appeared on the scene unexpectedly, outside normal channels, one might say.

I had become very close to one of my patients, a bright and vivacious young woman about my age named Chen Ping. We enjoyed each other's company so much that she took to waiting outside the ward for my shift to end. Then we could have a few minutes to chat as I walked to the nurses' station to check out.

One day I left the ward at the end of my shift to find Chen Ping waiting for me in her usual spot. "Hello, Ah Ping," I greeted her warmly, adding the familiar "Ah" to her given name after the fashion of close friends.

Her usual response was a cheerful hello. Today she burst out: "Do you have a boyfriend yet?"

I was put on the defensive by the bluntness of her question. It almost sounded like an accusation. "As of this minute, no," I said, trying not to let my chagrin show. Why ask me what she already knew?

"That's all right," she said, smiling at me in such a friendly fashion that I felt my irritation ebb away. "Don't be in a hurry. Someone will come along soon."

The next day, as I hurried through the main gate of the sanitarium with the last of the oncoming shift, I saw Chen Ping and her husband standing off to one side of the courtyard. With them was a small man dressed in a gray Chungshan jacket, like a Nehru jacket, and wearing glasses. I stopped involuntarily. *So this was what yesterday's conversation was about!* I realized. *Ah Ping was planning to introduce me to this shrimp and first wanted to make absolutely sure that the field was still open.* I felt my irritation with my friend rising up again. *Ah Ping could at least have asked me if it was all right before bringing this fellow over! That was the way introductions were supposed to be done.* By this time Chen Ping had spotted me and was calling my name and beckoning me to come over. *This is really not the time or the place for a meeting,* I thought. *I'm already a couple of minutes late for my study meeting. And here of all places! If my coworkers find out I am meeting young men in the sanitarium courtyard they will tease me for days.* Chen Ping was calling out my name louder now, and there was nothing I could do but obey her summons lest I call attention to myself. I decided that I would say hello and then excuse myself immediately.

As I crossed the courtyard, I took a closer look at the young man. He was decidedly short, perhaps no taller than I was. He was also slender and pale and had about him a bookish, even scholarly air. "Let me introduce you," Chen Ping said to me as I walked up. "This is Wei Xin. He is an engineer in my husband's factory."

"Hello, Nurse Yang," Wei Xin said politely. "Chen Ping has told me how well you've taken care of her." He was smiling at me in a familiar way, as if we had already known each other for a long time. I smiled back in spite of myself.

"You don't look like you're from around here," I said, stating the obvious. He was a good head shorter than most men in Manchuria, who were tall and robust, at least compared to short, skinny southern boys like him.

"Yes, I come from southern Jiangsu Province, near the city of Nanjing," he answered, the smile never leaving his face. "I have been here for several years. I came in 1970, after the—"

"I'm sorry," I interrupted him, remembering that I was late. "I can't talk right now. I'm already late for my study session." I said good-bye and hastened off, relieved that I had gotten away without committing to yet another "premarital encounter."

Ah Ping trailed behind me the entire day, continually feeding me little morsels of information about Wei Xin: "He is twenty-seven years old, the perfect age for marriage for a man." . . . "He is a graduate of Nanjing University, and is continuing to study to try and improve himself." . . . "He writes beautiful calligraphy." I refused to take the bait.

Ah Ping tried one last tidbit as I got off work. "Wei Xin is a southerner," she said. "Think what that means, Chi An. You know how good southern boys are to their wives. They are more willing to talk over disagreements. They even help out with the housework." I knew that Ah Ping spoke the truth. Manchurian men had a reputation for ordering their wives around and beating them if they didn't obey. My friends all said that they would marry a southern boy if they could. Most didn't have the opportunity. "Have a 'premarital encounter' with Wei Xin," Ah Ping was urging. "See if he isn't more refined and considerate than the other young men you've seen. See if he isn't a classic gentleman."

"I am not interested," I told her, trying to make my decision sound final. "He is even shorter than I am." Wei Xin might be a modern-day Mencius, a contemporary of Confucius's who was a paragon of virtue and filial piety, but I did not want to be let down again.

The next day I was called to the phone at work. I was more than a little irritated when I heard Wei Xin's voice on the other end of the line. Was the "refined and considerate" Wei Xin going to stalk me like some special prey? "I can't talk now," I snapped at him, "I'm at work."

"I only want to ask you one question," he said quickly. "Do you have time during the next few days to go to the zoo?"

Why I hesitated I'll never know. "How about next Sunday?" he pressed.

"Okay," I gave in. He *had* looked slender and pale, like a scholar. Maybe he would turn out to actually be one.

The "premarital encounter" went surprisingly well, perhaps because I didn't think of it as such. Our conversation flowed effortlessly along, from swift shared laughter through slower eddies of reflection, drifting easily from one topic to another. I forgot about my canned list of questions and simply enjoyed Wei Xin's company. Not expecting to find a husband, I made a friend.

Wei Xin had grown up in a village along the lower reaches of the Yangtze River in the lush, subtropical climate of central China. The stories he told about his home made it sound like a Garden of Eden, with teeming ponds stocked with fish, the fields burgeoning with crops of wheat, sweet potatoes, and vegetables year round, and rice—which was for me the staff of life—to eat at every meal.

I watched Wei Xin as he spoke, captivated by his stories. I have always regarded the eyes as a mirror of the mind. They reflect the honesty of the truthful and betray the dishonesty of those who dissemble. Wei Xin's eyes were lively and expressive, laughing when he laughed, smiling when he smiled. They were *shui ling ling*, like a "limpid pool of water." I was soon convinced that there was no guile in him.

All too quickly the afternoon ended. Wei Xin asked to see me again the following Sunday, and I agreed without a moment's hesitation. That night I told my mother all about him, at least what I had been able to find out that afternoon. After the generally gloomy reports of most of my previous dates, I must have sounded as if I'd completely lost my head. Mother listened in silence. When I had finished my long recitation of Wei Xin's virtues, her only comment was: "We'd better check this Wei Xin out."

Mother was a whirlwind of activity for the next few days. She soon struck pay dirt in the person of a former student of hers who worked in Wei Xin's factory. This man knew Wei Xin and thought highly of him. Not only that, he was close to an employee of the factory's personnel office. "I will ask him to take a look at Wei Xin's personnel file," he told my mother. "Come over to my house next Saturday. I will invite him over to tell you what he has found out."

"Wei Xin is well liked by everyone at the factory," Mother told me upon her return from that meeting. "The responsible officials are all full of praise for him. He has a college education and a good job as an engineer. People say that he is very even tempered and gets along well with everyone. And he is in good health." Mother's face wore an expression of triumph.

"Wei Xin's family background is not too complicated either," she continued. "There are a couple of minor problems, though. Wei Xin's father deserted the Red Army for medical reasons, and so this means that his 'family background isn't clear.' This isn't too important, because it involves the father, not Wei Xin himself. Wei Xin was a member of the Revolutionary Rebels. He was also investigated as a possible member of the 516 counterrevolutionary organization, but this history has been cleared. 'It's nothing to worry about,' the personnel clerk told me. 'There won't be any trouble over these old political charges.' "

I listened to my mother aghast. "Minor problems"?! Wei Xin's father had deserted from the PLA, which would make him a counterrevolutionary. Wei Xin himself had been investigated for participating in a major counterrevolutionary conspiracy. And why had Mother passed so quickly over his membership in the Revolutionary Rebels, which she usually referred to as "that band of hateful and violent barbarians"? Why was she ignoring what she had always told me were serious liabilities? One meeting with the personnel clerk, and she seemed convinced that Wei Xin was the perfect match.

"You should definitely continue to see him," she said. "He seems like a fine young man. And one more thing. I would like to take a look at him for myself."

I was to meet Wei Xin at the east gate of South Lake Park at 1:30 the following afternoon. I told Mother that she should go there at that time and pretend to be waiting for someone. "But bring along Ying-yue," I cautioned. "If you are standing there by yourself, you will stick out like a sore thumb." I deliberately did not come until 1:45 P.M., so that my mother could get a good look at Wei Xin while he waited for me. I hurried home after our date. "Well?" I asked my mother.

"I think this one is all right," Mother said straight out, without her customary caution. "He is a little on the short side, but he's a southerner, so what can you expect? You can tell he is a college graduate. He has the air of an intellectual, someone with a lot of ink in his stomach. He looks knowledgeable and forthright. All in all," she concluded, "I think he would be a fine match for you."

This was by far the best evaluation any prospective candidate had ever received from my mother. But I was beginning to feel a bit rushed. "How can you say that?" I objected, hoping to slow her down a little. "You haven't completed your investigations yet."

"I know," she said, "but the personnel clerk raved about him. Now that I have seen him for myself I can tell that he is a refined person. He reminds me of your father."

So that was it! "But he is so short!"

"That's all right," mother said. "So was your father. That means he won't beat you."

I had saved my best argument for last. "But Mother," I objected, "he was a member of the *zao fan* faction. You've always said, 'No Revolutionary Rebels.' "

She dismissed her long-standing opposition to the Rebels with a wave of her hand. "That doesn't matter," she replied airily. "Everyone was a little crazy during the Cultural Revolution. Just find out if he ever hurt anyone."

So it was that on our next date I reluctantly brought the conversation around to my least favorite subject. "What did you do in the Cultural Revolution, Wei Xin?" I asked. I tried to sound nonchalant, but I felt my breath coming faster. What if he started boasting about the high positions he had held in the Red Guard? What if he began bragging about the battles he had fought and won, like some of my previous suitors?

I need not have worried. Wei Xin told me that he had joined the Nanjing University Rebels in October 1966 and had worked in the broadcasting station. His first and only taste of violence had come when he broadcast an editorial accusing the municipal bus drivers of corruption. In retaliation a group of angry drivers had beaten him up so badly that he was left with a hernia. After corrective surgery he had sat out the rest of the Cultural Revolution at home.

What he really regretted about those years, he said, was the education he had lost. At the end of 1968, after only two years of formal instruction, his class was summarily graduated. He spent the next two years at an army farm in Inner Mongolia doing hard labor. When he was finally assigned to work in his field of mechanical engineering, he discovered that he knew next to nothing about it. Determined to remedy his ignorance, he began studying advanced engineering texts in the evening. It had taken him the next four years to master all the material that would have been covered in his junior and senior years at the university.

I was impressed by Wei Xin's drive and determination. The education of every student in China had been cut short as a result of Mao's disdain for book learning. The country was full of half-trained professionals, chemists who didn't understand catalysts, agronomists who didn't really grasp photosynthesis. Most of them tried to pick up on the job what they had missed in class and left it at that.

During my first months at the sanitarium I had floundered about, copying what the other nurses did without really understanding what I was doing. I jokingly described myself to my coworkers as a "barefoot" nurse. But my ineptness was really no laughing matter, for my patients sometimes suffered as a result. Wei Xin, to his credit, was not content to remain a half-trained, "barefoot" engineer like so many of those who had graduated with him. He had set out on his own to educate himself and he had succeeded. I found myself admiring him more and more.

We had talked for an entire afternoon about the Cultural Revolution, and for once I hadn't been put off by the subject, I reported to my mother. "Wei Xin never hurt anyone. He had a hernia and spent the most violent period at home. Just like I did."

Mother stopped what she was doing and looked anxiously at me. "You didn't tell him about your health problem, did you?" she asked. I knew she was worried that news of my poor health might cause Wei Xin to have second thoughts. Brides were expected to be healthy.

"No," I said. "The subject has never come up. When we are together, Wei Xin does most of the talking." Thereafter with Wei Xin I carefully skirted questions about my health. I didn't want to admit to him that I had a problem.

Soon I was counting the days until our Sunday outings. When we were together, we talked constantly. I wanted Wei Xin to *know* me, so I told him everything I could remember about my childhood. Then I listened in turn like a lovestruck schoolgirl as he described growing up in his distant southern village and recalled his father, whom he loved. A curious feeling came over me as I listened to his stories, as though I were a small girl again, sitting snug and warm on my father's lap.

Although Wei Xin and I were eager to be near one another, we rarely touched. When we accidentally brushed against one another while walking or sitting, I felt a rush of warmth and excitement. Once or twice, when we found ourselves alone in a relatively deserted corner of a park, Wei Xin would reach out and take my hand. But as soon as someone came, I would pull my hand back. Such open demonstrations of affection were frowned on in the puritanical atmosphere of the time. Kissing was out of the question, even if we had been able to find a place away from prying eyes.

The only thing that bothered me at all about Wei Xin was his size. He was scarcely taller than I was and lightly built to boot. I didn't like shortness in men or women, because it reminded me of my own past lack of stature. It annoyed me that when we walked down the street he was shorter than all the men and half the women we met. I took to wearing the flattest-heeled shoes I could find on our dates and resolved to concentrate on his good points. It seemed pointless to make his height an issue when everything else was going so well.

Fall came and the weather turned chilly. The crowds in the parks thinned out, and occasionally Wei Xin's gloved hand found its way into mine. "A few more weeks and we won't be able to meet out of doors," he joked. "Maybe it's time I met your mother." I smiled back, for inviting Wei Xin home to meet my mother was the next big step in courtship. There was even a name for it. It was called *Gu Yi Shang Men Yi Ci*, which means "cousin visits the family for the first time." Once my mother met my "cousin" she would have given her approval to the relationship. Wei Xin and I would thereafter be considered practically engaged—that is, unless Mother for some reason took a dislike to him and didn't invite him back for a second visit. Mother issued a formal invitation the following week.

When Wei Xin showed up at my door the following Sunday, I had never seen him look so carefully dressed. He had gotten a haircut, and his shoes were spit-polished to a glossy shine. He looked as if he were going for an interview to join the Party.

He also brought a friend, which was not unusual. The "cousin" often came in the company of someone, an older relative or a friend, who could objectively evaluate the home and offer a second opinion about the young woman. It caused a bit of confusion for my mother, though, who at first thought the friend was Wei Xin. I quickly straightened out the misunderstanding by having them both stand up, and everyone sat down again laughing.

The conversation centered on my mother's polite interrogation of Wei Xin about his background and family. I thought Wei Xin acquitted himself well. Chinese is a language of courtesy and grace and, in the politeness and good manners he showed my mother, he used the language to full advantage. I was pleased at how well he expressed himself. But what was Mother thinking? From time to time as Wei Xin was speaking I stole a glance over at her. I found her expression unreadable. I was sitting on the edge of my seat.

After an hour of conversation, my mother excused herself and went into the kitchen. This was a good sign. According to Shenyang custom, if the mother prepared a meal for the "cousin," she was welcoming him back for future visits. But if she prepared long noodles for the young man and her daughter, she was inviting him into the family as a son-in-law. Long noodles symbolized a long marriage. I got up and followed Mother into the kitchen. "What are you going to make?" I whispered.

"I'm going to make long noodles," she said smugly.

I took a step backward. "But that means we are engaged to be married," I protested. "Why are you moving so fast?"

"You don't understand anything," she whispered back. "He is a good match." She pushed me out of the kitchen. "You just go back and talk to Wei Xin while I fix the noodles."

When the two bowls of long noodles appeared before us, Wei Xin looked overjoyed. His friend hastily excused himself. ("I'm very envious of you," I learned later he had whispered to Wei Xin on the way out. "This is obviously a good family.") The noodles themselves were horrible. Perhaps flustered by the importance of the occasion, Mother added too little water and boiled the noodles into a gummy mass with almost no broth. Wei Xin didn't seem to notice, eating every last noodle in his bowl. Somehow I finished mine, too. It was unlucky not to.

Wei Xin was soon almost a member of the family. He spent every Saturday and Sunday at our apartment, even when I had to work. He would take the late bus back to his factory every Saturday night and be on the early bus back to our apartment on Sunday morning. He sought every opportunity to please my mother—running errands, helping with the housework, and tutoring my youngest brother, Ying-yue, in his junior high school courses. He even helped Liang-yue, my older brother, whose education had been cut short by my father's death, brush up on his math, science, and English. (Later Liang-yue went back to evening school, eventually graduating from a local university. Ying-yue, too, graduated from college. Both ascribe their success to Wei Xin's patient tutoring.)

Pleased by all this, Mother soon suggested to Wei Xin that he simply spend Saturday night at our apartment rather than make the expensive, three-hour round trip back to his dormitory. My younger brothers, who adored their new "elder brother," welcomed him into their room. I slept with my mother, as I had since moving back home after my illness.

I, too, was impressed by Wei Xin's behavior, but I didn't want to marry him right away. What if all his good-deed-doing was just a pose? What if he was just pretending to be agreeable during our engagement and revealed himself to be a monster as soon as we married? Then I would be stuck for life.

It was time to put Wei Xin to the test. I deliberately arrived late for dates to see if he would let his irritation slip. I feigned anger to see if he would snap at me in turn. I pretended to be hurt by something he had said to see if he blamed me for the misunderstanding. But he was always patient, conciliatory, and apologetic. He even made fun of himself for being such a pushover. "There is an old Chinese folk saying," he joked after I had once again gotten my way. "Men who are afraid of their wives prosper."

Wei Xin's most important trial, however, turned out to center on the "Criticize Lin, Criticize Confucius" campaign then under way. Each Wednesday and Thursday we were all required to report to work early for an hour of political study, which we spent reading articles from the *People's Daily* and *Red Flag*, the Party's theoretical journal. The Lin under criticism was Lin Biao, "Deputy Commander in Chief Lin," to whom we had all sworn allegiance in the late 1960s. We were shocked to learn that Mao's "closest comrade in arms" had betrayed him. Lin Biao had attempted a coup against Chairman Mao several years before, we were told, and had died while trying to flee to the Soviet Union. The other object of criticism was Confucius, China's ancient sage, whom up to now we had been taught to respect, if no longer to revere. Lin's double cross and Confucius's failings were supposedly explained in our study material, which we read out loud and then discussed in our political study groups.

From whispered conferences with my friends I knew they were having the same problem I was: What did China's ancient sage have to do with this modern-day traitor? Who, in short, was the real target? Uncertain of our ground, all of us were careful in what we said. During our discussion sessions, we took turns hectoring Lin Biao mercilessly. Our criticism of Confucius was more restrained. Few tried the political high-wire act of linking the two to the present situation. A slip could be ruinous.

Our writing assignments were even more difficult. Whenever a particularly important editorial appeared in the *People's Daily*, we would all be given copies and asked to "reflect" on it. This meant that we were to write a one- or two-page essay called a *shelun tihui*, or "editorial reflection." These were to be done at home and turned in at the next session, when they would be read aloud and discussed. My study group was chaired by the Party vice secretary of the sanitarium, who took our efforts very seriously.

I labored long and anxiously over each of my early essays. Since it was unclear where the campaign was headed, the only safe thing to do was to paraphrase the original editorial. It was a job that required both a large vocabulary and an acute political sensibility.

My first few efforts did not impress the Party vice secretary, and I decided that the writing of *shelun tihui* was a perfect job for Wei Xin. This was only partly a test of his love. I was more interested in knowing how well developed his political sensibilities were. Would he later get the children and me into trouble by an offhand remark or a carelessly written comment? If Wei Xin could hew to the correct political line during the "Criticize Lin, Criticize Confucius" campaign, when that line was not clearly drawn, then I would be willing to trust him with our future.

Wei Xin did not disappoint me. Not only did he cheerfully take on this new task, he turned out beautiful essays, filled with classical expressions and proper grammar. Neither did his *shelun tihui* contain any careless errors or evidence of latent rightist thought. The Party vice secretary was also impressed. He began asking me to write *zhongxin baogao*, "reports from the Party center" that were required reading for every study group in the sanitarium. Wei Xin's ghostwritten articles were not only polished, they were politically correct.

The mysterious link between Lin Biao the traitor and Confucius the philosopher only became clear after Mao's death. China's sage, who always sought the Golden Mean, had been a foil for Premier Zhou Enlai, the ultimate bureaucratic insider. Mao had come to distrust Zhou because of his behind-the-scenes efforts to douse the fires of the Cultural Revolution. In typically devious fashion, Mao was not willing to attack Zhou directly. But by linking Zhou to the traitor Lin, albeit in a veiled allusion to Confucius, he was trying to tar him with the same brush.

One final hurdle had to be cleared before we could get married: convincing Wei Xin's absent parents to approve sight unseen his choice of a bride. Wei Xin, who prided himself on being a systematic thinker, had devised a three-step plan. First he had written his parents and told them that he had met a young woman through mutual friends. Then, two months later, he had written and described his visit to my family. So far his parents' reaction had been positive.

The third and final step was for Wei Xin to write his parents and formally request their permission for us to marry. Once his parents gave their blessing, we would go to register our marriage with the civil authorities.

However, the real ceremony would not take place until we traveled south to Wei Xin's village. There, in the presence of his relatives and friends, we would kowtow first to Wei Xin's parents and then to his ancestors in the traditional gesture of respect and submission. Then, in my first act of service to my new parents, I would pour out two cups of tea and, kneeling, offer a cup to each. Only then, after I had performed all the duties required of a new daughter-in-law, would Wei Xin and I be considered properly wed.

Wei Xin had already drafted the third letter to his father, yet he held back from mailing it, not wanting his father to think that he was acting impetuously. For my part, I was starting to feel a little anxious, despite Wei Xin's reassurances that asking his parents' permission was just a formality. "My father will be overjoyed that I am getting married," Wei Xin said expansively, adding: "He is the only man over fifty in his village without a beard."

I gave Wei Xin a quizzical glance. What did our getting married have to do with his father's growing a beard? Wei Xin laughingly explained that it was the custom in his village for a man to grow a beard after the birth of his first "proper grandson." A "proper grandson" was the son of his son and carried his surname. Wei Xin's father was a grandfather many times over, but neither of his two sons had any sons of their own. Wei Xin's older brother, whose first two children were girls, was prohibited by the birth control regulations from trying a third time. "It's up to me to give my father a proper grandson," Wei Xin said seriously. "Many men in the village younger than my father are proudly wearing beards. My father is still clean shaven. I know he wants a proper grandson very badly. He will welcome you into the family." I said nothing, a little embarrassed by the unexpected turn the conversation had taken.

One day when I got off work, I unexpectedly found Wei Xin waiting for me at the entrance to the sanitarium. I smiled a greeting at him that he did not return. "Chi An, I have something to ask you," he said. His hands were shoved deep into their pockets and his manner was formal, even cold. "Chi An, tell me. Do you have any problems with your health?"

This was the question I had been dreading. There was no way I could continue to skirt the issue. *If I am honest with him,* I thought, *he may end our engagement. Who would want to marry someone with serious health problems? But to deny that I have a problem? That wouldn't be right. Besides, if he found out after we were married, it might sour our relationship forever. I will tell him now.*

"Sometimes my stomach hurts a little," I started, then bit my lip. Despite myself, I was putting the best possible face on things. I took a deep breath and continued in my best clinical manner, as if I were talking about one of my patients. "I have had to be hospitalized three times for a bowel obstruction. The hospital stays have varied from three days to three weeks. The problem is related to a narrowing of the small intestine and can be brought on by too much fiber in my diet. It can also be controlled by a diet of low-fiber food. For the past two years I have had only minor flare-ups, no hospitalizations." I attempted to end on a light note: "Aside from this I am in pretty good shape." It fell flat. Wei Xin only shoved his hands deeper into his pockets. We walked in silence for awhile.

"I have to tell you what I've heard," Wei Xin said at last. His face was grim. "Yesterday I was approached by one of your coworkers. 'Everything about Chi An's family and character is good,' she said to me. 'But she does have a serious problem with her health. I have heard that she has tuberculosis of the intestine. Think about

what you are about to do. She might not be able to have a baby.' "
Wei Xin ended his recitation of the woman's warning and looked at
me, saying nothing, watching my reaction.

The reason for Wei Xin's behavior was suddenly clear. Not just
my health was in question but my ability to bear sons. Not too many
years before, the first obligation of every man in China had been to
continue his father's line. This tradition had weakened in cities like
Shenyang, but it was still strong in the countryside. I didn't know if
Wei Xin saw it as his unbreakable duty to his ancestors to have male
children. But he was very close to his father and wanted, above all,
to please him. And what his father longed for was a "proper grandson," a grandson only Wei Xin could and would provide—unless he
married a woman who was barren.

I plucked up my courage. "I will tell you the simple truth, Wei
Xin. I do not know whether I will be able to have children or not. I
have had health problems—serious health problems—but nothing
specifically to do with . . . *that* area. But there could be a problem I
don't know about. Do you understand?"

Wei Xin understood all too well. I could see him struggling with
himself. Long minutes passed in silence. I longed for him to speak
but dreaded what he might say. When Wei Xin finally spoke, he
endeared himself to me forever. If I hadn't loved him already, I would
have from that moment on.

"After we get married," he began softly, "we will try to have a
baby. If we can, that's fine. If we can't, then we will find a little boy
to adopt. I will tell my father that the child is ours. We will have a
family, and my father will have a proper grandson. That way he can
finally grow a beard."

To me, at that instant, Wei Xin looked six feet tall. I pulled his
hand out of his pocket and clasped it tightly in mine. A passerby or
two cast us disapproving glances, but I scarcely took notice. "Wei
Xin," I said from my heart, "I have found my perfect match. You
are *shiquan shimei*, a perfect ten, complete and wonderful."

8

I Get Married—
After a Fashion

THE RESPONSE from Wei Xin's father was prompt and positive: The Wei family would welcome me into their clan. He suggested in his letter that we plan to come to the village the next May for the traditional wedding feast. This date was still six months away, but there was much to do beforehand. We had to obtain permission from our respective work units to marry, register our marriage at the local police station, and, most important, enter our names on the waiting list for an apartment.

Since I was over the minimum age of twenty-five, my Party secretary gave me permission to marry immediately. Wei Xin's factory, which had the responsibility of providing housing for us, was not so quick to approve. The factory's waiting list for apartments was already several years long. Wei Xin's department head explained to him that "the Party secretary wants us to discourage marriages until we complete a new dormitory." Since at the time no new dormitory was under construction, Wei Xin knew that it might be years before one was built. He turned again for help to his well-connected friend in the personnel department. Within the week he was in possession of an official letter, signed and sealed by the factory Party secretary, which stated that Wei Xin had permission to marry Yang Chi An.

Wei Xin and I walked bravely into the local police station the next day, letters of permission in hand, to register our marriage. Once that was accomplished we would legally be man and wife. However, our courage deserted us as soon as we were inside. We had always been very discreet in our relationship, and here we were about to announce to perfect strangers that we wanted to be man and wife. We stood awkwardly in the middle of the reception area, bumping gently into one another for reassurance, feeling like a couple of bank robbers caught in the middle of a heist—not that anyone paid the slightest attention to us. Police officers bustled about, people came and went, clerks behind counters shuffled papers, all totally oblivious to us.

Wei Xin walked over to the nearest counter. "Can you tell me where the . . . uh . . . registration clerk is?" he asked hesitantly.

The middle-aged female clerk looked up at Wei Xin and then over at me with the kind of bland hostility reserved for struggle objects at a political meeting. "Down the hall," she grunted, dismissing us with a wave.

"She treated us as if we were class enemies," I whispered indignantly to Wei Xin as we walked away. "This is what is called 'putting on official airs to crush the people,' *Guan Chi Ling Ren*. These clerks act as though they were high officials." Wei Xin shushed me as we approached a second counter, behind which sat a much younger but equally forbidding clerk. MARRIAGE REGISTRATION SECTION, the sign overhead read.

"We've come to register," explained Wei Xin.

"ID cards and letters of permission," the clerk said curtly, without so much as a word of welcome. We silently handed over our cards and the letters.

She looked them over briefly. "State your name, age, and birth date," she then ordered. She checked our response against the ID cards and the letters.

Her next question was directed to me. Without even the merest hint of feeling, she asked: "Do you really want to get married to Wei Xin?"

I was taken aback by her rudeness. Not even my mother had ever put the question to me so bluntly. Our close friends and family had always understood that the growing closeness between Wei Xin and me would lead to marriage, and it had never been necessary to state our plans to anyone in so many words. Now the clerk stared at me impatiently as I struggled to answer. "Y-yes," I answered finally, in a voice so soft it scarcely carried across the counter that separated us.

Turning to Wei Xin, she repeated the question: "Do you really want to get married to Chi An?"

Wei Xin, having anticipated the question, answered yes in a firm voice.

"Before I can officially accept your application to get married," the clerk said, not lightening up for a minute, "I must read you a document concerning the official policy on birth planning. Our Great Leader Chairman Mao has said that 'population must be controlled,' " she began. "Everyone must understand that struggle for family planning is part of the class struggle. Planned parenthood is essential for socialist revolution and socialist construction. It is in accord with the fundamental interests of the masses. Those who oppose the policy will be criticized and punished."

The regular cadence of her rote speech caused my mind to wander. I imagined the trip that Wei Xin and I would make to his village and the huge and boisterous wedding feast that awaited us. How I looked forward to meeting his father!

"Yang Chi An." The sound of my name brought me back to the present. The official was staring at me impatiently. "Please pay attention," she ordered. "To repeat what I was saying, the current policy is that every couple can have no more than two children. To further reduce the birthrate, these two children must be at least four years apart. You must obtain a quota from your unit before you get pregnant. And you must contracept until you receive a quota. No exceptions are allowed to any of these conditions. You must agree to abide by each and every one of them. Do you agree?"

"Yes," I said quickly, ready to say anything to get this unpleasantness over with. As she repeated herself to Wei Xin, I began to wonder exactly what it was I had agreed to. What was this about a quota for children? While working on the family planning program in the countryside over the past few years, I had never questioned the two-child limit. When the authorities said that under China's present circumstances, two children four years apart were enough, I accepted the argument. But a *quota* to have children? Were Wei Xin and I being told not only how many children we could have but when we could have them? My worst fear was that, because of my health problems, I would not be able to conceive a baby. *I want to start trying as soon as possible,* I thought, *not wait until the authorities give me permission. Just how many years would I have to wait, anyway?* My embarrassment at this whole proceeding began to be replaced by the first stirrings of anger. A quota!

The official was staring at me again. "Have you thought about how you are going to contracept?" I heard her say in her arrogant voice. *This is going too far!* I thought to myself. Wei Xin and I had never even kissed, and here we were being asked how we were going to avoid getting pregnant! I must have clucked my tongue disapprovingly, for her stare hardened. This time even Wei Xin couldn't bring himself to say anything. Out of the corner of my eye, I saw that his face was so red it was purple.

"How are you going to contracept?" she repeated after a few seconds, when we still hadn't responded. Irritation was written all over her face. "Have you heard anything I've been saying?" she demanded.

I worked hard to keep my own face expressionless this time. "Yes," I said evenly. "We have been thinking about it." I meant the exact opposite of what I said. It was having children that I daydreamed about, not years of barrenness. "I will talk to the leaders of my unit about birth planning as soon as we register our marriage."

"This is a very serious question," she continued, unmollified by my vague answer. "The new policy is that a couple must obtain a quota from your unit before you get pregnant. Until you receive a quota, you must contracept. Birth control pills or an IUD are the preferred methods." She started to read an official description of the policy on contraception.

"We know," said Wei Xin, finding his voice at last. "Chi An works in a hospital. Anything related to birth planning she already knows." This was not strictly true, since I worked not in a regular hospital but a TB sanitarium. What I had learned about the program came from my short stints in the countryside. But it was enough to cause the clerk to break off her recitation.

"It is not enough to know what the policy is," she said suspiciously. "You must demonstrate a positive attitude toward the birth planning policy." Passive acceptance of any given Party policy was not enough. Those personally affected by a particular policy were required to publicly affirm their support for the Party's decision. If we didn't agree that the planned parenthood program of the Party was wise and farsighted, she wouldn't marry us. "Well?" she added impatiently. "What is your attitude?"

"We support the leaders," I said with an earnestness I did not feel. "We will do whatever the leaders say."

"Since you already know what the policy is," she said, "it is not necessary for me to say anymore. Sign at the bottom of this document to acknowledge that you agree to abide by the two-child policy," she said, thrusting the paper and a pen in front of us.

I had not anticipated having to sign a formal agreement. My anger flared up again. How dare this officious little busybody tell us how many children we could have and when we could have them?! What business was it of the state how many children Wei Xin and I had? These were decisions that the two of us—and no one else—should have the right to make. I felt my face flush again, this time from anger at this intrusion of the state into my private affairs. *Besides*, I thought bitterly, *I probably won't even be able to have a child. Much less two.* I looked at the piece of paper on the counter in front of us. "Two-Child Agreement," it read. *I will not sign it*, I resolved.

Wei Xin was looking quizzically at my red face and resentful smile. The clerk had already turned away to busy herself with something else. Wei Xin picked up the pen and tried to hand it to me, but I shook my head violently. "I will not sign it," I whispered. "How can we sign such a thing?"

"It's only a piece of paper," Wei Xin whispered back. "What difference does it make?" Pulling the agreement to him he scribbled down the characters of his name, then slid it back in front of me. "It's only a piece of paper," he whispered again.

I understood what Wei Xin was getting at. Many policies in China were never enforced or were enforced for brief periods of time only. There would be a flurry of editorials, propaganda posters would appear everywhere, meetings would be held night after night. And within three months the entire affair would be forgotten. Perhaps this two-child policy would quickly come to nothing as well. Perhaps by the time we had children, the agreement we signed would have been forgotten. Still, I had a strong sense of foreboding as I signed my name under Wei Xin's. I felt as if I were signing the rights to my children away.

The clerk collected the agreement, and quickly filled out two marriage certificates. She disappeared briefly. When she returned, an official police seal was stamped across the lower right-hand corner of the certificates. She handed one certificate to Wei Xin and the other to me.

And that was that. Without fanfare, a word of congratulations, without a ceremony of any kind, Wei Xin and I were man and wife. We stood there stiffly for a second, waiting for some acknowledgment of our new status, but the clerk had returned to her paperwork. I ventured a thank-you. "*Hao le,*" she responded absentmindedly, without looking up. "Okay." We were dismissed.

I did not feel any different, I reflected as we walked back to my mother's apartment. I looked at my marriage certificate and then in annoyance at Wei Xin's copy. "Why did they give us two marriage certificates?" I asked him testily.

"One for you, one for me," Wei Xin answered lightheartedly.

I was unhappy about the way we had been treated and not about to let Wei Xin off that easily. "Don't you think it odd that there should be two marriage certificates?" I persisted. "After all, you and I are joining together, becoming one couple. For a divorce, two certificates are necessary, because the two people involved are going their separate ways. But for a marriage? One should be enough."

Wei Xin did not rise to my challenge. And I could not really let myself go and criticize the Party out loud, even now that Wei Xin and I were husband and wife. The consequences of speaking too freely or carelessly could be unpleasant. So I fumed to myself: *What kind of system marries a couple with a stern lecture about birth control instead of a word of congratulations? The whole experience was more like signing a contract than taking a wedding vow. What kind of system issues two marriage certificates?* The thought that Wei Xin and I were still divided in this way further blackened my already bleak mood.

The state now considered us to be married. The following week at work, the official in charge of birth planning for the sanitarium staff paid me a call. "Here are your birth control pills," she said matter-of-factly, handing me a bottle of pills. "The bottle contains sixty pills, a three-month supply. You take one pill every day for twenty days, and then wait until after your period has ended and start the cycle again."

So much for choosing my own means of contraception, I thought. But what I said was: "Thanks for your concern." I put the bottle aside. I was sure I would not need them until Wei Xin and I were married in the eyes of his family.

Over the next few weeks Wei Xin on occasion hinted that we could legally start living together as man and wife, but I ignored his overtures. The thought of our unhappy "civil ceremony" officiated over by that pompous clerk made me shudder. I made an effort to put the experience out of my mind, succeeding so well that I was soon totally unable to recall the date we had visited the police station. I really didn't consider us to be married. Our twin marriage certificates proved useful in only one respect: We visited the personnel office of Wei Xin's factory and had our names placed on the waiting list for factory housing. Wei Xin continued living in his factory dormitory, and I resided at home with my mother and brothers.

One time, at Wei Xin's insistence, I went over to "see" his dormitory room. As soon as I arrived, all his roommates excused themselves with knowing smiles. He was very excited and maneuvered me into sitting down on his bed beside him. He put his arm around me for the first time, but I quickly shrugged it off. We spent the rest of the afternoon talking at arm's length. The real marriage ceremony was yet to come. I wanted to wait until everything was perfect.

Preparations for the feast in Wei Xin's village went forward. His father, following a fortune-teller's advice, settled upon May 15, 1975, as the auspicious day. He wrote Wei Xin a long letter, detailing his plans to invite all of his friends and relatives from near and far. There would be twenty tables of guests. Since the tables were in rounds of ten, this meant that two hundred guests would witness our betrothal. "Father wants to invite everyone in Village of the Three Brothers," Wei Xin said to me excitedly, waving the letter at me. "The food alone will cost several hundred yuan. But he says that this is the big event of my life, and he wants to do right by me. Father also wants to know what the bride would like for her bride price." He looked at me expectantly, waiting for my answer.

It was the custom in China for the bride to ask the groom's family to buy her presents. The traditional bride price was six or nine ounces of pure gold in the form of heavy earrings, bracelets, and rings. Worn as jewelry during good times, they provided a hedge against famine during bad. After the revolution the Party forbade the buying and selling of gold. Now girls generally asked for "the three things that go round and the one that sounds," namely, a bike, a sewing machine, a watch, and a radio." Sometimes they also demanded the "forty-eight legs," a houseful of furniture, the legs of which totaled forty-eight.

I had never been much interested in material things. When Wei Xin pressed me to name my bride price I shook my head. "I am marrying you because I want to," I told him firmly. "Your family doesn't have to buy me any expensive presents."

Wei Xin looked pleased. "I know my father is worried about the bride price," he told me as he dashed off a letter containing my response. "When my elder brother got married six years ago, it nearly bankrupted our family. My sister-in-law made endless demands for clothes, jewelry, and furniture. It took us several years to pay back the money we borrowed." He looked fondly at me. "I am glad that you are not materialistic like that."

One Tuesday evening in late March Wei Xin showed up at our door. He rarely came over during the week, so I knew at once something must be wrong. He tried to speak, then burst into tears. He handed me a letter and gestured that I was to read it. It was postmarked Village of the Three Brothers, Jiangsu Province.

Dear Younger Brother:

Father has taken ill. For some time he has been having difficulty swallowing. He can eat only rice congee, and then only a little bit at a time.

I took him to see an herbal doctor, who prescribed yin muer [a white fungus that grows on trees]. He said that it would "absorb the poisons in father's body." We have been combing the country markets looking for it, but it is difficult to find. It is also very expensive, about twenty yuan an ounce. We have already spent one hundred yuan.

Following the doctor's instructions, we boil it into a broth for Father
to drink. He sips it slowly. The yin muer seems to help a little, but
it is hard to tell. Father has already lost a lot of weight.

I am sorry to have to share bad news with you. I know that your
wedding feast is less than two months away. But I think that you
should come home immediately.

Elder Brother

I looked up at Wei Xin, who sat hunched forward in his chair, staring down at the floor. How my heart ached for him. I knew that he loved his father as much as I had loved mine. "Wei Xin," I said, choosing my words carefully. "From your brother's letter it sounds serious. I think you better go see your father as soon as you can."

A look of almost physical pain passed over his face. "What would make it hard for Father to swallow?" he asked, looking up at me.

"Well," I said, "it sounds as if his esophagus is partially blocked. That would make it difficult for him to swallow. He may have a tumor, some kind of cancerous growth."

At the sound of the dread word *cancer*, Wei Xin's head sunk into his hands. "No, no, no," he moaned softly.

I spoke quickly to rekindle his hope. "If the cancer is still in its early stages, it is possible to remove the section of the esophagus where the tumor is located, replacing it with a piece of small intestine. But your father needs to be seen as soon as possible by a doctor of Western medicine, not just an herbal doctor, before the cancer spreads."

Wei Xin's strained expression relaxed somewhat at the thought that his father's condition might not be hopeless after all. "I will leave for Village of the Three Brothers tomorrow morning," he resolved instantly. "I will take a week of emergency leave. If I catch the first southbound train out of the station, I will be home within twenty-four hours."

"Of course you will stay here tonight," interjected my mother, who had been listening to our conversation. The station was only a short distance away from our apartment. "Why should you go all the way back to your dormitory tonight," she added emphatically, "and have to retrace your steps tomorrow? Of course you will stay here."

Wei Xin smiled his thanks at my mother, but his thoughts were elsewhere. "My father is a *good* man," he said to no one in particular. "Why must this happen to him?" He turned to me, emotion flooding his voice. "You will like him when you meet him, Chi An. Everyone does. He has a firm jaw, merry eyes, and cheeks that dimple when he laughs. He laughs a lot. He is strongly built, with a ruddy complexion from working out in the fields. And he is much taller than I. Last year he grew a mustache to get a start on the beard he will grow after the birth of his grandson." Wei Xin's eyes grew moist for a moment as he realized that now that day might never come. I reached out for his hand, which gripped mine tightly.

Wei Xin had been in such a wild, distraught state when he had arrived that I was frightened for him. Now, talking about his father, I could see the fear and tension leave his body little by little. "Tell me more about your father," I urged.

"Father joined the Red Army for a brief period of time after the Japanese invasion," Wei Xin continued. "But then he became ill and had to return to Village of the Three Brothers. Because he had experience with the Communists, the villagers asked him to serve as village head in 1948 when it appeared that the Red Army would win the civil war. Later, after collectivization began, he was elected to head the village production team, a post he kept for the next fifteen years.

"Things changed in 1968 during the 'cleaning of the class ranks' campaign. The work team that arrived in the village accused Father of being a deserter and a Nationalist lackey, and forced him to step down from his post. They held struggle meetings to denounce him and paraded him around the village in a dunce cap. They even declared him to be a counterrevolutionary. No villager joined in the denunciations, though, or even so much as laid a hand on him. They were all his friends. They knew he had left the Red Army because of his health. They knew he had served as village head during the last months of Nationalist rule only at his neighbors' insistence. My father had helped them all at one time or another, plowing their fields when they were sick or helping them to build a pigsty. Though they were all in his debt, he never asked them for favors in return.

"My father has a real passion for helping people with their problems," he continued, smiling for the first time that evening. "His motto was, 'Help others even when you have nothing to spare.' 'Remember that when you grow up,' he often reminded us. 'You must do as I do.' "

I smiled to encourage him.

"When he discovered that I had a head for books, he insisted that I study hard. He wouldn't let me work beside him in the fields any longer, even though I longed to spend more time at his side. No one from our village had ever gone to college. Without his encouragement I would not have gone either. I owe my father everything."

As we talked, out of the corner of my eye I saw my mother carrying my comforter into the storage room, which we used as an extra bedroom. A minute later she returned carrying two pillows, which she also put in the storage room.

I excused myself to Wei Xin and then ran into the storage room behind her. She was making up the bed for two people using *my* pillow and comforter. I hurriedly shut the door. "Mother! What are you doing?" I practically shouted at her.

"Can't you see?" she replied calmly. "I am getting the bed ready for you two to sleep in tonight."

"But . . . b-but," I stuttered, casting about for a reason why Wei Xin and I shouldn't sleep together. Since we were already legally married, this was not easy. "We can't sleep in the same room," I said at last in desperation. "What will my little brothers think?"

"Don't worry about them," mother responded. "I'll explain things to them."

"But we haven't had the wedding feast yet."

"That doesn't matter," Mother said gently, as if she were speaking to a child. "Wei Xin's father is dying, isn't he?"

"If he can't eat, then he can't live more than a few more weeks," I confirmed.

"So there won't be any wedding feast in May after all," she pronounced. "Stay with Wei Xin tonight. He needs you."

So it was that four months after we visited the police station, Wei Xin and I spent our first night together as man and wife. As we entered the tiny room that Mother had prepared as our wedding chamber, I was a little sad that we would not have the magnificent traditional wedding we had planned, bowing before Wei Xin's ancestors, serving tea to his parents, and receiving the congratulations of all his kin, near and distant. But later, as Wei Xin clung to me, I realized how right my very sensible mother had been. My husband's beloved father, whom he loved more than anyone in the world, lay dying. It was my responsibility as his wife to comfort him in his grief.

I went with Wei Xin to the train station early the following morning to see him off. We still didn't embrace when we said good-bye, but our eyes were sparkling as we clasped hands instead.

Wei Xin called me from the village two days later. "You were right," he told me, his voice breaking. As soon as he had arrived he had taken his father to the county hospital to be examined. The diagnosis was cancer of the esophagus. It was too late for an operation, the doctor told him. The cancer had already spread deep into the surrounding tissue.

I groaned inwardly, knowing that it was now just a matter of time. "Wei Xin," I said at last, "I have a suggestion. Instead of waiting until May to visit your parents, let's go together after you return. We could leave as early as next week. And why should we spend hundreds of yuan on a wedding feast when your father is ill? Let's just cancel the feast altogether. Instead of wasting the money on food and drink, we can use it on medicine."

"You mean you won't be disappointed?" he said slowly. "I know how much you have been looking forward to the wedding ceremony."

I was touched that even in the midst of his great anguish Wei Xin thought of me and my feelings. "What does all that matter now?" I said, and was surprised to find that it was the truth. "When we arrive, we can tell your father that we have already registered our marriage with the authorities.

"Oh, Wei Xin, I want to meet your father as soon as possible. I want to thank him for raising such a fine son. And I want to tell him that we have come for his blessing."

9

"Together Endure Hardship— Forever Be Close"

*T*HE FIRST DAY of our trip back to Wei Xin's village was a somber affair. Far from his usual talkative self, my husband spent long hours gazing silently out the train window. When he did speak, it was to despair over what we might find when we arrived. "I have only been away two weeks," Wei Xin agonized. "It seems such a short time. But to someone in my father's condition, two weeks is a lifetime. I should never have left his side. Maybe he is now in great pain. Maybe he has fallen into a coma. Maybe . . ."

Though he couldn't bring himself to say so out loud, I knew that Wei Xin feared he would never see his father alive again. "I want Father to approve of you," he insisted, afraid that death might intervene. "I want Father to accept you as his daughter-in-law."

We changed trains in Beijing, and by the afternoon of the second day had passed through Hebei and Shandong provinces into Anhui. As the train hurried southward the landscape grew greener and the weather turned warm, almost balmy. We crossed the Huai River into countryside terraced with rice paddies and thickly dotted with villages. I marveled at the sight of baggy-trousered peasants calf-deep in water transplanting tiny emerald shoots of rice. Though new to me, this was the terrain of Wei Xin's boyhood, and it gradually brought about a change in his mood. After we arrived in Nanjing and boarded a ferry heading down the mighty Yangtze River, he brightened up even more. We were now in his home province of Jiangsu, he told me, just thirty miles from his village.

The Yangtze was teeming with ferries, freighters, and cargo barges, many of them churning mightily to head upriver. But we were going with the current, and the lush, green riverbank slipped by quickly. We passed the mouth of a small tributary, really little more than a stream. "There it is!" Wei Xin shouted excitedly. "There's the Village of the Three Brothers!" I peered up the narrow inlet of the river. About a half mile away, barely visible through the late afternoon haze, was the gray outline of a small village. "The ferry will reach our county seat in a few minutes. Then we can take a smaller boat back upriver to the village wharf. We'll be home before dark."

We left the ferry in the county town. There we hired a small sampan, captained by an elderly man with ropy muscles and skin the color of burned leather. We sat amidships while he sculled his way upriver with surprising vigor and skill, staying in the shallows to avoid the pull of the current. The trip of four, maybe five miles back up the Yangtze was accomplished in only a little more than an hour. Still, it was nearly dusk by the time we turned up the small tributary that led to Village of the Three Brothers. The silver mist of evening had descended over the landscape, and we seemed to be sailing up a gray tunnel. The village remained hidden until we were almost on it, when it seemed to come flying at us out of a cloud, a dense cluster of low-lying buildings.

Only one structure stood out from the rest. Thick wooden columns, originally painted vermilion but now chipped and faded, reached up fifteen feet to support equally thick roof beams, on which rested the traditional upswept roof of a Chinese temple. "That's where I went to grade school," Wei Xin said proudly. "It was built eighty years ago as a hall to honor the First Ancestor." I looked at the stately building with renewed interest. Ancestral halls were rare in Manchuria, which had been settled by Chinese only in the first decades of the twentieth century. "Later," Wei Xin continued, "as the grandfathers of each succeeding generation passed away, names were painted on wooden ancestral tablets and placed on the altar. The Red Army gutted the hall, burning the ancestral tablets, and declared it to be a school. Of course, it had always been a school, but only for young members of the Wei clan. Now it also takes students from several surrounding villages."

Wei Xin led me up the nearest alleyway, past a half dozen houses with identical red clay walls and red tile roofs. In wide-open Manchuria peasants built their homes in different styles and some distance apart. Here the homes all came from the same mold and were packed so closely together that they were almost a solid mass. "Public health regulations say that homes must be built at least twelve inches away from one another," Wei Xin explained. "But everyone wants to squeeze the last few inches of space out of the building lot they have been given. So they are built with their walls practically touching."

We came to Wei Xin's house, and I followed him in through the flanking wooden double doors. The central room was deep in shadow. Wei Xin disappeared into the gloom and there was the click of a switch, but nothing happened. "The power comes on at dusk," I heard him say. "It shouldn't be long now." I stood blinking on the threshold, trying to make out my surroundings. The floor of the rather large room was of hard-packed earth. Furniture was sparse and starkly utilitarian—a table, four chairs, two short benches along the walls. In the very center of the room, resting on wooden sawhorses and dominating all else, was a seven-foot-long pine coffin. Openings in the side walls were covered by curtains.

"Father," Wei Xin called out, "I'm back!" For a second there was no response, then one of the curtains moved. A tiny woman word-lessly beckoned us to come in.

Just as Wei Xin and I stepped into the side room the power came on. Light from a single twenty-five watt bulb suspended from the rafters weakly illuminated a pale man as thin as a matchstick, sleeping on a bed. He lay on his side, with his angular arms and legs—no bigger than a child's—drawn tightly to his body. Hunger had dug great hollows beneath his high cheekbones, and his eyelids were stretched tight over protruding eyes. His ribs—for he was clad only in trousers—could easily be counted. He bore absolutely no resemblance to the ruddy, robust peasant Wei Xin had so often described to me. "Father," Wei Xin called out, more softly this time. "I'm back."

The eyelids fluttered and opened. The hollows widened into a smile of welcome that was painful to behold, for it seemed the grin of a death's-head. With an effort Wei Xin's father lifted his head off the pillow and turned to look at me. "So this is the bride," he said in a cracked voice.

"Yes, Father," Wei Xin said. "This is Yang Chi An."

"Well, let me get up so that we can introduce Chi An to our relatives," his father responded with false heartiness. On Wei Xin's last visit, his father had still had enough strength to walk slowly around the village. He had taken great pride in showing his son, the engineer, off to the rest of the clan. This time, his skinny arms scrabbling for purchase on the bed, he still managed to heave himself up into a sitting position. He scooted himself carefully over to the edge of the bed and set his feet on the floor. Then, taking Wei Xin's hand, he tried to stand, but his eyes rolled up in his head, and he crumpled. Wei Xin caught him as he fell, picking him up easily and putting him back in bed. "He is as light as a child," Wei Xin said to me in an anguished voice. I looked again at the emaciated figure on the bed. So much flesh had already wasted off his body. As a nurse I doubted if he would live out the week. As a wife I said nothing.

Wei Xin's mother hovered anxiously. She had an oval face, delicate features, and was tiny, no more than four feet ten inches tall or so. I saw that Wei Xin took after his mother in his general appearance and lack of height, though her personality seemed as reserved as his was outgoing.

After Wei Xin's father recovered from his fainting spell, the first thing I did was serve tea. While Wei Xin's mother sat beside her husband on the bed, I went through the several steps of the ceremony that would mark my formal entry into the Wei household. First I prepared a tray containing a full teapot and two small cups. Then I knelt on the ground in front of my new parents and poured out two full cups of tea, being careful not to spill any. Then I humbly offered up the cups to each of them in turn, keeping my eyes lowered as a sign of my respect for their new position. "Please have a drink of tea, Father," I said, handing the teacup to Wei Xin's father with both hands. "Please have a drink of tea, Mother," I repeated, doing the same with his mother.

Wei Xin helped to support his father's head while he lifted the cup and took a tiny sip. He immediately grimaced, for the act of swallowing had become very painful. "Please, Father, you don't have to drink it all," I pleaded.

Wei Xin's father took one more small sip and then let his head fall back upon the bed. "Very good, very good," he said with a haggard smile. "You are a good daughter-in-law." Wei Xin and I looked at each other happily. With those words his father had just sealed our marriage. Wei Xin's mother drank her tea in silence.

The next day Wei Xin and I hired a sampan and took his father to the county hospital. Wei Xin was hoping against hope that something could be done to slow the progress of the cancer. I was not optimistic on this count, but I thought that if they could put him on an intravenous drip, giving some nutrition to his starved body, it would extend his life a few days.

We were sent first to the radiology department, where Wei Xin's father was to have a chest X ray. The line outside the department stretched down the hall and out into the courtyard. Nearly two hundred young peasant women, accompanied by several older women, who I gathered were members of the Women's Federation, were waiting for pelvic X rays.

Wei Xin was surprised when I told him what they were there for. I had never shared with him my own experience with the population control campaign in the villages. Before we were married, it hadn't seemed a fit subject for conversation. "You mean all these women are here to have their pelvises checked by X ray?" he said in a low, quizzical voice.

"To make sure their IUDs are still in place," I confirmed. "Steel IUDs are bad for women. They cause pelvic inflammatory disease in the uterus. Plastic IUDs would be better, but they wouldn't show up on the X rays."

"My older brother complained to me last night that they were putting a lot of pressure on him and his wife to agree to sterilization," Wei Xin said thoughtfully. "He said that the birth planning program is really being pushed here in Jiangsu Province, which always tries to be one step ahead of the other provinces politically. I had no idea that it was this stringent already."

The line moved forward slowly. I tried to talk the technician into letting Wei Xin's father go to the head of the line, but he shook his head firmly. "Birth planning comes first," he said. "Orders from the hospital director."

Late that afternoon, after the chest X ray had been taken, I called on the hospital surgeon to see if anything could be done. "Look here, Nurse Yang," he said, holding the developed plate up to the light. It was dominated by a large grayish mass that overshadowed the lungs and heart. "The main tumor is as big as a grapefruit. It is nearly twice as large as it was last month and has branched out to the lungs and stomach. There is no point in trying to remove the main tumor surgically. Mr. Wei has only weeks to live."

I was glad that Wei Xin and his father were waiting outside. "Doctor," I said slowly. "He has not been able to eat for several weeks. Can he not be admitted and put on an IV—at least until he gets a little stronger?"

An exasperated look came over the doctor's face. "There is no point in *either* admitting him *or* putting him on an IV," he said impatiently. "He will not survive much longer whatever we do. We have no beds available for hopeless cases. Besides, as you can see, we are in the middle of a population control campaign. All our beds are occupied by women awaiting birth planning procedures."

"What if you loan me an IV?" I countered. "I would be able to give him glucose at home."

"Out of the question," he interrupted. "We have limited resources here in the countryside. This is not Shanghai—or Shenyang for that matter. There is nothing I can do for you except advise you to keep him comfortable."

Wei Xin's father had long been unable to eat solid food. His only nourishment was rice congee, boiled into a kind of thin glue. This he was able to drink, albeit slowly. He would take a teaspoon-size sip, wait for a minute or two while it trickled down past the obstruction in his throat, and then take another.

After the cancer spread to his stomach, Wei Xin's father experienced ever-greater discomfort after every tiny meal. When the pain of digesting food became too intense to bear, he would put his finger down his throat and gag himself into vomiting up what he had eaten. Then his aching hunger would return, and with it the temptation to eat again. He was soon refusing all nourishment.

Wei Xin's mother continued to give her husband *yin muer* tea to sip, though it was having no perceptible effect on his steadily worsening condition. Wei Xin and I took to combing the hills north of the village in search of this expensive fungus, which grew on rotting wood.

On one of these walks, Wei Xin led me up the hill overlooking Village of the Three Brothers, until the homes below grew small in the distance. "The traditional Chinese description of rural life says it all," he said when we stopped to catch our breath. *"Tian, yuan, mu, lu,* 'Fields, gardens, graves, and stoves.' My ancestors were born beneath those roofs down there. They survived by working those tiny fields and gardens." His face clouded for a minute, and I knew he was thinking of his father. "Did you know that all my ancestors are buried on this hillside where we are standing? It is a perfect site. From here they can look down on the village, gardens, and fields where they spent their lives. They can see the children and grandchildren they left behind."

There was a gray grave marker nearby, and Wei Xin squatted down to carefully brush away the dirt from its base and pull out a few encroaching weeds. "This is my great-grandfather," he explained to me. "I never knew him. But father would take my older brother and me here each spring for the grave-sweeping festival. He always told us if the ancestors were content the descendants would prosper."

Wei Xin's voice caught in his throat. He had to take several deep breaths before he could continue. "My father asked me this morning to do something for him," he said hurriedly. "He said it was time that we decided where *his* grave site was going to be." He looked briefly down at the village below and then turned his gaze back to the slope ahead of us. "Come on, Chi An," he said, taking a step upward. "Let's walk to the very top of the hill, where the view is the best."

On April 29, 1975, Wei Xin's father died. He was conscious until almost the very end, though speaking took a great effort. His last words to me concerned Wei Xin. "Daughter-in-law," he whispered wearily. "Take good care of Wei Xin. He left his home and family as a small boy. He never really came back to us again."

"Yes, Father Wei," I answered, tears springing to my eyes. "Your heart may rest easy. I will take very good care of Wei Xin."

Wei Xin's father closed his eyes. An expression of peace came over his face and he lay still. We thought he was gone. But then his countenance was illuminated by a truly celestial smile. Eyes still closed, speaking so softly that we had to lean forward to hear, he quoted an ancient Chinese poet named Uzyouzi: "Everyone knows that the tiny blades of grass / Can never pay back the sun for the gift of light."

And so Wei Xin's father breathed his last.

The tradition of centuries now took over. The body was washed, dressed in new clothes of black cotton, and placed in the waiting coffin. Family members took turns standing vigil over the coffin. A lamp was lit and kept burning twenty-four hours a day before the funeral, lest the soul of the deceased lose its way.

Wei Xin's elder brother was now the head of the family. After consulting a fortune-teller, he decreed that the funeral would take place two days hence. The grave site Wei Xin and I had selected was located directly above the Village of the Three Brothers, on the very crest of the hill. Wei Xin's brother found it good, and instructed the gravedigger to dig "deep and wide" upon the spot. Wei Xin was told to purchase a grave marker. Wei Xin and I went into town together and watched as the stonecutter skillfully chiseled the characters of his father's name into a two-foot-square granite slab. *"Wei Li-An,"* the marker read when he had finished: "Establish Peace Wei."

On the morning Father Wei was buried, the entire village turned out. Ritual mourning was required by custom, but this time the heads of many of those who straggled up the hill were bowed with real grief. There was no pretense in their keening and wailing. Widows and orphans, the sick and the lame, there were few in the Village of the Three Brothers who had not been touched by one or another of Father Wei's kindnesses over the years. He had been much loved.

After the casket was in the ground and the burial mound was piled high and tamped down, Wei Xin and his brother carefully marked its head with the gravestone. A few feet away they planted a pine tree. It was a tiny thing, only a foot tall and with a trunk no thicker than a match, but the soil here was deep, and Wei Xin's brother had promised to look after it until it was well rooted. When the two brothers had finished, they looked with satisfaction upon their work. "*Wan nian chang qing*," they repeated hopefully to each other. "Green for Ten Thousand Years." In their minds' eye, the little evergreen was already shading this spot with its overhanging boughs, as it would for centuries to come.

Early the next morning, before leaving the village to return to Shenyang, Wei Xin and I visited Father Wei's grave one last time. We picked our way to the top of the hill in the darkness and then sat down by the small tombstone to await the dawn. The land below was wrapped in a black mantle of shadow.

A half hour passed in silence. The light breeze that heralded morning began to play as a crescent of color slowly fanned across the eastern sky. The blackness retreated before the gray light of pre-dawn, revealing fields, gardens, and homes. After only two weeks, the outlines of the Village of the Three brothers were as familiar to me as if I had spent a lifetime there.

"I am grateful that, except for his aching hunger, Father's only discomfort was a feeling of pressure in his chest," Wei Xin said at last. "He was himself to the end, and was never in great pain."

"Because he was such a good man," I added.

"That's what my elder brother says, too," Wei Xin nodded. "He believes that because Father's life was spent doing good for others, he was allowed to die without the pain that normally accompanies cancer."

I ran my fingers over the characters carved into the granite grave marker. The sun burst over the distant hills, its rays setting the crystals in the granite on fire. Only heaven knew for certain, of course, but it seemed to me that the life of Wei Xin's father had paid back the sun in full.

There is a Chinese saying: "Together endure hardship, forever be close." The hardship of this time was Wei Xin's alone, though I felt his anguish as acutely as if it were my own. He told me later that without the solace of my company, the death of his father would have snapped his nerves. During our first few weeks together as man and wife we grew closer than many couples do over two decades. By the time we returned to Shenyang we were no longer newlyweds.

10

I Have Happiness

THE DAY AFTER Wei Xin and I slept together the first time, my ever-sensible mother went down and applied for a birth quota for us from the street committee. She happily informed me of this news when I returned from Wei Xin's village.

"Why so fast?" was my response.

"Better to apply for a quota than to lose a baby," she came right back. Having grandchildren was a hope dear to my mother's heart. My older brother and his wife had so far disappointed her, though not through any fault of their own: His factory had yet to issue them a quota. "What if you are already pregnant?"

Little chance of that, I thought. I hadn't told Mother about the birth control pills I had started taking the morning *after* my first night with Wei Xin.

"You don't understand how strict this planned parenthood business is becoming," she continued. "I went to see my friend on the street committee. She told me that target birthrates and even quotas are now being handed down from higher levels." Mother's friend, a retired teacher named Liu Jiazhen, was the head of the Eastern Gate Street Committee where we lived. She was a paid employee of the municipal government, responsible for pushing, prodding, scolding, and nudging the two hundred-odd families of her "street" into accepting Party policies. She was supported by seven or eight core volunteers, all retired women like herself.

"You ought to see the walls of her office," Mother was saying. "There are charts for everything: how many women are in their reproductive years, how many women must use contraceptives, what kind of contraceptives they use, and who has had an abortion. She also showed me her newest chart: It shows how many birth quotas are available for the coming year and who has applied for them. 'The Shenyang municipal authorities are demanding results,' she told me. Street committees that meet their quotas will be hailed as progressive. Their leaders will be publicly praised and promoted. Those committees that exceed their targeted number of births will be criticized as backward and told to strengthen their leadership."

"What is the quota for our street?" I asked.

"That's the problem," Mother said. "The quota for next year has been set at eight. Can you imagine!" Mother's right hand chopped the air for emphasis. "Only eight babies for more than two hundred families! I couldn't wait for you to return. Twenty-two couples had already applied for a quota. You and Wei Xin are couple twenty-three. The cutoff date is fast approaching."

"Cutoff date?" I queried.

"The cutoff date for being considered for a quota for next year. All interested couples must apply to the street committee by May 30. That's only a few weeks away."

"What happens if I don't get pregnant right away?" I asked, my old doubts about my ability to conceive a child resurfacing.

"The quota is only good for 1976," mother answered. "The baby must be born during the coming year. All couples with quotas can start trying to get pregnant right away. They must get pregnant by next March at the latest. That's so the babies will be born before the end of 1976. Any couple not pregnant by March will lose their quota. They will have to reapply for the following year."

That will be me, I thought, *applying for a quota year after year, unable to get pregnant. Oh, well.* Out loud I said, "I probably won't receive a quota this year anyway, since Wei Xin and I are just married."

Mother went on talking as if she hadn't heard my objection. "They will announce the lucky couples by the beginning of June, Teacher Liu told me. That way the babies are sure not to arrive until January, even if they are conceived at once and are born a month or two prematurely."

A few days later I walked in the front door to find my mother beaming at me. "Congratulations," she said.

"Congratulations for what?"

At this she turned mysterious. "Go see for yourself," she replied. "Look on the bulletin board in front of the street committee office."

People stood ten deep in front of the street committee office, craning their necks to read a big-character poster as tall as a man. Whatever was written on it was happy news, for the black characters had been brushed on bright red paper. Had it been an execution, a government order, or a political essay, it would have been printed in black ink on somber white paper. "What good deeds did these people do?" I heard one little girl ask her mother as I made my way to the front of the crowd.

"These people have received their quota," he mother answered.

"What quota?" she asked.

"Run along and play," her mother told her.

The headline of the poster came as no surprise. PLANNED PARENTHOOD QUOTAS FOR 1976, it read. The first paragraph was an explanation of the birth quota system. I had heard all that already from my mother. I quickly scanned down to the bottom: "The Eastern Gate Street Committee has determined to award a 1976 birth quota to the following eight couples." A short list of names followed. The last two names on the list were Wei Xin and me!

As I turned to leave, I was recognized. "There's Yang Chi An!" someone called out. "Her name is on the list!" A shout went up from the crowd, many of whom had known me since I was a child. Nearly all the families in the area monitored by the Eastern Gate Street Committee had lived there since the early fifties. Repeatedly over the years the street committee had called us together: to hold political study meetings, to promote the pantheon of Communist heroes, to discuss public health issues, or changes in the system of rationing grain and other food. Most of the residents knew one another, at least by sight. Now neighbors and friends crowded round me. "*Gongxi!* Chi An, congratulations!" "Good luck!" "Don't waste any time!" "Congratulations! *Gongxi!*"

I was embarrassed by all the attention. I hurriedly thanked everyone and turned to go. Just then an elderly woman whom I scarcely knew hailed me. "Chi An," she cackled. "Tell your man to get busy!" I practically ran back to my mother's apartment, followed by gales of laughter.

I had underestimated my mother's persuasive powers. Besides her friend, she knew almost all of the old busybodies on the street committee. At one time or another she had had their children or grandchildren in her fourth-grade class. She had gone to see all of them, she later told me, and got them all to agree to back me for a quota. Where there were old debts to be paid, my mother did not hesitate to collect.

The son and daughter-in-law of the cook who lived upstairs were not so well connected. Their names did not appear on the red poster.

My mother, who had long been friends with the cook's wife, decided that she would go cheer up the young couple. "I will tell them that they can always apply again next year," she told me as she disappeared up the stairs. "What is twelve months when you're young?"

She came back half an hour later looking distressed. "The daughter-in-law is already pregnant," she said, shaking her head sadly. "She conceived two months ago. The baby is due in January. She and her husband were hoping that they would receive a quota so that they could keep this child. Now it is impossible. 'The baby will not wait another eighteen months to be born,' the cook's wife told me.

"Her entire family is very upset," Mother went on. "And I don't blame them a bit. To tell someone to destroy a growing baby for lack of a quota seems unnecessarily harsh. But that is what the authorities will do, as soon as they find out the daughter-in-law's condition. They will instruct her to take remedial measures."

I felt a stab of guilt. "Remedial measures" was the standard official euphemism for an abortion. *What if the quota that Mother wangled for Wei Xin and me was originally intended for her?* I thought. *And what if I am unable to become pregnant? I will have caused her to sacrifice her baby for nothing.* "Maybe I should give her my quota," I pondered out loud. "Then she could keep her baby."

"Don't talk foolishness," Mother rebuked me. "It is against regulations to transfer a quota from one couple to another. Otherwise people would be buying and selling them on the black market."

I was off the next day when my mother's friend from the street committee dropped by. "Congratulations," she said when I opened the door. "I came by to give you your authorization to conceive and bear a child. We call it a *Shengchan xuke zheng*, a birth permit." She handed me a pink slip of paper. "Be sure you keep the birth permit in a safe place," she cautioned. "You will need to present it to the hospital when you go in to have your baby. Otherwise the hospital will have to take remedial measures."

She stood up to go. I offered to see her to the entrance of the apartment building, but she politely declined. "I have one more call to make in this building," she said, starting up the stairs to the cook's apartment. I watched her disappear up the stairs, cringing inwardly. I knew that the next message she would deliver would not begin with congratulations.

I looked down at the pink birth permit in my hand. It was dated 1976. The old woman had been right. The clock was now ticking. I had roughly the next ten months in which to conceive a baby. My baby, if there was to be one, had to be born in the coming year. The old woman had joked that Wei Xin should get busy. She didn't know that I was the one with the problem, not Wei Xin.

I was relieved to be able to stop taking the "pregnancy prevention medicine," as birth control pills are called in China. During the month

I had been on them, I hadn't been myself at all. The physical symptoms caused by the pills were bad enough—dizzy spells, periodic nausea, and heavy, prolonged bleeding at menses. Even worse was their effect on my emotions. I had always been a cheerful, even-tempered person, but once on the pill I started experiencing wild mood swings. One minute I would be giddy, the next close to tears. It required all my willpower to keep my emotions in check. Once I was off the pill my problems disappeared virtually overnight. A doctor later told me that Chinese "pregnancy prevention medicine" contained dosages of the hormone progesterone that were higher than many women could safely tolerate, especially those who, like me, were on the small side. The authorities had wanted to make absolutely sure that all pregnancies were in fact prevented.

After we returned from Wei Xin's village we lived with my mother, sleeping in the tiny storage room that had been my makeshift bridal chamber. Knowing that a double bed would never fit between the walls, Wei Xin purchased a twin bed instead. Even this was such a tight squeeze that we had to walk on top of it to get to our portable closet, which itself took up the last few square feet of floor space next to the far wall. As newlyweds, we told each other, we did not need a lot of room.

Living at my mother's apartment seemed the sensible thing to do. The apartment was close to my work, though not to Wei Xin's. When I had to work on weekends, my brothers would be good company for Wei Xin and vice versa. The arrangement made sense economically as well. Food was by far the biggest item in every family's budget. By eating out of the same big pot, we would all save a lot of money.

It was the custom in Shenyang for young people living at home—married or not—to turn every last cent of income over to their parents. After talking it over, Wei Xin and I agreed that I should continue to honor this custom. Come payday, just as I had done for the past six years, I would hand over my pay envelope to Mother.

Wei Xin's pay, on the other hand, we would keep back. Part of it we would send home to *his* mother; the rest we would save.

I had thought that Mother would be pleased by this arrangement. I couldn't have been more wrong.

Payday fell on the last day of the month. I handed Mother my pay envelope, unopened. "Good child," she said absently. Then she turned to Wei Xin. "And where is your pay envelope?" she asked.

Wei Xin looked at her in astonishment. "Here in my pocket," he answered reluctantly.

"Well, give it to Mother," came the reply.

I was dumbfounded that Mother would demand that Wei Xin hand over all his earnings to her. But my gentle, good-natured husband slowly put his hand in his pocket and drew out his pay envelope. Opening it, he took three ten-yuan bills—a little more than half his salary—and handed them silently to my mother. "Give me the rest as well," she demanded.

Wei Xin looked at me in exasperation. "I will gladly give my mother-in-law *part* of my salary every month," he said. "But I will not give her all. I am not her adopted son. I did not marry into the Yang family, like a *ru zui*, giving up my family name for yours." His voice grew louder until he was practically shouting. "I have responsibilities to my mother! How can she demand everything I make?!" Wei Xin threw his pay envelope down on the floor and went into the storage room, slamming the door behind him.

Mother was not in the least nonplussed. "Chi An, give me Wei Xin's pay envelope," she ordered, holding out her hand.

I had to support my husband. For the first time since I was a small child I talked back to my mother. "You're being too unreasonable," I said. I picked up the pay envelope, but instead of putting it in Mother's outstretched hand, I put it in my pocket. Then I followed Wei Xin into the storage room. The next week Wei Xin and I moved to his dormitory.

———

Living at Wei Xin's dormitory presented one major drawback: It was on the other side of Shenyang from the sanitarium. Suddenly my commuting time was quadrupled. From my mother's apartment it had been an easy twenty-five-minute bus ride to work. Now I faced a grueling one-hour-and-forty-five-minute commute, requiring no fewer than three bus transfers. As if that weren't bad enough, I had to stand most of the time. The seats on the buses I rode were usually taken.

Chinese public transportation is terribly overcrowded. In Shenyang as many as one hundred people often crammed their way into a bus built to hold half that number. At the bus stops it was every man, woman, and child for him or herself. Instead of forming a line, those waiting would position themselves in a row along the stretch of curb where the bus stopped. As soon as the doors opened, they would swarm up the steps like angry hornets, pushing, shoving, and elbowing their way on board. At the same time, those passengers who wanted to disembark would be pushing, shoving, and elbowing their way off. While the buses were jam-packed with people all year round, riding them was particularly uncomfortable in the summer heat— and it was early June when Wei Xin and I moved to his dormitory. After nearly two hours standing in a hot, crowded, noisy bus, I would arrive at work and return home at the end of the day exhausted.

Wei Xin's third-floor dormitory room resembled a cell in a Buddhist monastery. There was no kitchen, so we took our meals in the factory cafeteria. The toilets were communal, shared with several dozen other workers. The room's single, soot-stained window looked out on a dreary industrial landscape of factory yards. But it had two twin beds, although we slept together in one, being used to close quarters. Moreover, it had a desk and a wardrobe and was exactly twice the size of the tiny storage closet we had been sleeping in. We joked that we were twice as well off as we had been.

In truth, we were so engrossed in each other that we were largely oblivious to our surroundings. The part of the city where we now lived was given over to huge, state-owned enterprises, yet we walked past the grimy buildings and potholed streets without a second glance. Heavy trucks roared by, belching black smoke; our conversation went on without pause. The clang and throb of the mills and factories did not stop even at night, but through it all we slept peacefully in each other's arms. Because our joy was rooted in our hearts and not in the world around us, it could not be reduced by living in poverty and exile. When Wei Xin surprised me with my favorite snack, a bag of fresh-steamed shrimp, it became a feast of regal proportions. With every mingled breath and laugh we shared, we seemed to grow closer.

As soon as I stopped taking my birth control pills my period was late. Mornings I would wake up feeling tired and out of sorts. My appetite was off. The next time Wei Xin surprised me with a bag of steamed shrimp I couldn't eat a single one. I found even the sight of the bulgy-eyed, pink-skinned, many-legged, fishy-smelling creatures revolting.

At first I thought that this was simply some weird aftereffect of the birth prevention medicine. I was sure that the pills I had been taking had thrown my system off. It did not cross my mind that I might be pregnant. My past health problems had left me convinced that, at best, it would take me a year or more to conceive a child. I often despaired that I would not be able to get pregnant at all. *You are barren*, a small, cold voice would whisper to me during these lows. *You will never have any children.*

Several weeks passed, and still my period did not come. Then one morning as I was getting ready for work I was overcome by a rush of nausea—real nausea that made the bile rise in my throat. I barely made it to the bathroom at the end of the hall before I fell to my hands and knees and threw up. I had only had a light breakfast, and my stomach emptied in a second. *Why is this happening to me?* I thought frantically. *I have no fever, no tenderness in my stomach, so it can't be the same old problem.* A fresh wave of dry heaves hit me, and suddenly I knew. *I was going to have a baby! With all my health problems, with all my fears of barrenness, I was pregnant!* Fortunately Wei

Xin wasn't home, or he would have been bewildered to see me retching and rejoicing at the same time.

I went to see my mother immediately. I was sure that she would be thrilled by my announcement. The rift caused by our moving out—we had not spoken since then—would be healed. "Wei Xin and I are going to need our quota," I announced to her as soon as she opened the apartment door. "I have happiness." To have happiness, *you xi*, is Chinese for "expecting a baby."

Mother's eyes opened wide, and she gave me one of her rare smiles. "So when do I get to hold my grandbaby?" she said instantly. When Wei Xin and I had lived at home, Mother had made me crazy with her constant talk of "holding grandbabies." Now the phrase rang pleasantly in my ears.

"Next year," I answered. "Probably around the end of March."

Mother took me by the hand and led me into the kitchen. "Sit down and rest for a while, Chi An. Let me fix you a cup of tea." I was touched by this gesture, since I had always been the one to fix tea for her, never the reverse. She bustled around the kitchen, chatting happily as she went. "So I am going to be a grandmother. Just wait until Teacher Liu hears the good news. You are the first of the quota couples to conceive!"

Mother placed a cup of hot tea in front of me and then sat down facing me across the table. "Chi An," she said, regarding me with a serious mien. "You are my only daughter. I want you to move back home. I want to take care of you. And one more thing: Don't worry about money."

I could not believe what I was hearing: She was telling me what I had longed to hear since I was a little girl. Not only that, she was putting me ahead of the budget that she agonized over each month. I tried to speak, but emotion had made a fist in my throat.

Mother interpreted my silence to mean that I was unconvinced, and continued her urgings. "You need someone to take care of you, Chi An. Have you had any morning sickness? You need more rest these days, now that there is a child growing inside you." Her words flowed like a healing balm over deep wounds. At last I was able to speak. "Maybe later . . . when I am farther along . . . ," I said haltingly. "First I have to tell Wei Xin. He doesn't yet know that I have happiness."

Sharing the good news with Wei Xin proved more difficult than I had anticipated. Each time I started to speak, I was overcome by an acute sense of embarrassment. The words "I have happiness" just wouldn't come out. It may be hard for someone not raised in the puritanical Cultural Revolution to understand, but I found the subject of pregnancy and childbirth impossible to talk about with a man. Old women who had borne three or four children and grandmothered half a dozen more could speak frankly of such things; I, a newlywed, could not.

Even without a doctor's confirmation, I knew that a child was growing inside me: Morning bouts of nausea left me weak and lightheaded, and it was all I could do to drag myself off to work. Riding on the hot, crowded bus, the nausea would often return with a vengeance. Weight started dropping off my already slender frame at an alarming rate, and in the mirror my face looked pale and haggard.

Despite my misery, I had no choice but to continue working. Simply being pregnant did not qualify me for medical leave. Once I gave birth, I would be eligible for sixty days of maternity leave. My only consolation was the thought that Wei Xin would quickly notice my distress. He would probably even guess its cause.

Weeks passed, and Wei Xin noticed nothing. I woke up gagging and stumbled down the hallway to the bathroom; he slept peacefully on. I rejected the treats he brought home for us to nibble on; he shrugged and ate them himself. I was baffled and hurt by what I read as indifference. *How can Wei Xin not see that I am carrying his child?* I thought. I began sleeping in my own twin bed. I knew I was being childish, but I was too weak and miserable to care.

I was three months along before Wei Xin finally sensed that something was up. I returned from my fourth trip to the bathroom one Sunday morning to find him waiting at the doorway to our room. "Are you feeling all right, Chi An?" he asked. "You look paler than normal. Do you need to go see a doctor?"

I didn't know whether to laugh or cry. I had been sick for weeks on end. I had lost a total of nine pounds. I opened my mouth to give vent to three months of hurt feelings, but the look of loving concern on Wei Xin's face stopped me. My anger faded. "Wei Xin," I said softly, "I have happiness."

"Really?!" Wei Xin burst out. "Truly?!" He leapt to his feet and was almost dancing around the room, talking a mile a minute. "We need to be good parents, Chi An. I want to treat my son the way my father treated me. I want to help him to grow into a fine, upstanding man."

"It may be a little girl, Wei Xin," I cautioned.

"What? A girl?" Wei Xin dismissed the thought with a wave of his hand. "No, I don't think so. I am sure it will be a boy. My father was a good man, a just man, and now he will have his grandson." A look of pain passed across his face. "I only wish he were here to see his first grandson come into the world."

Wei Xin brightened up against almost immediately at the thought of the coming birth. "We need to begin saving money, Chi An. We need to plan for our son's future. We need to make sure that our son receives a good education. We need to make sure that he gets into a first-rate university." Wei Xin was striding up and down the room now, chest out and head erect, the picture of a proud father. "We want our son to go to Nanjing University or even Beijing University."

"The child isn't even born yet, Wei Xin," I broke in, giggling. "Isn't it a little early to start worrying about what college he attends?"

Wei Xin stopped his pacing and burst out laughing. "I *am* being silly, aren't I? But it's just that I'm so happy for us." He sat down beside me on the bed. "I knew you were going to have a baby, Chi An. I knew there would be no problem. *Hao shi you hao bao*, as my father used to say. 'Those who do good will be rewarded.' And you have helped a lot of people."

He put his arm around me, and I leaned back into the comfort of his embrace. "Who was it who said you were barren?" he whispered with mock indignation. His arms tightened around me, and I forgot the heaviness, the discomfort, and the pain of the past few weeks.

From this day forward Wei Xin once again became a model husband. Each day after work he would bring me a large thermos bottle full of stew from the cafeteria. Called *bao jian cai*, or "protect health" food, it was chock-full of chunks of meat or fish. I would tuck into this stew with a real hunger. After my morning sickness passed, I quickly gained back the weight I had lost, and then some.

When I was in my fifth month of pregnancy I was ordered, along with the rest of the sanitarium staff, to go on a "class-education" field trip. Such field trips, designed to improve our class feelings and stir up our class hatreds, had become a fixture of post–Cultural Revolution life. I had already taken part in several and found them loathsome. On one occasion we visited a Japanese prison, now called a "museum of class education," where we were shown barbaric instruments of torture, including pliers used to pull out fingernails and toenails.

This time we were to visit the site of a famous Japanese massacre of Chinese workers, the Ravine of the Ten Thousand, *Wan Ren Keng* in Chinese. When I heard that we would be traveling the entire 150 miles by truck, I went to see the Party secretary. He was a round little man who affected a hearty bonhomie that could disappear in an instant if he was crossed. "I am five months pregnant," I told him. "I've had a difficult pregnancy so far. I am afraid this trip will be too tiring for me."

"Don't worry," he replied patronizingly. "All you have to do is sit on the truck for a couple of hours, walk around at the memorial site, and then ride back. It will be an easy day for you. It is important for you to go. We have arranged this field trip to deepen your understanding of the class struggle. Everyone must take part." My sensitive antennae seemed to detect a snide undercurrent in his voice. *You lack class feelings*, it whispered, *otherwise you would be eager to go.*

The following Sunday morning I and the other off-duty staffers, some sixty people in all, assembled in the courtyard. Soon a single large truck pulled up, and I realized with a sinking feeling that the trip would be standing room only. I scrambled aboard and managed to squeeze my way up to where the front rail provided a handhold. It was lucky I did. The dirt roads of the countryside were heavily rutted from the summer rains. The truck lurched and bounced along, throwing us every which way. I hung desperately onto the rail and flexed my knees, using my legs to absorb the worst of the jolts.

The trip to the Ravine of the Ten Thousand took three hours. My legs were trembling from exhaustion by the time we arrived. I stumbled along behind the group as the guide took us through the museum and out to see the huge mounds of bleached bones in the ravine itself. Already I felt a certain heaviness in my abdomen, but I decided that it was probably just tiredness.

When our visit to the Ravine of the Ten Thousand was over there was a rush for the truck. I was slow boarding and so had to stand in the very back, with nothing to hang on to. The ride back was a nightmare of exhaustion and pain. It was all I could do to keep my feet as the truck pitched and bounced down the road. My legs began to buckle under the strain of absorbing a thousand shocks. The heaviness in my abdomen deepened into an dull ache, and I felt a seeping wetness.

Then, when we were still an hour out of Shenyang, I felt the sharp, stabbing pain of a contraction. *Dear heaven, don't let my labor begin now!* I cried out inwardly. *It's too early!* But a few minutes later I felt another, even sharper pain and then another. I was miscarrying.

Wei Xin, who was waiting for me at the sanitarium, rushed me to the hospital. The doctor on duty did a quick pelvic examination; then he gave me an injection of muscle relaxant. "This should stop the contractions," he told me. "But we will have to wait and see if the heavy bleeding stops. If it doesn't, then we don't want this fetus. We will have to abort."

Fetus . . . abort. The words came as a shock. How could he talk of aborting my baby?! My contractions ended a short time later, but the bleeding continued into the night. Despite my tiredness, I could not sleep. I lay awake waiting for the nurse to come in and check my pads, as she did every hour, hoping that they would be dry. By the following morning no fresh blood was visible. I began to relax a little. "Stay where you are, baby," I whispered, patting my tummy lightly. "It's not time for you to come out yet."

"I think we should stay with your mother until the baby is born," a haggard Wei Xin said to me the following morning. He was as good as his word. After I was discharged, he took me straight to my mother's apartment. Over the next few days he brought over our clothes and other personal items. Nothing more was said about money.

I rested at home for two weeks, spending my time dreaming about the child that I would have. Nearly losing this child had made him— or her—all the more precious to me. I knew that Wei Xin was determined to be a good father. I was equally determined to be a good mother. Wei Xin hoped we would have a boy, but in my mind's eye I saw a little girl with two pigtails. I would not ignore my little girl the way my mother had ignored me. Each day after I returned home from work I would take my little girl on my lap and comb out her long hair. I would even occasionally buy her candy. Not so often as to spoil her, of course, but often enough to let her know that she was loved.

The day after I returned to work, the Party secretary summoned me to his office. I had absolutely no desire to see the man who, in my mind, was responsible for my near miscarriage. I wandered about the sanitarium for half an hour before I overcame my aversion sufficiently to report to him. "I have been very concerned about your health," the Party secretary began in his most solicitous manner. "I know that you are pregnant with your first child. I understand you are feeling better now."

I nodded briefly, having decided to speak as little as possible during the interview.

"Of course," he went on offhandedly, "it was nothing more than a coincidence that you started bleeding on the field trip. It could have happened anywhere. Riding on the truck had nothing to do with it. Your fetus is probably not in the best position. Don't you agree, Nurse Yang?"

I was suddenly angrier than I had ever been in my life. I wanted to scream that he was talking nonsense. *Hu shuo ba dao!* If six hours bouncing over back roads in a truck hadn't caused the bleeding, what had? By insisting that I join the field trip, he had almost cost me the life of my child, yet now he was denying that he was to blame. Worse yet, he wanted me to *agree* that he was not to blame!

"Don't you agree, Nurse Yang?" he repeated, glancing sharply at me.

"No," I started to say, but then my political conditioning took over. The Party secretary of my unit was too important a figure to alienate. If I openly accused him of nearly causing me to miscarry, I would pay for my defiance for years afterward. "I mean . . . the trip had nothing to do with my problem," I stuttered awkwardly, despising myself for my cowardice. "Besides, everything is better now." I tried my best to sound humble and earnest.

Now that I had come around, the Party secretary was all smiles. "If you ever need to take any time off, Nurse Yang, just let me know," he said pleasantly. He held out his hands in a gesture of comradely concern. "I'll be glad to approve medical leave for you."

11

"The Eighteenth Level of Hell"

*T*HE SECOND HALF of my pregnancy was as uneventful as the first had been miserable. There was no longer anything wrong with my appetite. Aided by Wei Xin's daily thermos of "protect health" stew, I gained weight steadily week after week, in the end packing forty pounds onto my slender frame. My stomach grew to enormous size, until my mother began clucking over the difficult delivery I was sure to have. I myself had no such worries. Aside from working, all I did was eat and sleep. As my due date approached I was sure everything would go smoothly.

I was already in bed one evening at nine o'clock when I felt my first contraction. Wei Xin and I quickly gathered together the things I would need and rushed off to the hospital. By the time we arrived the contractions were coming so close together that I was sure the baby would arrive any minute.

The results of the pelvic examination were doubly disappointing. "I can't admit you," the head of the maternity ward said. "Your cervix is only two and a half centimeters dilated, and your water has not yet broken. According to our rules, you have to be dilated to at least four before we can give you a bed." He pulled off his rubber gloves and turned to go.

"Isn't it possible to be admitted early?" my mother asked hopefully. "We live some distance away."

"What would be the point?" he responded. "This is your daughter's first child, so it is going to be quite a long time before she gives birth. Maybe as long as a day. Take her home, and let her sleep for a few hours. Bring her back tomorrow morning, and we will take another look to see how she is progressing."

My contractions were coming so frequently now that I was sure the baby would be born tonight, not tomorrow. "Why go home now?" I insisted to Wei Xin and my mother after the doctor had left. "If I walk for an hour or two I will surely dilate enough to be admitted. Then I can stay here until the baby is born."

My mother was doubtful, but Wei Xin readily agreed that we should stay in the hospital. He did not want to take any chances with either his wife or his child.

I started walking up and down the corridors of the hospital, certain that the exertion would bring my labor to a speedy end. The hours passed and my contractions continued, but to no avail. Several times I asked a maternity ward nurse to check my progress, but each time her answer was the same: I had yet to reach the four centimeters necessary to be admitted. By dawn my entire lower body was swollen from a night on my feet. And I was exhausted.

"Failure to progress," the head of the maternity ward said after examining me in the morning. "You are still only two and a half centimeters. I still can't admit you." Wei Xin started to object, but the doctor rudely cut him off. "We have a shortage of beds here, comrade," he said as he walked away. Since the Cultural Revolution traditional bedside manners had disappeared, and many doctors had become surly and abrupt.

I spent the rest of the day sitting outside the maternity ward, unable to be admitted and afraid to go home. Toward evening the nursing supervisor took pity on me after discovering that I was a fellow nurse. She persuaded the doctor in charge of one of the hospital's general wards to admit me. At last I had a bed and was able to rest, though not to sleep. My painful contractions continued as regular as clockwork, waking me each time I dozed off.

When she went off duty, the nursing supervisor wrote orders that I was to be given a sedative at 8:00 P.M. to ensure that I would get a good night's sleep. When I later asked for the medication, however, I was told that the order had been countermanded by the assistant head of the nursing department. I would get nothing to help me sleep. For the second night in a row, I was unable to do more than catnap. My contractions continued to keep me awake.

For all the medical attention I received over the next twenty-four hours, I might as well have gone home. No doctor or nurse came near me. I was given no pelvic examinations and received no medication. Wei Xin and my mother began to protest this neglect to the hospital staff. I myself grew frantic with worry. What if something went wrong with my baby during my interminable labor? I asked for the nursing supervisor, only to learn that she was not on duty that day.

My mother finally cornered a ward nurse, who reluctantly revealed what the underlying problem was: The head of the maternity ward was upset that I had been admitted to the hospital without his approval. As a maternity patient, I was his responsibility, but now he wanted nothing to do with me. He and the nursing supervisor who had admitted me were old enemies, having been on opposite sides during the Cultural Revolution. Although the Red Guard factions who had once battled for control of the hospital had been disbanded, their members continued to wage guerrilla warfare on one another. They fought over patients and treatments, attacking one another's diagnoses and countermanding one another's orders. The chief of the maternity section had a reputation as a particularly vicious political infighter. The nursing supervisor, a onetime leader of the *baobuang* faction, was only one of many who had drawn his fire over the years.

"Why do you think the nursing supervisor's order for a sedative for your daughter was canceled?" the nurse explained to my mother. "The assistant head of the nursing department is an ally of the doctor in charge of the maternity ward, that's why. They are both former Rebels who hate the nursing supervisor and are constantly on the lookout for ways to spite her and her *baohuang* friends." My mother was angry to learn that I had become a pawn in a political grudge match, but what could she do?

On the morning of my third day in the hospital the head of the maternity ward finally deigned to come and see me. Without examining me, he ordered that I be given a drug called pitocin by intravenous drip. Pitocin, I knew from nursing school, was often given to women who failed to dilate to the 10 centimeters necessary for childbirth. Its usual effect was to immediately strengthen the contractions of the uterus. I reacted differently though, when the pitocin began flowing into my body. My contractions, instead of becoming stronger, merely became erratic and unbalanced. Added to this was a constant cramping feeling that had not been there before.

That afternoon the nursing supervisor, back on duty, stopped by to see how I was doing. She listened closely as I described my contractions and then gave me a thorough pelvic examination. "You have not dilated any more, Nurse Yang," she said when she finished. She reached over and turned off a small valve beneath the IV stand. "There is no point in continuing the pitocin drip. The head of the maternity ward has allowed you to remain in labor too long. Your cervix is no longer sensitive to the touch."

She sat down on the side of my bed and started sketching a figure on the palm of her hand. "This is your uterus," she explained. "Your unbalanced contractions mean that it has taken on the shape of a *hulu* gourd." She drew a picture that looked like a dumbbell, with bulbous ends and pinched middle. "When the lower half contracts, the upper half rests, and vice versa. The problem is the middle, the narrow part here. The middle of your uterus is continuously contracted, putting pressure on the baby. The pitocin was only making this worse."

She took out her stethoscope and listened for the baby's heartbeat.

Her face clouded. "The heartbeat is much too slow," she said. Then, after a pause to time beats against her wristwatch: "Only 57 beats a minute and dropping. It should be about 160 beats per minute. Your baby is in distress, Nurse Yang."

I suppose the nursing supervisor was treating me like a fellow professional, but in my exhausted state I wasn't capable of dealing with this news. All the anxiety, fear, and pain of the last three days welled up inside me, fighting to get to the surface. I was on the verge of hysteria. I put my hands over my ears, trying to shut out the voice of the nursing supervisor. But her final words came through faint but clear: "If this continues, we will lose the baby. This baby has got to come out by cesarean section, and it has got to come out now. I am going to summon the chief surgeon."

The chief surgeon came on the run. He listened briefly for the baby's heartbeat and then took Wei Xin and my mother aside. He was an older man with a shock of white hair. His face wore an expression of the utmost gravity as he spoke. "Do you want to save the mother or save the baby?" I heard him say softly.

I knew that, because I had already been in labor for three days, the chief surgeon wanted to avoid the trauma of a cesarean section. If Wei Xin said he didn't want the baby, then the chief surgeon would continue giving me pitocin until my uterus was dilated, even if this took another day or two. Then he would crush the baby's skull and remove it piece by piece.

"Save the mother!" my mother cried out immediately. The chief surgeon nodded and then looked at Wei Xin, waiting for his response. When it came I could have cried for joy. "Save both of them," Wei Xin said firmly.

"You realize that we may lose the baby anyway because of the effect of the anesthesia," the chief surgeon said. "Or we may find it necessary in surgery to sacrifice the baby to save the life of the mother."

"Just do your best, doctor," Wei Xin said without hesitation. "My wife and I want this baby very much." A nurse brought a consent form for surgery. With trembling hands, Wei Xin signed it on my behalf.

A few minutes later I was being wheeled into the operating room, Wei Xin's words still ringing in my ears. "My wife and I want this baby very much." I felt myself being lifted onto the operating table.

The chief surgeon stood nearby, explaining the upcoming procedure to a young intern. A nurse was laying out his surgical instruments. *This baby is too important to Wei Xin and me to be sacrificed*, I thought. *I must do everything in my power to save my baby. But what?*

An anesthesiologist approached, hypodermic in hand. Suddenly, I knew what I had to do. I pulled my arm away from the needle. "Doctor," I whispered hoarsely to the surgeon. "Could we use acupuncture anesthesia for the operation?"

The chief surgeon broke off his conversation with the intern and gave me a sympathetic glance. He knew what I was thinking: With acupuncture anesthesia my baby would not be exposed to a chemical anesthetic, which in his current weakened condition might be fatal. "Yes," he said gently, "I believe we can." He shook his head almost imperceptibly at the anesthesiologist, who withdrew.

"You are aware, aren't you, of the limitations of acupuncture anesthesia?" the chief surgeon said. "Acupuncture will not completely insulate you from the pain. In fact, on some people it has very little effect. Even if it works perfectly, you will still experience some discomfort during the operation."

"I know," I answered calmly, firmly set upon the course I had chosen. "This is what I want to do."

The acupuncturist came in and set straight to work, inserting needles into the flesh between thumb and forefinger, into my little toes, and into two places on my lower legs. I recognized all these points from my training in acupuncture. The point between thumb and forefinger was *He Ba* ("With Father"), *Tai Chong* ("Grand Flux") was on the outside of the little toe by the nail, and *San Yang Jiao* ("Triple Potent Connection") and *Ding San Li* ("Three Miles Fixed") were both midway up the outside of the calf. All were well known for their efficacy in controlling pain.

By this time the feeling had already left my feet and hands. Now the acupuncturist connected the needles to a six-volt battery to increase the analgesic effect. A tingling sensation—like a thousand tiny pins and needles—climbed rapidly up my arms and legs, leaving numbness everywhere it passed. My ankles, calves, knees, and lower thighs lost feeling in a matter of seconds. My arms and neck tingled and went numb. The pins and needles advanced down my shoulders and up to my upper thighs—and stopped!

A nurse was already prepping me for surgery. The chief surgeon looked impatient to begin. *Hurry up!* I mentally urged the tingling on. *Move up higher!* But nothing happened. The area of numbness had ceased expanding. My limbs were dead to pain, but the skin of my torso was alive to the touch. I felt the cool air of the operating room as the nurse uncovered my abdomen. I felt the scrape of the razor as she shaved off my pubic hair. I felt the coarseness of the sponge as she wiped off my lower abdomen and the chill of the disinfectant alcohol as it evaporated. *Oh, dear God*, I thought, panicked, *I'm going to have to go through this operation without an anesthetic!*

The nurse put a cloth screen in front of my face so I would not see the actual operation. Then she slipped an oxygen mask over my nose and mouth. The oxygen was for my baby, but it had the unwanted side effect of erasing my exhaustion. I was instantly wide awake. Even the numbness in my arms and legs seemed to retreat a bit. My nerves were on edge, alert to every passing sensation. Soon they would be screaming.

I felt the chief surgeon lightly trace a vertical line down my stomach, and my abdominal muscles quivered. *He is showing his intern where he is going to make the incision*, I thought, breaking out into a cold sweat. In seconds I would feel the knife. I grabbed the metal rails on each side of the bed with my hands. I clenched my jaw shut. *Whatever happens, I must not make a sound*, I thought. *Not a sound. I must not upset the surgeon who is going to save my baby.*

All at once someone thrust a fiery poker deep into my vitals. I went rigid with pain and the effort not to cry out. The poker began to move upward, sending shock waves of pain throughout my body. I must have blacked out for a few seconds, for when I came to the fiery poker had stopped moving. I was still in agony. It felt as if I had been laid open from throat to groin. But at least the pain wasn't getting any worse. *The first incision is done*, I told myself, trying to relax my cramped muscles.

"I don't think the incision is quite long enough," I heard the chief surgeon say—too late. Before I could brace myself, the fiery poker was back. The surgeon flicked his scalpel against the upper end of the incision, each flick opening the gash a little more. It felt as if I was being sawn in half by inches. Mercifully I lost consciousness again.

A baby's cry pierced the darkness. I turned away from the sudden brightness of the sound, but something in the cry drew me upward. *Whose baby is crying?* I wondered listlessly. The cry came again. A sense of urgency came over me. I had to find out whose baby it was. The light above me was so bright it hurt my eyes now, and pain once again gnawed at me. I heard voices, but the words were too faint for me to make out their meaning.

I fought my way to the surface. The vast, burning hole of my incision took my breath away. I opened my eyes to find a nurse wiping my forehead with a damp cloth. I tried to ask about the baby I had heard, but no sound came out. "It's a boy," she said, smiling.

I thought my heart would burst with happiness. My baby was alive! I had a little boy! I was so thrilled that for a second I even forgot about the pain.

Then the chief surgeon instructed the intern to remove the placenta. It was as if he was tearing a piece of live flesh from my body. *Think about something else!* I commanded myself. I focused on the white ceiling tiles six feet above my head and started to count them. One, two, three, four. . . . I had reached tile number seventeen when I felt the final wrench of the placenta ripping free. All at once the strength began to drain out of my body. I tried to keep my eyes open but I could no longer focus. The last thing I saw was the ceiling tiles, which now seemed to be splattered with drops of blood.

When I next opened my eyes, I saw that I was receiving a blood transfusion. The ceiling swam hazily into view, and I realized with a start that it had not been my imagination: The white ceiling tiles *were* covered with bright red drops of blood. "How is the patient doing now?" I heard the chief surgeon ask in a tense voice.

"Her blood pressure has stabilized and is climbing," the intern replied. He sounded shaken. "I am very sorry about what happened."

So I passed out from loss of blood, I thought weakly. *What went wrong?*

The chief surgeon gave a loud sigh of relief. "Don't blame yourself," he said, as if in answer to my unspoken question. "I should have waited a little longer before having you detach the placenta. The large artery supplying the placenta shuts down naturally a few minutes after the baby is born. I hurried the procedure. That's why when you pulled out the placenta the artery ruptured."

"I didn't know that performing a cesarean section could be so dangerous for the woman," the intern said in a low voice.

"Every surgical procedure carries with it an element of risk," the chief surgeon replied. "Otherwise we wouldn't require the patient to sign a consent form."

"The patient was very fortunate that the chief of surgery himself was here," the intern said. "When the artery ruptured, you found it immediately and pinched it off. If it had been someone with less experience the patient might not have made it."

"That may be true," the surgeon said with a self-deprecating chuckle. "But always remember one thing: If we had been a little more patient, the problem wouldn't have occurred in the first place. It was touch and go as it was. Here, help me close up."

I knew then that I had almost died from loss of blood. I must have fainted at this point, for I did not feel them stitch me back together.

The next time I opened my eyes I was back in a hospital room. A nurse was placing a fresh unit of blood on the IV stand, replacing one that had already emptied into my body. When she saw I was awake, she gave me an injection of morphine. For the first time the excruciating pain of the incision subsided, and a pleasant feeling of languor came over me.

I asked to hold my baby—and found that I was still caught in the middle of a political firefight. Even after my cesarean, the head of maternity had denied me a bed in his ward. While my baby was taken to his nursery, I myself had been returned to the general ward. This "revolutionary leftist" now refused to allow his nurses to bring my baby over, saying that it was against hospital regulations to expose a newborn to the infectious diseases common to the general ward.

After all I had gone through to give birth to my baby, I was to be denied access to him! I found it difficult to control myself and lashed out at the doctor and the politics that had produced him. The Cultural Revolution had not only destroyed the bedside manners of certain doctors but also their common decency, I sobbed to Wei Xin.

These were dangerous opinions to be voicing, and Wei Xin quickly sought to calm me down. "The important thing is that we have a big, healthy boy," he said, patting my hand. "What you need now is rest. Go to sleep, Chi An. I'll watch out for Tacheng." Tacheng, which meant "great endeavors," was the name Wei Xin and I had decided on. When I heard our son's name on Wei Xin's lips, fresh tears came to my eyes.

"I saw him while he was being washed and weighed," Wei Xin continued, unable to keep the pride out of his voice. "He's a big boy, Chi An, rosy and plump. He weighs eight pounds and four ounces. I think he's going to be tall, not short like me. He has a thick mop of black hair already, and his skin is very white, like yours." I was comforted by Wei Xin's description of Tacheng and began to relax. I was asleep before Wei Xin finished talking.

When my artery had ruptured I had lost a staggering 2,400 cc of blood, or nearly half the blood in my body. Yet, after I had received my second unit of blood, the nurse came to remove the IV setup. Wei Xin knew I had lost a lot of blood, although he didn't as yet know why. He protested that I needed additional blood transfusions, but she told him that no orders had been written for any—nor for pain medication, antibiotics, or anything else. "I haven't seen orders for your wife's postoperative care," she told Wei Xin. "I don't believe that the doctors have written any."

By the wee hours of the morning the morphine had worn off, and I awoke groaning in pain. Wei Xin went to the nurse's station and begged the charge nurse for another injection of morphine. She gave him a couple of codeine tablets. "I cannot give her anything stronger without orders from a doctor," she said apologetically. The codeine helped a little, but I was still in such pain that I could not get back to sleep.

Several doctors made their rounds through the ward the following morning. None paid the least attention to me. When my mother arrived at noon, Wei Xin complained that I had not been examined by a doctor since the operation. "Somebody is responsible for this neglect," Mother declared. "I intend to find out who."

Although I was staying in the general ward, the doctor in charge told my mother that he had admitted me only as a favor to the nursing supervisor. "Your daughter is a maternity patient," he told my mother. "She should be under the care of the head of the maternity ward." With some misgivings Mother went to see this "revolutionary leftist," who adamantly denied any responsibility. "I neither admitted your daughter nor performed surgery on her." He scowled. "See the chief surgeon if you are unhappy with the care she is receiving."

The chief surgeon listened sympathetically to Mother's complaints about my care. "So the head of the maternity ward has not once been in to examine your daughter," he said when she finished, shaking his head in disapproval of his colleague. "It is his area, you know. He is in charge of all maternity cases. He is the one who ought to be providing postoperative care to your daughter."

"But he refuses!" Mother cried out, unable to restrain herself. "Please come and examine my daughter. She is in great pain."

The surgeon took a step back. "I cannot extend my hand too far," he said quickly, "I cannot *shen shou tai chang*. It really would not be appropriate for me to examine your daughter." In response to my mother's pleading, he did write out an order for a stronger pain medication. But that was as far as he would go. He never came to examine me. We later learned that the chief surgeon, tainted by his advanced training overseas, had been a prime target of the Cultural Revolution. Ever since he had been careful not to overreach himself, especially in matters involving his primary antagonist of those days, the head of the maternity ward.

On the third day after my operation the head of the maternity ward appeared in the doorway of the ward. "It looks as if you are doing pretty well," he said, his lips curling in a sardonic smile. "When are we going to release you?"

My mother, who had been upset by her earlier failure to obtain proper medical care for me, could not restrain herself. "How can you talk about releasing her when you haven't even examined her?!" she shouted. "Where have you been for three days? Why don't you look at her chart, which is here at the foot of the bed? Why don't you examine her?"

"Why should I?" he responded haughtily, not moving from his position in the doorway. "I am not the one who admitted her. Nor am I the one who performed the operation. The chief surgeon should be taking care of her, not me." He turned and disappeared.

As the pain of my incision gradually subsided, I discovered other minor injuries from surgery, mostly self-inflicted. I had gripped the rails of the operating table so tightly that my palms were bruised a dark shade of purple. My hands hurt for days afterward. My tongue and the inside of my cheeks were so badly chewed up that it hurt to eat. I must have been biting myself to stop my cries, though I had no recollection of it.

A week after the operation the chief surgeon's intern removed my stitches. As soon as he finished, I announced that I was ready to go home. Wei Xin and my mother couldn't have agreed more. "I can take care of you better at home than they do here," Wei Xin harrumphed.

I was still weak and in considerable pain when I went home, and shortly thereafter I came down with a low-grade fever. A pelvic examination—my first since the surgery—revealed that I had developed an infection in the lining of my uterus, probably because I had been given no antibiotics after the cesarean. It took several weeks of penicillin to clear the problem up.

The head of the maternity section was later forced to step down, though his problems had nothing to do with me or medical malpractice. He had seduced a whole series of young, unmarried nurses with promises of marriage, and two of his conquests eventually turned against him. The first testified that, when she had been ordered down to the countryside, he had falsified a medical excuse for her so that she could remain at the hospital where they could continue their relationship. The second testified that he had gotten her pregnant and had then performed an abortion on her. Unbeknownst to her, he had at the same time inserted an IUD so that he could continue their liaison without fear of further pregnancies.

Later, when the doctor had developed a new romantic interest, both of these nurses went individually to the authorities and complained. After a brief investigation he was found guilty of "destroying the down-to-the-countryside movement" and "destroying the birth control program." He was sentenced to one year of labor reeducation. More important, his license to practice medicine was permanently revoked. I, for one, thought that the punishment fit the crime.

Only after I had been home for several days did I tell Wei Xin the full story of the operation. His eyes grew wide as I told him about choosing acupuncture anesthesia, about the excruciating pain I had endured, and about the arterial hemorrhage that had almost taken my life. By the time I finished talking, he was as pale as a ghost.

"I had no idea . . . you had to go through all that," Wei Xin said haltingly. "I wanted to be with you when you went into surgery, but they made me wait outside. I felt helpless. . . . I breathed a sigh of relief when I heard Tacheng's first cry. But then a long period passed when I heard nothing, and I became very anxious again. Finally I heard him cry again. But you, Chi An. . . . After all you went through . . . I never once heard you cry out."

"I didn't dare," I said. "I was afraid the doctor might change his mind about using only acupuncture. I was worried that a chemical anesthetic might hurt Tacheng."

Wei Xin said nothing for a long time. When he finally spoke, he sounded almost angry. "After all you went through, Chi An, Tacheng had better be a respectful son. If he disobeys you even once, I'm going to box his ears. He owes you everything. You endured the eighteenth level of hell so that he could be born."

12

"Remedial Measures"

THE USUAL MATERNITY leave was sixty days, but because Tacheng was delivered by cesarean section, I received a full one hundred days' time off. I needed every bit of it. It was a month before I could walk without pain, and my long, ragged incision was tender for weeks afterward.

I cherished every moment with my tiny baby, who was a constant source of wonder to me. Wei Xin shared my joy over our son and made good his promise to be a model father. When, at two months of age, Tacheng began fussing at bedtime, Wei Xin constructed a wooden cradle at work and suspended it from the ceiling of our bedroom. A few swings, and Tacheng would be asleep. When Tacheng began waking up at night with a wet diaper, Wei Xin would get up and change him while I slept.

Wei Xin even went with me and Tacheng when I returned to work on the night shift, for he was afraid that his son would not be comfortable in the nursery. He placed a chair next to Tacheng's crib, so that if his son happened to awake he would see a familiar, loving face. He was still sitting there when I got off shift the following morning, surrounded by a crowd of my coworkers who were ribbing him for being so "motherly."

Two weeks after I was released from the hospital, before I went back to work, the tall, gaunt figure of the sanitarium's population control worker appeared on my doorstep. Unlike other officials, who tended to cloak their real purpose in mock camaraderie and tedious political diatribes, she was all business. After perfunctorily congratulating me on the birth of Tacheng, she came straight to the point of her visit. "I am here to ask you to sign a one-child agreement," she said. "Under the current regulations, if you agree to have no more children, you will receive a monthly bonus of five yuan and a wash-basin. You understand that if you sign a one-child agreement, it is best if you undergo sterilization—just to make sure that there are no accidents." Her tone was so matter-of-fact she could have been talking about the weather instead of this most intimate of human affairs. "Your husband can always be sterilized in your place—that is, if he is willing," she added. "Most men aren't. They think it interferes with their potency."

I felt my ears begin to burn. I wanted to respond with equal frankness and tell her that there was no way Wei Xin or I would agree to sterilization right now, but my political inhibitions—not to mention my innate modesty about sexual matters—won out. It was always better to be vaguely agreeable in the face of authority. "I will consider signing a one-child agreement," I said. "But my husband has mentioned that he might like to have a second child."

"In that case," she went on, "you have two choices. You either have to have an IUD inserted or start taking birth control pills."

I didn't want to do either. Birth control pills would reduce my milk supply, I explained, and I had a hungry baby boy to nurse every hour or two. As far as the IUD was concerned, I told her, I had developed an infection in my uterus. Until the infection was healed, I could not wear an IUD. "Besides," I ended, "you know that it is not easy to become pregnant while nursing a baby."

She seemed a bit put off that I had not agreed to begin contra-cepting immediately. She and I both knew that nursing mothers did sometimes become pregnant. Her sour expression deepened. "You do know that the mandatory waiting period between first and second births is now four years?" she queried.

"Yes," I replied.

"And that even after this waiting period, you will have to have a quota before you can give birth?" she pursued.

"Yes."

"And that remedial measures are required for those who violate the waiting period?"

I assented again, and she left.

This visit filled me with a sense of foreboding. No sooner had I had my first child than the authorities wanted to foreclose the possi-bility of my having a second. I had been deliberately vague with the population control worker, but there was no doubt in my mind that I wanted a little girl. I was willing to wait four years—even longer if necessary—but I hoped eventually to have a baby sister for Ta-cheng. But the policy was becoming ever stricter. Even if I kept my end of the agreement, would the authorities keep theirs?

When Tacheng was seven months old, I unexpectedly became pregnant. I knew almost immediately, for I missed my period and shortly after that began feeling tired, out of sorts, and sick to my stomach. Before the month was out, the same violent nausea had once again taken over my body, and I began losing weight. If any-thing, my second pregnancy promised to be even more physically taxing than my first.

But even more than the physical problems I would face during pregnancy, I found the thought of a confrontation with the authorities emotionally overwhelming. When the sanitarium's population control official discovered that I was pregnant, she would surely demand that I undergo remedial measures. She would remind me that a birth quota system was now in force—and that I did not have a quota. She would point out that Tacheng and this baby would be only sixteen months apart in age, far less than the recently mandated four-year waiting period between first and second children. She would produce a copy of the birth control agreement that Wei Xin and I had signed at the police station, whose terms limited us to two children born at least four years apart. "You have entered into a sacred compact with the state," she would say, ignoring the fact that we had signed only under duress, "and you must abide by its terms."

At the same time I knew that the birth control policy was not yet written in stone. Of course, even with all my mother's connections, a second quota would be impossible to obtain. And there was the agreement Wei Xin and I had signed. Yet if I straightened my spine and stubbornly insisted on carrying my child to term, no one would force me to have an abortion. Officials from the street committee and my work unit would visit Wei Xin and me at home in the evenings. We would have to listen humbly and earnestly to their tedious sermons on the merits of population control. The Party secretary of the sanitarium himself might call me in for a long lecture laced with veiled threats, or even command that I be publicly criticized in a staff meeting. If I kept my child, I might have to spend the next ten years working the night shift. But in the end the decision would be mine.

The stakes were high: My unborn child's life was at stake. Yet the very thought of playing cat and mouse with Party officials filled me with dread. All my political conditioning had taught me to take the path of least resistance. "When the wind blows, the grass bends" had become a byword of my generation. I had seen it happen again and again: Those who did not bend to the will of the Party were broken by it.

I would not report my pregnancy to the population control official, I decided. *Let her figure out for herself that I was pregnant.* I would volunteer for the night shift, so I would be home for my worst episodes of nausea and vomiting, which generally occurred in midmorning. My next pelvic examination was not scheduled for another four months, by which time I would be more than halfway to term. What would happen once I was discovered to be pregnant I preferred not to think about. Would I succumb to the threats and blandishments of authority? Or would my unborn child, by then six months along and making her presence felt, give me the strength of will to resist?

Such was my plan, but things did not work out that way. Months before my pelvic examination would have given me away, an attack of morning sickness made my condition evident to everyone at work. One morning, shortly before my shift ended, I was suddenly overcome by nausea. I clapped my hand over my mouth and tried to make it to the restroom, but it was too late. I threw up in full view of a wardful of patients and the charge nurse.

The population control official caught up with me as I was walking out the gate to go home. She didn't mince words. "I heard you got sick this morning," she said. She looked me up and down with a frown on her face, as if I had contracted some loathsome disease. "Not to mention that you look pale. I want you to go to the hospital tomorrow for a pelvic examination. Such matters are best dealt with promptly."

I meekly did as I was told, telling myself that there was no point in disobeying her order. It would be good to have a physical examination and check the progress of my pregnancy. There would be time enough to resist later—when I was ordered to report for an abortion.

A nurse took my medical history and performed the pelvic examination. "The cervix is soft," she told me when she had finished. "All the signs of pregnancy are present." She estimated from the date of my last period that I was ten weeks along. "Your due date is around July 21," she concluded. "You also have an infection of the cervix, probably from your recent cesarean section."

The news of my condition was delivered in a clinical tone of voice without the barest hint of a smile. Unplanned pregnancies no longer elicited congratulations. The nurse knew I did not have a quota for a second child. And I knew that she would report my condition back to my unit by phone as soon as she left the examining room.

The next day the population control worker again accosted me at 7:30 A.M. as I was getting off shift. "We must take care of your situation without delay," she said, forgoing any small talk. "You should take remedial measures within the week."

I had carefully rehearsed what I was going to say to her. *The official limit is still two children*, I would say, *despite the recently introduced quota system. No one can force me to have an abortion. Besides, with my ongoing infection, it would be dangerous for me to have an abortion. All things considered, I have decided to have this baby.*

Now, face to face with this representative of the authorities, my instinct to go along, to avoid confrontations at all costs, reasserted itself. I said nothing.

"Well, Chi An?" she again demanded after a moment. "Do you agree?" I found myself nodding in spite of myself, promising an abortion I had no intention of getting.

I consoled myself with the thought that my cowardice had bought a little time. But all too soon my weeklong grace period was up, and the population control worker came looking for me again. "Why have you not yet been to the hospital?" she scolded me. "You have worked in the area of birth control. You know what the policy of the government is. You must not violate your agreement. If you do, you'll bear full responsibility for the consequences."

Each day after work she continued to harangue me, her threats becoming more and more transparent. I was angry and yet at the same time intimidated. I never once talked back.

I had no sanctuary from this relentless pressure to abort. Not even my mother's apartment was inviolable. Teacher Chen, the head of the street committee, visited me there each and every day. Sometimes she would be waiting for me at the entrance to our building when I arrived home from work. Other times she would stop by in the evenings, when my mother and Wei Xin were home. Her argument never varied: "Because of my friendship with your mother I did you a favor," she would remind me. "I gave you a quota out of turn. Now you have a son, rosy and chubby. If you have a second baby outside the quota system, I will be criticized. You owe it to me to take remedial measures."

"Ignore her scoldings," Wei Xin scoffed each time she left. "If things get too bad we can always move back to my dormitory room." I found it impossible to follow his advice. My natural inclination was to please people by doing what was asked of me, which made me an easy mark for this kind of political arm-twisting and guilt-mongering. The threats and the scoldings replayed themselves endlessly in my mind, until they began to eat away at my resolve.

I longed for my baby to move so that I would know it was really there. It was one thing to know with your head that you were pregnant. It was another to feel your unborn baby alive within you, using arms to push and legs to kick. *If I could just feel a kick*, I thought to myself, *even one, no amount of pressure would make me give in*. But the quickening was, I knew, at least a month away.

For two weeks the population control official continued her barrage of threats; then one day after I got off work she gave me an ultimatum. "I have made an appointment for you at the hospital tomorrow morning at 8:00 A.M.," she said to me. "Don't miss it. If you do, the Party secretary swears that the consequences for you will be very serious." Without waiting for a response, she turned to go. "One more thing," she tossed over her shoulder as she walked away. "I intend to accompany you to the hospital after you get off work. There will be no more delays."

"This is sheer coercion!" Wei Xin said angrily that night, after I recounted to him the words of the population control official. He threw down the English-language textbook he had been reading and jumped to his feet. "How can they do such things?!" It was the first time I had seen him really furious over our situation.

"If I don't go in tomorrow, they will increase the pressure," I said.

"The Party secretary will get involved. The street committee will hold public meetings to denounce me. Do you think the daughter-in-law of the cook, who had to have an abortion after we took her quota, would hesitate for an instant to attack me? Our personal business will be *mancheng fengyu*—wagging tongues throughout the city."

"It already is," Wei Xin said. "Today I was visited by the population control worker in *my* factory. She told me that it would be best if we took care of our problem immediately. So much for moving back to my dormitory to avoid this pressure."

I was stunned by this news. Our only escape route had been blocked. "Oh, Wei Xin, what are we going to do?"

"What *can* we do?" he responded, sounding defeated. "If the authorities are going to make an issue of this, what choice do we have but to go along? How can an egg break a rock?"

My eyes began to fill with tears. The outcome of my pregnancy was now a foregone conclusion. In a few hours my baby would be taken from me. Wei Xin put his arms around me and held me close. "I am so sorry, Chi An," he whispered.

For long minutes I struggled to accept the inevitable. "I don't know why," I said at last, my voice breaking with emotion. "But I am absolutely certain that I am carrying a little girl . . . Tacheng's baby sister."

The following morning, escorted by the population control official, I went to the hospital. All too soon I was lying on an operating table. I screwed my eyes tightly shut, trying to block out all sensation. The doctor, an older man with a kindly manner, inserted a speculum to hold my vagina open while he visually examined my cervix. I heard him cluck his tongue in disapproval. The pressure of the speculum suddenly released. "You may get dressed," he told me gently. "You have an infection of the cervix. Moreover, I don't think the cesarean section you had last year ever healed properly."

He turned to the official standing nearby. "I would advise against this procedure," he said. "If we dilate the patient's cervix and suction out the contents of her uterus there is a possibility of a rupture of the uterine wall. Even if there is no rupture, it is possible that the procedure will aggravate her infection to the point where generalized sepsis sets in. That would force us to perform a hysterectomy."

A thrill of hope surged through me: *Perhaps I will be able to keep my baby after all*.

"This abortion *must* be performed," the official said flatly.

The doctor's eyes went hard. "The patient's condition does not permit it," he expostulated. "She—"

"If you won't do it," the official interrupted harshly, "then find us a doctor who will!"

The doctor turned on his heel and left without a further word.

Ten minutes later I was back on the operating table. The door opened and in walked the head of the maternity section. A chill came over me at the sight of the leftist ideologue whose malpractice had almost cost me Tacheng's life, not to mention my own. He sat down between my upraised legs and, without bothering with a pelvic examination, set right to work.

I had always regarded myself as a strong person. Though soft and malleable where other people were concerned, I was strict and unyielding with myself. I had not cried out when Tacheng was born, despite the prodigious pain I had endured. But now I utterly lost control. When the doctor began to suction roughly at the inside of my uterus, I could not hold back my tears. The physical pain was nothing compared to my cesarean section, but it felt as though my heart were being torn into a thousand pieces.

The doctor paused in his suctioning and glanced off to his right, *where the glass bottle was hanging!* my mind screamed at me. He is checking to make sure he got all of her!

He finished suctioning and withdrew. It was over. The population control official led me into the postoperative room, where she gestured that I was to climb onto the bed. I didn't have the energy. I fell on my hands and knees to the floor and sobbed. "Please forgive me," I moaned. "Heaven, if you can hear me, please forgive me for what I have done."

The next few days passed in a haze of bleeding and pain. The doctor had damaged the already fragile lining of my uterus, and I bled profusely, soaking through one pad after another. Worse than the weakness and disorientation that followed the bleeding was the emotional pain. I stopped paying attention to my surroundings, even ignoring my beloved son, Tacheng. One question and one question only occupied my thoughts: *Who is the* xiongshou, *the villain, of this episode? Is it the doctor responsible for my daughter's death? Is the population control official the villain? Is the policy itself to blame? Am I the villain?*

However much I despised the head of the maternity ward, I couldn't really blame him for what happened. Had I refused to go to the hospital, my daughter would still be alive. Neither could I blame the population control official. She, like the doctor and Teacher Chen of the street committee, was only an instrument of the official policy on spacing children. I had been in their position myself, forced to carry out orders I found distasteful. Neither could I with confidence condemn those who set the policy, for what if they were unaware of the cruel way it was being carried out? I found it impossible to apportion responsibility for this tragedy. Of those who had played a part, I was certain only of my own guilt. I could not absolve myself just because I had been under duress. I had been willing to be crucified to save Tacheng's life. Why, I moaned over and over to myself, had I given in so easily this time?

Wei Xin had little time to console me. Although he had stood by me during my confrontation with the authorities, once I returned from the hospital he had no time for me. He was too busy boning up on engineering and English. The Ministry of Education had announced that the nation's graduate schools, closed after Mao condemned them for "training spiritual aristocrats," were about to reopen. Graduate students were to be chosen based on their performance in a nationwide entrance examination, to be held in March 1978. Candidates would be tested in English, Chinese, Communist ideology, and their field of specialization, which in Wei Xin's case was mechanical engineering. Those who did well enough in all four areas would be admitted to advanced-degree programs at China's universities in the fall. The Cultural Revolution in higher education, which had glorified ignorance and incompetence, was about to end.

Wei Xin, whose college education had been cut short ten years before, saw his chance. As soon as he learned of the March exam, he dug out his old university textbooks and began poring over them. Much of his time he devoted to improving his reading comprehension of English, the area he felt weakest in. Although literary works had been burned, the shelves of the Shenyang University library were full of English-language books on engineering and technical subjects. The librarian, who had known my father well, was delighted to loan them out to his former friend's son-in-law, even though he was not yet a student. Wei Xin usually stopped by the library on Saturday mornings after getting off work, returning home with a armload of musty-smelling books with titles like *The Properties of Metals*, *Newton's Laws*, and *General Thermodynamics*. Then he shut himself in our tiny cubicle and read each of these books from cover to cover, pausing only to eat, as if they were kung fu thrillers instead of arid technical treatises.

Wei Xin's studious nature was one of the things that had first attracted me to him. Now, when I most needed his love and support, he had vanished into an airless world of old science books with foreign titles. He read like a man possessed. Even his beloved Tacheng couldn't entice him away from his books for more than a few minutes at a time. As for me, it was as if I didn't exist. I had had an IUD implanted following the abortion to make sure I wouldn't have to repeat that horrible experience, but I needn't have bothered. All of Wei Xin's energy went into his books. If Wei Xin responded at all to my attempts at conversation, it was in monosyllables. One Sunday evening at bedtime, after another long weekend of silence, I had had enough.

Instead of quietly getting into bed alongside Wei Xin and falling asleep, I took a position directly in front of him. "Wei Xin!" I said in a loud voice. "Don't forget that you have a wife and a son!"

Wei Xin looked up in surprise at my outburst, so out of character for me.

"What good is all this?" I sulked, gesturing disdainfully at the pile of English books by our bed. "I still have a son, this I know. But I have lost my unborn daughter to the population control program. And now I have lost my husband to his books. Is it worth it? That's what I am asking myself. Is it worth it?"

For once Wei Xin put aside the book that he was reading, though not without carefully marking his place. "This is not just about graduate school, Chi An," he began quietly. "Old heaven knows that I don't want to spend my life in a machine factory. But going back to school is only the first step. China is opening up to the West. I have heard rumors that the government is preparing to send students to America and Great Britain for advanced training in a year or two. The competition will be fierce. Only those who are fluent in English will be selected." A note of excitement had entered his voice. "I must be ready, Chi An. Think of how wonderful it would be to study in the West!"

China had been closed to the outside world for so long that I was tempted to dismiss Wei Xin's plan as sheer fantasy. Yet with the death of Mao and the reemergence of Vice Premier Deng Xiaoping in Beijing, China was gradually waking up from its long Maoist nightmare. For the first time since 1966, college entrance examinations had been held in December 1977. The national graduate school examinations, for which Wei Xin was preparing, were a short month away. "Do you really think that you have a chance to go abroad?" I asked, struggling to maintain my skepticism. Wei Xin's excitement was proving contagious.

"Absolutely," Wei Xin answered. "If I pass the examinations in March—and I think I have a good chance—then I will spend two years in graduate school at Shenyang University. Without a degree from a Western university, I would then begin teaching as an assistant lecturer. I would advance up the academic ranks slowly, taking perhaps twenty or even thirty years to reach professor. If, on the other hand, I am able to study abroad on a government scholarship, chances are I will be given an associate professorship as soon as I return. Think of what that would mean for us."

It would mean a great deal, I knew. The jump from lecturer to associate professor was a big one. It brought with it not only a much larger salary but access to the best housing on campus. As a lowly assistant lecturer Wei Xin would be assigned quarters in a junior faculty dormitory—if we were lucky. If we weren't we would still be living with my mother in five years. It might be twenty before we qualified for an apartment of our own. In China it was easier to find a spouse than a place to live. I was proof of that. But as a professor . . .

"Of course, completing a Ph.D. at an American university will take at least four years," Wei Xin went on, more soberly now. "We will be separated during this time. I will be in the United States. You will be here, living with your mother. But our time apart will pass quickly. When my studies are completed"—here Wei Xin laughed—"I will 'return home robed in imperial silk,' *Yi jin huan xiang*, like a successful candidate in the imperial examinations of dynastic times. I will be given an associate professorship. I will be recognized in my field. We will be assigned a spacious two-bedroom apartment on campus."

By this time I was thoroughly caught up in Wei Xin's vision of the future. I could see our new apartment in my mind. Wei Xin would be writing in his study, surrounded by shelves of books, some of them written by him. The children's room would have two beds, for by then Tacheng would have a baby sister. To make this dream a reality, any sacrifice seemed worthwhile, including long hours of loneliness while my husband prepared for his exams. "When you succeed, *Guan zhong yao zu*," I said to Wei Xin excitedly, " 'you will have your ancestors smiling in their coffins.' The old fortune-teller, who prophesied when you were a baby that you would one day 'travel by horseback and eat fish at every meal,' will have been proved right."

Wei Xin, who had always done well on written examinations, easily passed the graduate entrance examinations in March 1978. Most important for our plans, he did especially well on the English portion of the exam, receiving the highest score of his entering class. He matriculated at the graduate school of engineering of the Shenyang Institute of Science and Technology. Classes began immediately, enthusiastically taught by professors who had been in intellectual cold storage for the past ten years.

China ended its self-imposed isolation even faster than Wei Xin had optimistically predicted. In April it was announced that China would send its first small group of scholars abroad for advanced study in the fall. Other, larger contingents would follow. In theory at least, scholarships for study in the West would be awarded on merit, not class status or family connections. The main selection criteria were two: proficiency in one's academic specialty and an excellent command of English.

Wei Xin achieved nearly perfect marks in his first engineering courses at Shenyang University, winning his professors over to his cause. Only one hurdle remained: the national English-language proficiency test, slated to be held in Beijing and other major cities in August. Shenyang University was allowed to send a total of twelve candidates to Beijing. Nine of those selected were junior faculty members, who had been teaching since before the Cultural Revolution. The remaining three were chosen from among the new graduate students on the strength of their entrance exam results. Wei Xin was one.

Once the semester ended in early July, Wei Xin redoubled his efforts to prepare for the Beijing exams, now less than two months away. I once more relinquished him to his English books, though voluntarily this time. I even suggested that he sleep at his university dormitory during the week, so that he would not lose two hours of precious time commuting each day. Tacheng and I saw him only on weekends, when he returned home carrying his usual armload of books and promptly disappeared into our bedroom to read.

His feverish preparations paid off. In October the university announced that Wei Xin was one of four Shenyang University candidates—and the only graduate student—who had passed the examination. Since government scholarships were given preferentially to those in scientific and technical fields who could help China's modernization, we knew then that it was only a matter of time before Wei Xin would be going abroad. We were overwhelmed with excitement.

My only regret about Wei Xin's impending departure had to do with my hope for a daughter. The guilt I felt over my last pregnancy had not diminished with the passage of time. Only the feel of a newborn girl in my arms could assuage my pain and help me forget her precursor. Nearly three years of the mandatory four-year waiting period had already passed. Another year, and Wei Xin and I could apply for a second quota.

Now that Wei Xin was going abroad, I had to rethink my plans. I didn't want to conceive a second child on the eve of Wei Xin's departure, with or without permission. The prospect of raising Tacheng as a single parent for the next five years was daunting enough as it was. I would wait until Wei Xin's return. *I am still young*, I consoled myself. *Tacheng will be eight years old when his father returns. The next time, no one will be able to accuse of us failing to observe the four-year waiting period. Obtaining a birth quota shouldn't be difficult.*

Early in 1979, I and several other young nurses from my ward were summoned to a mass meeting. The summons arrived in the person of the population control official, so I suspected, though I could not be sure, that we were in for a lecture on birth control. The official, with the irritating penchant for secrecy characteristic of her kind, refused to say, remarking only that the meeting would be the occasion of an "important address by the Party secretary."

Waiting in the assembly hall for the meeting to begin, I suddenly realized what those present had in common. All sixty-odd of us were young married women who had not yet been sterilized. This discovery made me uneasy, though I could not say why.

Secretary Wang arrived and took up a position in front of the assembly. His round little face, normally the picture of conviviality, was set in an expression of the utmost gravity. "Today we have a matter of extreme urgency," he began, "a *toudeng dashi*, to discuss. It concerns the population of the motherland. The People's Republic of China has within its borders nearly a billion people, or one-fifth of the world's population. This is a big burden for the people's government. Our major error in regard to population policy was to turn to the Soviet Union for advice. Our so-called Soviet elder brothers taught us that overpopulation, like unemployment, was only a problem in capitalist countries. During the 1950s we had a policy of encouraging women to give birth and discouraging abortion. As a result our population grew very rapidly during those years, and we now have too many people. Our population must not be allowed to continue to increase. If it does the consequences will be catastrophic.

"Having children is not a question that we can afford to let each family, each household, decide for itself," he went on. "It is a question that should be decided at the national level. China is a socialist country. This means that the interests of the individual must be subordinated to the interests of the state. Where there is a conflict between the interests of the state in reducing population and the interests of the individual in having children, it must be resolved in favor of the state. Socialism should make it possible to regulate the reproduction of human beings so that population growth keeps in step with the growth of material production. This is especially important now that China has embarked upon the Four Modernizations program. Whether or not we are able to control our population will determine whether the Chinese revolution succeeds."

There was nothing new in what the Party secretary was saying. *People's Daily* editorials in recent weeks had been stressing the need to lower the population growth rate. A major speech on the subject by Qian Xinzhong, the minister in charge of the State Family Planning Commission, had been reprinted in full on the front page of the *Shenyang Daily*. I shifted in my chair, trying to find a comfortable position for what promised to be a long, boring recitation of the Party line on population control.

"The Shenyang provincial authorities have determined to do everything possible to reduce the population increase rate," Secretary Wang continued. "New goals have been set. We in Shenyang must lower the population increase rate of our province from last year's 14.2 down to 10 per thousand this year. By 1985 the rate must be further reduced to 5 per thousand, while by the year 2000 the natural increase rate should be zero." Here he paused, looking around the room to make sure he had everyone's complete attention. "This means that fewer babies must be born.

"A new law has been promulgated by the provincial authorities requiring all couples to practice family planning," he said. "This law mandates severe financial penalties for having unauthorized second or higher-order births. The bearing of second and higher-order children is to be discouraged."

I sat bolt upright. The setting of such stringent limits *was* new— and worrisome. Maybe the authorities were ready to increase the waiting period for second children beyond four years. One thing was clear: A major shift in government policy was in the works.

Secretary Wang fixed us with a stern glance and then slowly and deliberately said, "We here in Shenyang city must set an example for areas of the province more backward in family planning. The city government, responding to the call of the provincial authorities to reduce the birthrate, has come to the following decision: The bearing of second or higher-order children is to stop immediately. No couple in Shenyang city is to be allowed more than one child. This one-child policy goes into effect today. We must all wholeheartedly support the new policy of the Shenyang city government! I want all women of child-bearing age to sign a one-child agreement!"

I was so stunned by this news that for an instant my whole body went numb. Only gradually did I became aware of the anguished whispers of those around me: "We are really unfortunate. . . . No more second children at all. . . . I have a daughter and now I won't be able to have a son. . . . One child and that's it. . . . What are we to do?" Such grumbling was unheard of in China, where political conditioning usually choked people into silence. Several women were quietly dabbing their eyes. I, too, felt words of anger and tears of frustration welling up inside me, but I instinctively clamped down on my emotions. My habit of self-censorship was too deeply ingrained to allow me openly to question Party policy at a public meeting.

But all around me women were doing just that. I was amazed when their muffled comments and complaints began to grow louder. Instead of acting out their support for the new Party policy, as the "masses" were expected to do, they were for once expressing their true feelings, which were decidedly, overwhelmingly critical. Secretary Wang seemed taken aback by this minor rebellion and stood uncertainly on the stage, making little quieting motions with his hands.

All at once the shrill voice of the population control official cut through the discontent like a buzz saw. "We must all support the new policy of the Shenyang city government!" she said. She was standing next to the Party secretary, looking like a chopstick next to a dumpling. "I believe the local government is right. The only way to reduce the birthrate to the level required by the provincial authorities is to limit everyone to one child. The one-child policy is good for China!

"Besides," she went on, less stridently now that the hall had quieted down, "all you women know how difficult it is to raise children these days. The men don't help. Mothers-in-law have their own jobs. With all the pressures of work and home, it is best to stop at one child. Everyone should sign a one-child agreement without delay. The new policy is not just good for China, it is good for us women."

I didn't know which irritated me more: her parroting of the Party secretary's new line or her portrayal of herself as an advocate for women. I knew from firsthand experience that when it came to enforcing the dictates of the population control program, she was without scruples. Her mock sympathy was just a ploy to win us over.

Secretary Wang, having recovered his poise, now broke in. "We will now break up into three discussion groups headed by myself, the Party vice secretary, and the population control cadre. We will go over the new one-child policy in detail. Everyone must express an opinion about the new policy." The phrase "express an opinion" was typical Chinese Communist Party doublespeak. The only opinion the Party really wanted to hear was wholehearted, unqualified endorsement of its latest scheme.

I landed in the group led by the dour-faced population control official. The first thing she did was go around the circle and, in her most forbidding manner, ask each woman to "express her opinion" about the new policy. Stripped of the anonymity provided by the crowd, everyone was quite subdued. Those who had earlier spoken out now retreated to the safe position that, while they themselves had no objection to signing a one-child agreement, they would have to talk it over with their husbands. I followed their lead. It was obvious from her expression that the official didn't like this answer, but she could hardly fault us for it.

While no one openly dared to oppose the one-child policy, neither did anyone applaud it. Only three women in my group indicated any willingness to go along. The official took these three prospects briefly to one side. When she returned, the trio in tow, she looked almost happy for once. "These three staff members have responded to the call of the Party," she announced, a triumphant expression animating her sour face. "All have agreed to sign one-child agreements and undergo sterilization. As pioneers in the population control program, they will receive generous rewards and large cash bonuses." She continued to lavish praise on her three victims for several minutes, obviously hoping that others of us would follow their lead.

I listened without enthusiasm to her repetitive spiel. I was more interested in studying the three women. Each, I knew, had their own personal reasons for going along with the official's blandishments. All had one child already. One was married to an army officer stationed along the Soviet border and saw her husband only once a year, at Chinese New Year's. The second, who was now living with her parents, had left her husband after she discovered that he was having an affair with another woman. I didn't know the family circumstances of the third, except that she had a son about Tacheng's age, but I imagined them to be equally unhappy. None of the three seemed outwardly happy over her decision. In fact, their grim and joyless faces formed a marked contrast to the official's forced gaiety.

As a result of that first meeting thirteen women agreed to sign a one-child agreement. After these women had all been sterilized (to ensure there would be no reneging on the agreement), a second meeting was called in their honor. One by one, in a solemn ceremony, they were called up on the stage to be congratulated by Secretary Wang. As the population control official introduced each one by name to the assembly, the secretary pinned a paper rose, a scarlet monstrosity some six inches in diameter, on the lapel of her jacket. Then he handed her a large commendation, the size of a folded newspaper, and shook her hand. It was left to the population control official, her gaunt face in a tight smile, to distribute the prizes: a transistor radio and one hundred yuan. These were handsome gifts indeed, with a combined value equivalent to three months' salary for most of us.

As the women, several of whom looked wan and pale from their recent surgery, stood awkwardly on the stage, Secretary Wang hailed them as models for the rest of us. "These women have responded to the urgent call of the Party," he said. "They are activists in the family planning program, helping to solve the problem of excessive births that China faces." After reiterating the new policy once again in te-dious detail, he concluded by saying, "Each of you must express your opinion. Whether you agree with the policy or not, you must abide by it." Afterward we once again broke up into small groups to be grilled by our leaders about our "opinions." Another dozen women agreed to sign one-child agreements.

A third meeting was held two weeks later. The second batch of "volunteers," now sterilized, was called up to the stage. They were congratulated by the Party secretary as the first had been, although this time there were no paper flowers or printed commendations. Their prize, a set of bedsheets worth perhaps fifteen yuan, was a vast step down from those awarded to the first group. Another lengthy meet-ing followed, producing a third, still-larger crop of "volunteers." One concession was made to overcome their reluctance to sign a one-child agreement: Some of them were allowed to wear IUDs instead of undergoing tubal ligations.

After this third meeting, the population control official sought me out privately for the first time. "You might as well express your opin-ion now," she said. "This current group is the last that will be re-warded. Everyone after this . . ." She left the sentence unfinished and waited for my reaction.

I had given up my first little girl (I was still sure that the baby had been a girl) too easily. This time I would not be so pliable. "I am not going to agree to have only one child," I said flatly, surprising even myself. "I would like to have a girl. It's true that I have a little boy, but now he is growing up and I want another baby. I am hoping to have a baby girl in a few years. Besides, Wei Xin doesn't consent to my signing a one-child agreement." This last was not strictly true. I had only hinted to Wei Xin of the pressure I was under, not want-ing to distract him from his intense regimen of course work and study, which continued to consume all his energies.

"Well, Chi An, we have been through all this before, haven't we?" she said coldly. "You know in your heart that you will have to agree sooner or later. The Party secretary is determined that everyone in his unit will sign a one-child agreement. If you wait until the end, you will become very . . . *passive*."

This was another instance of Chinese Communist Party double-speak. What she meant by "passive," in Chinese, *beidong*, was that in the end the pressure would grow so intense that I would have no recourse but to sign a one-child agreement. The Party preferred to maintain a pretense of choice when it imposed its policies on the people, but in the end they would stop at nothing to enforce compliance.

The third group received a set of dish towels, the four and fifth groups nothing. By then only a handful of women continued to hold out. I was one of them. The population control official came to see me every day now. I knew what she was going to say even before she opened her mouth, having heard it all dozens of times before: "Chi An, almost everyone has signed a one-child agreement. The Party secretary is eager to report to the city government that his unit is in 100 percent compliance with the directive on population control. Why do you continue to resist the inevitable? You know in your heart that you will have to agree in the end. If you wait until the end, you will become very *passive*."

Despite her constant harassment, I bore up well. That is, until the day the official dropped her bombshell. "Chi An," she began, "I know that you want to have a second child, but at what cost? I have been talking with the population control cadre over at Shenyang University. I understand that your husband has qualified to go overseas. Do you know that your continuing refusal to sign a one-child agreement may affect his chances?"

I stared at her in horror. I had expected to suffer for insisting on my right to have a second child. I had prepared myself for all manner of unpleasantness—public criticism, heavy fines, a job demotion. But how could I make Wei Xin suffer alongside me? His one dream was to study abroad. It was all he had worked for, had hoped for. . . . I heaved a secret sigh and inwardly conceded defeat. *How could I have been so naive as to think that I would outlast the authorities?* I thought sadly. *What was it Wei Xin had said the last time I was pregnant? How can an egg break a rock? Well, the egg has shattered for good this time. There will be no more children. This is the new reality. I must accept it for Wei Xin's sake.*

"I may be willing to sign a one-child agreement," I told the official finally. "But I cannot agree to a tubal ligation." I was gambling that she was so eager to report 100 percent compliance to the Party secretary that she would not insist on sterilization. "What happens if I lose my only child?" I pointed out. "If I have been sterilized I will be unable to have another."

"Such operations can be reversed," she said quickly, sensing that victory was near.

"Such reversals are usually not successful," I countered. "Often they are not even attempted. Remember, I have worked in the population control program, too. I will sign a one-child agreement, but no sterilization. Is it agreed?"

There were no paper flowers or commendations for me, of course, because I was one of the last to sign. All I received was a Birth Planning Honor Card: Only Son (*Jihua Shengyu Guang Rong Zheng: Dushengzi;* those whose only child was a girl received cards that read: Birth Planning Honor Card: Only Daughter), which the population control official handed me without comment. Inside the red plastic cover, beside my name, age, and occupation, was printed the following: "This certificate is issued to those families who voluntarily decide to have only one child. If the holders of this certificate have another child, this certificate will be withdrawn by the issuing organization."

The very language of the agreement was a mockery of the truth. The authorities had browbeaten me into signing an agreement that perversely stated that I had "voluntarily decide[d] to have only one child." As for talk of having another, the controls over childbearing were being ratcheted tighter day by day. Most of the "holders of this certificate" were incapable of conceiving another child in any case, since they had already been sterilized. The more I reflected on it, the more I regretted not having been stronger two years before. There would have been penalties to pay and criticism to endure, but in the end I would have held my daughter. Now I probably never would.

That night I silently handed the little red booklet to Wei Xin. He looked down at the official document in his hand, and then up at me in bewilderment. "You mean you already signed a one-child agreement," he blurted out. "Why, Chi An? Why didn't you wait?"

"Why didn't I wait?" I retorted, struggling to control my irritation at his reaction. "The one-child campaign has been under way for months. I was ordered a dozen times to 'express an opinion.' In the end they forced me to sign."

"But why didn't you tell me how much pressure they were putting on you?" Wei Xin pursued. "I would have stood by you." His words were sympathetic enough, but they were spoken with an undertone of disapproval.

"Why tell you?" I sneered, raising my voice for the first time. All my hurt and frustration of the past weeks and months spilled over. "What can you do? Can you convince the authorities to let us have two children when everyone else is limited to one?"

Wei Xin blinked in surprise at my uncharacteristic anger and fell silent. Then he heaved a great sigh. "Why didn't we keep our second baby, Chi An?" he asked sadly. "If we had disobeyed the authorities, everything still would have worked out in the end. Now it's going to be impossible for us to have another child."

I felt the same sense of regret—perhaps I had killed my only chance to have a baby sister for Tacheng—but coming from Wei Xin it sounded like an accusation. I reacted angrily. "And whose fault is that?" I retorted. "I still remember how you *stood by me* the last time. Your great plan was to move back to the dormitory. One visit from *your* population control worker and you surrendered. 'What can we do?' you said. 'What choice do we have but to go along? How can an egg break a rock?' "

I continued to vent my pent-up frustration and grief at my husband: "Why should I have kept the baby, Wei Xin? You don't deserve another child. You haven't been paying any attention to Tacheng and me for the last two years. And you are about to go overseas for how many years? Five? Six? How could I take care of a second child with you studying abroad? I only signed this agreement because they threatened to withdraw your scholarship—" I gasped and put my hand over my mouth. I had not intended to tell Wei Xin why I had given in.

Wei Xin went pale.

"I am so sorry," I said quickly. "I had not intended to tell you."

Wei Xin looked again at the little red booklet he held in his hand, reading the embossed gold characters: Birth Planning Honor Card: Only Son. "I guess we should consider ourselves lucky," he murmured. "We already have a little boy. Other couples have girls."

I nodded, anxious to put our confrontation behind us, but in my heart I didn't believe it. I didn't consider myself lucky at all because I had a boy instead of a girl. Not for one minute.

13

Return to the Village
of the Three Brothers

On JANUARY 15, 1979, Shenyang University nominated Wei Xin to the Education Ministry in Beijing for a scholarship to study abroad. His destination would be the United States, which had just established diplomatic relations with the People's Republic of China two weeks before. Wei Xin was ecstatic over this news and had letters of application off to a number of American universities within the week. By April he had been accepted by schools in New York and Texas. He decided in favor of New York.

Wei Xin's selection was greeted with a great outpouring of joy by his friends and acquaintances. The news that Wei Xin was to go to America provided a pretext to celebrate something larger: China's long-awaited opening up to the West. Wei Xin was living proof to his friends that the wall of isolation that Maoist xenophobes had built around China was cracking and crumbling. A more open and just society could not be long in coming.

The applause died away as the months passed without word from the Education Ministry. Winter gave way to spring, and spring in turn to summer. Wei Xin had originally intended to enroll in the fall quarter of 1979 but had to abandon his plans when August ended with his scholarship still unapproved. The problem, he learned from friends in the university administration, was political. The Education Ministry had balked at sending the son of a known counterrevolutionary abroad on a government scholarship. It made no difference to the ministry that Wei Xin's father was now dead or that the charge itself was ludicrous. Wei Xin's "family background was not clear," disqualifying him from consideration.

Wei Xin, who was flying high after his selection, became despondent when his scholarship was put on hold. For two years he had dedicated his every waking moment to realizing a dream: being one of the first Chinese scholars to study in the West since 1949. This prize had been almost within his grasp when, through no fault of his own, it had been snatched away. My mood was equally melancholy, though for a different reason. If Wei Xin was to be denied his scholarship, then the huge sacrifice I had made in signing a one-child agreement lost all meaning. I had forgone the consolation of a second child for nothing. I tried to conceal my sadness from Wei Xin, not wanting to add to his dejection.

The only good news was that Shenyang University, for the moment at least, was resisting pressure from the Education Ministry to withdraw Wei Xin's name. My father's former colleagues had something to do with that. When the ministry hinted that the university might want to select another candidate in place of Wei Xin, a group of senior professors paid a call on the university president. Wei Xin had been selected on the basis of professional merit, they told him, and was the best candidate available. The president, himself a recently rehabilitated victim of the Cultural Revolution, promised to continue supporting Wei Xin until the case against his father could be reviewed by the Party authorities in his native Jiangsu Province.

In the meantime, since Wei Xin had already completed his master's degree, the president approved his appointment as a junior lecturer.

Fortuitously, Mao's theory of class struggle, which had frozen Chinese society into good and bad classes for thirty years, was about to lose its paralyzing power. In November 1979, Hu Yaobang declared a general amnesty for all class enemies. Those who for decades had worn the "hat" of a landlord or counterrevolutionary or whatever were to be allowed to rejoin the people. They were to have, in Party parlance, their "hats" taken off. Only those who had committed "blood crimes against the people" would continue to wear them. Several million victims of past campaigns were rehabilitated virtually overnight. Wei Xin's father was one of them. In early December, Wei Xin received a brief letter from the Party committee of his home county, stating that "Wei Li-An's class status has been changed from counterrevolutionary to poor peasant." When this news was conveyed to Beijing, the Education Ministry reversed itself and approved Wei Xin's scholarship.

Wei Xin was still hoping to arrive at the State University of New York at Stony Brook in time for the winter quarter, which was now only two weeks away. The university administration agreed, releasing him from his teaching duties and putting him on extended leave. Wei Xin hand carried his request to the Education Ministry in Beijing, only to have lead-footed bureaucrats there balk in horror at the thought of expediting his departure. We have already reserved passage for you on March 6, they told Wei Xin, and have you scheduled to begin classes in the spring quarter. As far as speeding things up, they went on, it is impossible for us to make the necessary financial arrangements to pay your tuition, room, and board in the United States in less than two months' time. While in Beijing, Wei Xin was issued a plane ticket and an allowance of seven hundred yuan for miscellaneous expenses in the United States. At the official exchange rate this sum was worth only $470, but it was a small fortune to us, about the equivalent of a year's income.

The next few weeks dragged by. Wei Xin was home every day after being released from the university, but he was not himself. He had originally thought to brush up on his English but found himself unable to concentrate for more than short periods at a time. There had been enough setbacks and changes of schedule that he remained on edge even now that his scholarship had been approved. He kept worrying out loud that something might go wrong. Perhaps an official of the Education Ministry would show up on our doorstep and tell him that his scholarship had been revoked, or the Party would resurrect the old charge that he was a foreign spy, or the ministry would decide to delay his departure until the fall.

"Chi An, I have been thinking," he said to me one day. "I would like to use part of my allowance to visit my family in Jiangsu. I will be away for many years. I must see my elderly mother one last time before I go. Besides, she has never seen Tacheng, her only proper grandson."

I needed no convincing. "That's a wonderful idea!" I responded, clapping my hands in delight. I was tired of Wei Xin's jitters and was sure that a visit to Jiangsu would calm him down by taking his mind off his fears. We would have one last chance to spend time together as a family before Wei Xin disappeared from our lives for five years or more. After talking over our plans, Wei Xin and I decided to leave for the Village of the Three Brothers two days before the beginning of the Lunar New Year and stay on with his mother for two weeks.

The train was crowded with travelers (and their baggage) homeward bound for the Lunar New Year. The Party, in a slap at tradition, had shortened this ancient celebration from two weeks to three days and changed its name to the Spring Festival. But it couldn't erase the equally ancient drive of all Chinese to return to the bosom of their families for the beginning of the year, whatever the holiday was called.

In our hard sleeper car, the aisles were packed and most of the berths had two or three people crammed into them. Even so, we traveled in relative comfort, for Wei Xin had splurged and purchased two separate berths, a middle and an upper. Tacheng and I lay side by side on the middle berth, looking out the window. My four-year-old son, who had grown up in a narrow world of gray concrete buildings and red-brick walls, was entranced by the wide-open spaces of the countryside.

When we arrived in the Village of the Three Brothers, the entire community came came pouring out of their homes, greeting us in a friendly chorus. The women formed a happy gaggle around Tacheng and me, embarrassing him by lightly pinching his white, chubby arms and cheeks and remarking on his size. "He is a good half head taller than other boys his age," Wei Xin's mother clucked in surprise. "Such a grandson to come from my diminutive son. . . ." The men surrounded Wei Xin, loudly congratulating him for having fathered such a "little dragon." There was real warmth in their voices.

Toward the end of my first stay I had begun to make some headway in the local dialect. Now, chatting pleasantly with Wei Xin's relations, it quickly came back to me. Some phrases Wei Xin still had to translate, and I still had to reply mostly in Mandarin, but I could now understand what was being said. I could even make sense of most of Mother Wei's thick Yangtze brogue. She seemed a different person from our first visit, when the shadow of Father Wei's illness had hung over her like a shroud. Her earlier reticence had vanished, and she was delighted to have her first proper grandson under her roof.

The New Year's feast was a time of visiting, which by custom commenced with calls on one's closest kin and moved out through more distant relatives and friends. We spent our evenings with Wei Xin's best friends from the village, who came over once the formal calls of the day were through. During long, meandering conversations around the table, there was much good-natured ribbing of the village boy who had made good and was about to make even better. "Our village has finally produced a *zhuang-yuan*," a companion of his from childhood chortled, "someone who scored first in the imperial examination—even if he is shorter than a dwarf barbarian!"

"Even when he didn't study," a bucktoothed friend of his from elementary school remarked, "Ah Xin here always did well on his exams. I always sat behind him to copy his answers. He was so short that it was easy to see over his shoulder!" The men in the circle broke up, with Wei Xin unself-consciously joining in the general laughter.

It did my heart good to see Wei Xin relax in the company of old friends. For two years he had been going full blast at his studies. Just a few days before he had been agonizing over the possible loss of his scholarship. Now he had returned to the secure world he had known as a boy, listening in amusement as the companions of his boyhood poked gentle fun at him.

As the days passed in a happy blur of visiting and feasting, I reflected how happy I was to be back among these gentle and kindly folk. They were so free and natural in their speech and sentiments that they made the city dwellers with whom I had grown up seem evasive, even deceitful, by comparison. Their red clay houses may have been poor in material goods, but they were rich in human kindness and other gifts of the spirit. It was not only Wei Xin who had come home.

The one thing that took a little getting used to was the traditional segregation of men and women. "Come in and sit down, come in and sit down," Wei Xin would hail each new arrival. If the visitor was a man, he would answer Wei Xin's greeting in a hearty voice and join the circle of men gathered around the central table in loud conversation. A woman, on the other hand, would nod demurely at Wei Xin and go quietly to the benches along the walls where the other women were seated, chatting among themselves. Mother Wei would promptly pour a cup of hot tea for her new guest. A man would accept the cup wordlessly, as if it was his due, downing it with loud slurps and smacks to show his appreciation. A women, on the other hand, would accept the cup with a word of thanks but then sip it noiselessly. Wei Xin periodically pressed the men of his circle to accept cigarettes but would not think of offering any to the women. Smoking, in public at least, was frowned on in women. Loud talk and self-assertiveness were also considered unbecoming. For all Mao's talk of remaking Chinese society, these attitudes had survived the last few decades of revolutionary turmoil intact.

Only Mother Wei, whose age put her above criticism, moved easily between the women's circle and the men's. She sat where she liked, along the wall with the women or at the table with the men. Now and again, as the fancy struck her, she even lit up a cigarette. I envied her freedom. I would have liked to sit beside Wei Xin during our last days together.

Besides Wei Xin's good fortune, the one other staple of conversation was the population control campaign. The one-child program was at that moment in full swing throughout Jiangsu Province. Officials everywhere were running roughshod over pregnant women and their husbands as they scrambled to meet their birth quotas. Virtually every visitor came bearing news of fresh outrages. The laughter would stop and the mood would grow somber as we listened to their stories of women forced into abortions, sterilizations performed without consent, and infants killed at birth.

The most shocking tale I heard came from Wei Xin's mother, who recounted it to me in a horrified whisper. It happened that in a hamlet not far from the Village of the Three Brothers there lived a couple with only one child, a doe-eyed five-year-old girl. When she was born her parents were disappointed, for like most villagers they preferred a boy. This was a simple matter of peasant economics. A son would stay by their side forever, carrying on with the farm work after they retired, looking after them in their old age. Their newborn daughter would not. When she married she would leave them for her husband's family and would no longer have any responsibilities toward them. They named her Zhaodi, which means "bring in a younger brother," in the hope that she would be the harbinger of a son. The years passed without a younger brother, though, and the couple grew increasingly desperate to have a son.

Finally, in late 1979 the wife became pregnant again. But their joy turned to ashes in their mouths when the authorities announced that all couples would henceforth be limited to one child. The prying eyes of family planning officials had not yet spotted the wife's condition, but they both knew that detection was only a matter of time.

A friend told them of a "sex prediction chart"—the same kind of chart I remembered from nursing school—that would tell them the sex of their unborn child. You plugged in the age in years of the mother and the father, plus the exact month in which the baby was conceived. The chart would then reveal whether you were carrying a boy or a girl.

They eagerly checked the chart. Sure enough, their unborn child was a boy—the son they had longed for these five years. They *must* keep this child at all costs, they decided. The one-child program was tightening daily. If they lost this child to the family planning workers, they might never have another chance. They devised a feverish scheme to save the life of their unborn son, ignoring all scruples.

One moonless night the couple woke their daughter at midnight. "Come with us, dear," they said quietly. "We are going to take you to a nice place to play."

The little girl, sensing by their weird behavior and wooden smiles that something was wrong, started crying. But her tears could not soften her parents' hearts. They had already set their feet on their chosen path and were determined to follow it to the end.

They led the girl, still weeping, into the hills behind the village. After half an hour of hiking through increasingly wild terrain, they came to a lonely and deserted spot earlier selected by the father. There, beside a huge camphor tree, yawned a black hole some five feet deep. It had been dug by the father the previous night, after he and his wife had decided to bury their daughter alive.

"Climb into the hole, child," the father commanded his daughter.

The little girl shrank back from the black circle and fell to her knees. "Don't kill me," she pleaded, clasping her hands together in a gesture of supplication. "I beg you!"

"But you must die, dear," the mother said coldly. "That way your parents can have a son to care for them in their old age."

"But *I* will care for you in old age," the little girl said to her mother. "I promise. I will never marry." She shuffled across the ground on her knees and tried to hug her mother's legs, but her mother pushed her roughly away.

The little girl turned to her father. "I will help to take care of my little brother," she pleaded, lifting up her arms to embrace him. "Please let me live, Father."

He grabbed her uplifted arms and threw her into the hole that was to be her grave.

Realizing that she could expect no mercy from her parents, the little girl clawed her way out of the hole and tried to run. She got no more than a few steps before her father was upon her. His heavy shovel rose and fell, splitting her skull open, killing her instantly. Her parents buried her body in the hole as they had planned, carefully tamping down the soil and scattering leaves around the top to conceal the grave site.

They returned home, where the sight of their daughter's empty bed struck them like a dagger to the heart. The voice of their conscience, so long denied, thundered, "Murderers! Child killers!" "Our daughter begged us to spare her life," they cried out to each other in their anguish. "How could we have so hardened our hearts so as not to hear?" They fell into a hellish orgy of self-condemnation and began to wonder if they had been possessed. "What kind of demon must have possessed us," the man later remarked in horror, "for us to have done such a thing? What manner of evil spirit sank its claws so deep into our brains that we murdered our only daughter, our own flesh and blood?"

The couple stopped going out to work in the fields and kept the door and windows of their house tightly shut day and night, something no village family ever did. On the rare occasions they emerged from their seclusion, usually to fetch water from the village well, they acted like zombies. They averted their eyes from passersby and when greeted responded in monosyllables. This bizarre behavior did not go unnoticed.

As the days passed and the couple's little girl did not appear in public, the neighbors became increasingly concerned about her. One of their number recalled that, a few days before she vanished, her parents had begun to mistreat her. She had been seen sporting a black eye and bruises. Several neighbors formed a small delegation and went over to the couple's house together. Where is your daughter? they asked the couple point-blank. The two tripped all over each other trying to answer: "We think . . . she's run away . . . or gotten lost . . . we don't really know." This halting jumble of words convinced the neighbors that something really was amiss. The police were called.

The couple at first denied any knowledge of their daughter's whereabouts but soon broke under questioning. Once they had admitted their crime, they eagerly confessed every last horrific detail. They seemed to want to prove their guilt beyond a shadow of a doubt, so that the authorities would have no choice but to put them to death. They even said as much. "Even the tiger, though vicious, does not devour its own young!" they cried out to the police. "We do not deserve to live. Execute us and put an end to our suffering."

The trial in the county court took only a few hours. As expected, the couple pleaded guilty and were sentenced to death. The execution took place within the week and was carried out in the usual fashion: a single bullet to the back of the head. Everyone in the county thought that justice had been served. Wei Xin's mother, a nominal Buddhist who believed rather vaguely in the sanctity of life, had only one regret. While the parents deserved to die, she maintained, the child in the woman's womb—the hoped-for son—most certainly did not. "That baby was an innocent little life," Wei Xin's mother told me in a distraught tone of voice. "He should not have been executed along with his parents. The people's government shed innocent blood."

Over the course of my stay in the village I was to hear of other little girls being killed to make way for boys. Nearly all these cases involved newborns, who were drowned or smothered at birth before they had a chance to draw their first breath. What was true of Jiangsu Province was also true of other parts of China. The situation in Anhui Province, immediately to the north of Jiangsu, was among the worst. The Anhui Women's Federation reported that in one small village alone, forty girls had been drowned in 1980 and 1981. Friends returning from the countryside told me that in some more remote villages there were almost no surviving female infants.

The Party, alarmed by the widespread resurgence of female infanticide in the countryside, began attacking it in the pages of the *People's Daily* and elsewhere. These articles blamed this barbarous practice on the survival of feudal attitudes toward the sexes among the peasantry. They called on local population control officials to educate the peasantry out of their ancient prejudices against daughters. The real culprit—the one-child policy—was rarely mentioned. But I knew that couples whose first child was a girl faced a cruel choice. They could keep their daughter and forfeit their chance for a son who would support them in old age. Or they could sacrifice her to the hope that their next child would be a boy.

Not all illegal pregnancies I heard about during our stay in the Village of the Three Brothers ended in tragedy. One of our visitors, a former schoolmate of Wei Xin's, told of how he and his wife had defied orders to have an abortion. Their first child had been a girl, and they were desperate to have a son. "I declared to our village Party secretary that we were determined to keep this child," he said. "He said that we would pay a heavy price for violating the one-child policy. 'To keep this baby,' I boldly replied, 'we will pay any price.' "

He smiled ruefully at the recollection, taking another drag on the cigarette that Wei Xin had lit for him. "The officials levied a fine of *five thousand* yuan," he continued. "We were shocked speechless. Five thousand yuan is roughly twenty times our yearly income. But still we obstinately refused an abortion. We put our heads together and managed to come up with about five hundred yuan—most of that amount borrowed from my brothers. 'We will make installment payments for the rest,' we said. The officials laughed at our offer and carried our pig to the slaughterhouse and our chickens to the butchers. Then they returned for our furniture, auctioning it off in the village square to the highest bidder. We were left with nothing but bare walls and dirt floors. The officials would have sold our house, too, but for the fact that it was built condominium-style, sharing walls with the homes of my brothers on both sides.

"After all our possessions had been sold," he went on, "the officials told us that we were still three thousand yuan in debt. A struggle meeting was called. I was publicly denounced for having violated the Party policy on having children, and for not paying the three thousand yuan we owed the village. How could we pay that debt? We had nothing left but four walls and the clothes on our backs."

"Once someone has been made a struggle object, he has no place to put his face," Wei Xin's mother remarked to no one in particular.

Wei Xin's friend shook his head in disagreement. "I refused to admit any wrongdoing, Mother Wei. 'Are you guilty or not guilty?' they asked me. 'Not guilty,' I said. They roughed me up a little bit, but they dared not be too harsh with me. After all, my three brothers were in the audience. And most people in the village were secretly sympathetic with our desire to have a son."

Wei Xin's friend had the guts to do what I should have done, I thought to myself. *Defy the authorities*. I had to know if he thought it had been worth it. I spoke up from the bench where I was sitting: "Are you sorry about the decision you made?"

"Well, moneywise it has been very difficult for us," he said. He held up the cigarette he was smoking. "This is the first cigarette I've had in months. And we've had to take down the doors to our house and use them as beds. But, no, I'm not sorry." He turned to Wei Xin. "You and your wife should come over to our house and see my son. He is now two months old. He is a big, healthy boy. We are both very glad that we have him."

I heard of other couples who successfully evaded the one-child policy. The oddest case involved a teacher in a country school who had gotten pregnant with her second child while wearing an IUD.

(This news, relayed by a friend of hers, caused me to perk up my ears.) As months went by without a period and her waist started to thicken, she surmised that she was pregnant. But how could she make sure of her condition without at the same time revealing it to the population control official at her school?

After careful deliberation she decided to take a calculated risk. When she was, according to her calculations, about five months pregnant, she went to the local clinic and requested an X ray. "I want to make sure that my IUD is still in place," she told the technician. The resulting plate showed her IUD clearly evident, though somewhat off center. The technician noted this result, and she went home happy. Her baby, its bones not yet well developed, had been invisible to the bored eyes of the technician.

It was not until the teacher was in her final months that the official became suspicious of her bulging waistline. "I don't know why I am putting on all this weight," the teacher responded, feigning perplexity. "I thought earlier I might be pregnant, but my IUD is still in place. I suppose I have just been eating too much." The official, who knew what the X ray had showed, accepted her explanation. The teacher's IUD indeed remained in place, and there it stayed until she gave birth, when it was expelled with the afterbirth.

Everyone howled with laughter at the teacher's unexpected success in foiling the population control official. The new one-child policy was deeply unpopular in the countryside, and those charged with carrying it out had already made many enemies. The general attitude was expressed by a middle-aged farmer with three children. "Now that the communes are being disbanded we have our own land," he said. "We grow our own food with our own two hands. We don't eat the state's rice the way you city people do. So why should the state tell us how many children I should have?"

The village woman whose struggle with the population control officials touched me the most deeply was the one I came to know best. Wei Xin's brother's wife, Aiming, was a small, fragile-looking woman with a bubbly, outgoing personality. Wei Xin had hinted at Aiming's difficulties, but it was from her own lips that I heard the whole story of all she had had to endure to give birth to her son.

Aiming told me that her husband, as the oldest son, felt responsible for giving his father a grandson. Conceiving children was not easy for them, however, because he did not work in the village. Shortly after they had married in 1967, coal was discovered in the hills north of the county seat. A government mine was opened, and two thousand village men were recruited from around the county to be trained as miners. Her husband was among those selected. The entire family rejoiced at this news, for it meant that he would be enrolled in the ranks of government workers, receiving a fixed salary, free housing, medical care, retirement benefits, and a host of other perquisites not enjoyed by peasants. There was only one drawback: Aiming, his wife, was not allowed to transfer her household registration. Though her husband was now classified as a worker, she remained a peasant. Among other things, this meant that she could not join her husband at the mine. Instead, as custom demanded, she went to live with her husband's parents in the Village of the Three Brothers.

Aiming and her husband were eager to have a child, but as a miner he had only one day off a week. It frequently took him half a day of hitchhiking and walking to cover the thirty miles from work to home—and he had to return to the mine the following night. Although the mine was not far from the village as the crow flies, it lay well off the main roads, and there was no public transportation directly linking it with the village in the south. Tired of wasting so much time on the road, he stopped trying to come home every Sunday. Instead he would work twenty-five or thirty days straight, allowing his days off to accumulate, and then take them all at once. This new schedule made it even more difficult for them to conceive children. "I had to time my husband's visits carefully," Aiming said with a laugh, "or I would never have gotten pregnant." Their first two children arrived in 1969 and 1973. Both were girls.

After the birth of her second child, she was visited by the head of the local woman's federation. "She wanted me to wear an IUD or agree to sterilization," Aiming recalled. "I refused. At the time the official limit was two children, but this was not strictly enforced. I still had to prove myself, you see. In the countryside people look down on you if you cannot produce sons. I wanted the people in my husband's village to respect me. My husband didn't beat me after I gave birth to girls, as some women are beaten by their husbands. But I could tell he wasn't happy. I wanted to give my husband a son."

After Tacheng was born in March 1976, Aiming's husband's longing for a son intensified. "When we received the letter saying that you and Wei Xin had a son," Aiming remarked, "my husband was happy for you. But then he looked at me and said, 'Aiming, my younger brother had a son on his first try. Why can't we have a son?' "

With two children already, Aiming and her husband knew that they had at most only one more chance at a son. The pressure to submit to sterilization would grow irresistible after a third child. A fourth was out of the question. In 1977, after long months of carefully scheduling her husband's visits home to correspond with the fertile portion of her cycle, Aiming became pregnant. She and her husband secretly rejoiced. Then, at four months, she miscarried. They were devastated.

Meanwhile, the population control strictures continued to tighten. In February 1978, Party chairman Hua Guofeng declared to the Fifth National People's Congress that China's provinces should reduce their population growth rate to 1 percent or less within three years. The Jiangsu provincial authorities declared that no couple could have more than two children. Third children were outlawed.

When Aiming became pregnant in October 1978, she knew she could not openly carry this baby to term. She would have to conceal her condition from the Women's Federation as long as she could, then go into hiding once she was exposed. As soon as the weather turned cold, she donned a bulky winter coat two sizes too big for her. She wore it indoors and out for the next six months. It was not until early May, when the arrival of warm weather forced her into cooler clothes, that she was discovered to be pregnant. "The local head of the Women's Federation was very unhappy to learn that I was already seven months along," Aiming laughed. "She immediately designated me a 'primary target for remedial measures.' "

Months before, Aiming and her husband had devised a plan for this moment. A room had been rented in a remote hamlet a couple of miles from the mine. It had been stocked with clothes, bedding, and other essentials. This would be Aiming's hideout until she gave birth. All Aiming had to do was travel there, and she would be safe.

Aiming had planned her escape route carefully but had not reckoned with how quickly the Women's Federation would move. The night before Aiming was to travel to the mine, she and Mother Wei were awakened at 1:00 A.M. by the sound of someone banging on the front door. They looked out through the bars of their bedroom window to see the Women's Federation head at the door. She was backed by five militiamen armed with rifles. A horse-drawn cart stood down the street. Aiming knew at once that they had come to take her to the commune medical clinic, by force if necessary.

"I bolted for the back door," Aiming recalled, "wearing only my nightshirt. Behind me I heard Mother Wei loudly arguing with the head of the Women's Federation through the door. 'What do you want at such an hour?!'

" 'Open the door! This is a matter of state business!'

"I ran across the alleyway and hid myself quickly inside a pigsty. I did not want to wake up the dogs of the village. I waited and listened to see what would happen when they found out that I was missing."

As soon as Mother Wei opened the door a crack, the militiamen forced their way inside. "Where is she?" Aiming heard the head of the Women's Federation shout.

"I don't know," Mother Wei's voice came back coolly. "She left some time ago."

"We'll see about that," the official responded. "Search the bedrooms," she ordered the militiamen. There was the sound of trunks being opened and furniture being moved. After a minute the voice of the official could be heard again. "Where did she go?" she shouted, angry that her quarry had eluded her. Mother Wei's response was too soft to make out, but the official's strident voice could be heard loud and clear: "In that case we will wait here for her until she returns."

With the squad of militiamen apparently encamped in the house for the night, Aiming knew she couldn't stay in the pigsty. At any minute the head of the Women's Federation might order a search of the village. Besides, she was being tormented by great clouds of mosquitoes, undeterred by her thin nightshirt and her careful efforts to wave them away. She considered setting out for her distant hiding place under cover of darkness, but abandoned the idea for fear that the roads were being patrolled. Instead, she decided, she would leave the confines of the village and conceal herself in the surrounding paddy fields. There, where it was safer, she would wait out the militiamen.

Aiming slipped out of the pigsty and moved quietly down the alleyway, taking care to remain in the shadows on this moonlit night. In a minute she had passed out of the village onto the narrow pathways that divided the individual paddies, placing her feet carefully on the muddy, slippery ridges to avoid a fall. She came to a small rock outcropping about a hundred yards from the village—close enough to see what the militiamen were up to but providing enough cover to avoid being seen—and squatted down to wait for the dawn. "There were even more mosquitoes in the rice paddies than in the pigsty," Aiming recalled wryly. "The mosquitoes stung me until I was covered with welts. Maddened by the constant bites, I got down from the rock into the paddy itself, squatting down in the cool water, feeling my feet sink into the mud below. I smeared thick mud over the exposed parts of my body. The cool wetness helped to relieve some of the itching, but as soon as it dried the mosquitoes would return, biting me through the layer of mud. I felt a tickling on my legs and kept having to slap off hungry leeches. I was miserable, hungry, and tired. I refused to give in to self-pity, though. I was not going to give myself up, no matter what happened." She gave me a fierce look, which seemed out of character on her usually friendly face. "If they discovered me, I was ready to fight them to the death for the life of my son."

Aiming hid in the fields for two long days, until the militiamen grew tired of waiting and drove off in their cart back to the commune seat. That evening she dragged herself back to the house. Mother Wei was shocked by her appearance. Most of her body was covered with a thick layer of dried mud. In the places where the mud had cracked and fallen off, great red welts stood out on her skin through streaks of dirt. "With my great big belly and my dirt-matted hair and face, I must have looked like some alien creature," Aiming recalled with a smile. "Mother Wei said I resembled neither human nor ghost."

Aiming hid inside Mother Wei's house that night and the following day, resting and regaining her strength. Then she set out under cover of darkness for her hiding place. It took her most of the night to walk to the county seat. From there she took the morning bus to the market town nearest her destination, covering the last five miles through the hills to the hamlet on foot. She was at the end of her strength when she arrived at her hiding place. Her husband, who had gotten word through a friend that she was coming, was waiting for her. She collapsed into his arms, exhausted but triumphant.

For several days after Aiming's disappearance the head of the Women's Federation busied herself striking other "primary targets for remedial measures." Nine women from the Village of the Three Brothers and surrounding communities—all five or more months pregnant—were arrested during successful midnight raids and taken to the commune medical clinic for abortion and sterilization. Then she turned her attention back to the still-missing Aiming.

Having failed to capture her quarry by surprise, the Women's Federation head resorted to bullying. She and two assistants invaded Mother Wei's house like an occupying army, arriving early each morning and staying until late each night. Throughout the day they took turns browbeating her about Aiming:

"If you don't tell your daughter-in-law to come back, we will sit here until she does."

"We have never seen anyone with skin as thick as yours, but we will wear you down."

"Unless you tell us where your daughter-in-law is hiding, we will have to hold a struggle meeting to criticize you."

Other times they would threaten her with heavy fines. "It is your fault we are wasting our time sitting here," the official said a dozen times a day. "You are responsible for our salary. For every day we spend on your daughter-in-law's case, you owe the Party six yuan. You are also responsible for feeding us."

Mother Wei did her best to ignore her unwelcome visitors, saying nothing in response to their taunts and threats. Nor did she refuse outright their demands to be fed. But at mealtimes she prepared only enough food for herself and her two granddaughters, which they hurriedly gulped down in the kitchen. Her visitors had no choice but to take their meals elsewhere. At mealtimes they would head out the door, grumbling as they went about her tightfistedness. For an hour or so at lunch and dinner Mother Wei had a much-needed respite from the constant pressure she was under to turn in her daughter-in-law.

Sixty-five days after the officials had come in the dead of night for her and her unborn baby, Aiming went into labor. She was assisted by a local midwife, who was bribed into helping with the delivery. She gave birth to a healthy eight-pound boy.

As soon as Mother Wei received the glad tidings, she broke her long silence. "I have a grandson," she proudly told the Women's Federation officials. "There is nothing more you can do. Now you can leave."

Without a word, without even a backward glance, the three officials got up and walked out the door. But the head of the Women's Federation, who had earlier vowed that the Wei family would pay for the trouble they had caused, soon proved that she had not been making empty threats. A few days later Mother Wei received a bill from the Women's Federation for 390 yuan for sixty-five days of "work."

Aiming's husband promptly paid this fine, though it took all their savings. Still, he feared that the matter might not end there. " 'Don't come home yet,' he told me," Aiming recalled. "He didn't think that the Women's Federation would harm me or the baby, but after everything that had happened, he couldn't be sure. We agreed that I would continue in hiding for the time being."

Word of the Wei family's new arrival spread swiftly through the Village of the Three Brothers. Under normal circumstances Mother Wei's central room would quickly have filled with callers. Neighbors and kin from miles around would have come to offer their congratulations. But there was a rumor afoot that the Wei house was being watched, and this time most people stayed home. The few close kinsmen willing to brave the wrath of the authorities waited until after dusk and knocked on the back door. After a hurried visit, they left the same way they had come.

When the next few weeks passed without incident, Aiming's husband decided that it was safe to bring his wife and son back to the village. By design they arrived on the eve of his son's one-month birthday. The following day virtually the entire village poured into Mother Wei's for the full-month feast. Aiming and her husband moved proudly among the guests, showing off their tiny, pink-cheeked son. Mother Wei followed close behind, handing a scarlet-colored egg to each of the assembled guests so that they would "have a share in our good fortune." "Full-month wine" flowed freely, and the house rang with toasts of "*Gongxi! Gongxi!*" late into the night. Thus was the youngest member of the Wei clan officially welcomed into the family. Only the local Party secretary and two members of the local Women's Federation boycotted the feast. From them there was an ominous silence.

After this show of support, Aiming and her husband hoped that they would be left in peace. But the head of the Women's Federation was not yet finished with them. A week after Aiming returned home, the militiamen came again, this time in broad daylight. Aiming's husband was at the mine. "I thought they were coming for my son," Aiming recalled. "I gave him to Mother Wei in a panic and told her to escape out the back door. But it was me they were after. They grabbed me and put me on the cart. I was so surprised that I put up no resistance."

Aiming was taken under guard to the commune medical clinic. There, on orders from the head of the Women's Federation, she was given a tubal ligation the same day.

"Do you regret not putting up more of a struggle?" I asked. "After all, you can never have any more children."

"At first I was upset," she confirmed. "They carted me off like a pig to the slaughterhouse. But then"—she paused in midsentence and looked down at the pink-cheeked little boy playing happily at her feet, then she looked up at me—"then I thought of our little treasure. I decided that it was not too high a price to pay."

I had become very fond of Aiming and was horrified to learn that she had been forcibly sterilized. Much though I had suffered, I had never been subjected to the kind of open and crude coercion that she and other village women had experienced. Peasant women were being treated almost like subhumans, it seemed to me, with no regard for their rights or feelings.

But as I looked at Aiming's three children, the two older girls and her young son, I discovered that my sympathy for my sister-in-law was not entirely unbounded. She had claimed the family that I had always dreamed of and would now be denied. So desirable and so unattainable was her achievement that I started feeling twinges of something akin to envy. *It isn't fair*, I caught myself thinking more than once. *Aiming has two daughters, yet I am forbidden even one.* I disliked finding these ungenerous feelings in me. I felt guilty about them.

I went to great lengths to hide them from others, even Wei Xin. But I could not entirely subdue my new mood. I was suffering from the red-eyed disease.

On March 6, 1980, Tacheng and I went with Wei Xin to the airport. It was not a proper parting. My husband did not mask his eagerness to be off. He kept glancing at his watch, as if he were afraid that his plane might take off without him. He was out of his chair with the first announcement that the plane was ready for boarding. He hurriedly kissed Tacheng, gave me a quick squeeze, and then bolted for the gate. Tacheng and I were both crying as we watched him walk briskly up the ramp and disappear into the plane without a backward glance. The plane taxied onto the runway, picked up speed, and was airborne. In a minute it had dwindled to a tiny silver dot on the horizon. Then it was gone. I looked out into the clear eastern sky, feeling abandoned. Tacheng and I were alone.

I bent down to console my small son. "When will Daddy come back?" four-year-old Tacheng asked through his sniffles.

"Soon," I responded automatically. "He'll be back very soon."

In fact, it was five years before either of us saw Wei Xin again.

14

The Little-Boy-
Who-Wouldn't-Die

After Wei Xin left for the United States, my life came to center on my young son. My normal sense of maternal responsibility for Tacheng was compounded by a feeling akin to pity for this four-year-old, who was to be without a father for more years than he had yet been on this earth. We were both, in our own way, fatherless. I had been orphaned by my father's death, while Tacheng had been orphaned by his father's ambitions. I resolved to be both mother *and* father to him. I brought home treats for him from work and read him stories at night. On my days off I took him to the zoo or for a walk in one of Shenyang's many parks. My little man delighted in all this attention, and his joy at our newfound companionship dulled the painful edge of my own loneliness.

I had never liked the ten-hour workdays and the irregular work-week of the sanitarium, which meant I rarely had weekends off. Worse still were the frequent shift changes—every month or so we rotated from day to swing, or swing to night, or back to days again. This unpredictable schedule, which had been difficult enough to manage with Wei Xin's occasional help, became impossible now that I was a single mother. Tacheng was too old to stay in the sanitarium nursery, and it was hard to find a neighbor willing to watch him with my schedule changing from day to day and week to week. I refused to even consider sending him off to a boarding nursery, remembering the many miserable months my brothers and I had spent in such institutions when we were small.

Unhappy with my situation, I started considering possible alternatives. My thoughts turned to the health clinics run by large, state-owned enterprises, all of which provided free medical care to their work forces. A job in such a clinic seemed ideal to me. Clinic nurses, like most other factory workers, kept regular hours, working Monday to Friday and a half day on Saturday. I would be home every night and on Sundays to take care of Tacheng. I could even take him to work with me, since such enterprises always had day-care centers.

I did not underestimate the difficulty of transferring from the sanitarium to a factory health clinic. Life in China's socialist welfare state, with its cradle-to-grave job security, was undemanding as long as one did not deviate from the authorities' rigid plan. Work assignments followed graduation from school and, unless the needs of the state dictated otherwise, were intended to be for life. Midcareer transfers for personal reasons were definitely outside the plan and were dauntingly complex to arrange. For my transfer to go through, I had to clear three major hurdles. First, I had to find a unit willing to hire me to fill a nursing position. Second, the sanitarium had to be willing to sign a release, even though they could expect no immediate replacement. Finally, I had to have a letter from the municipal employment bureau approving the transfer.

I shared my hopes for a transfer with my mother, who, with her widespread contacts throughout the city, was indispensable to my plans. She agreed to help, and immediately swung into action. Once again she began making the rounds of her former students and their parents, asking whether there were any openings for nurses in the factories where they worked.

Finding me a spouse and a birth quota had not been easy, but finding me a new position proved even more difficult. Several months of calling on former students produced few leads and zero offers of employment. Only the larger state enterprises in and around Shenyang had their own medical clinics, and it turned out that most of these did their hiring from within. When workers retired, their places were taken by their own sons and daughters. Mother was at her wit's end. Then she remembered that a former schoolmate of my father's—they had attended middle school together—was the director of the Liaoning Truck Factory. Located in the industrial suburbs to the north of Shenyang, the factory was a small city unto itself. Its sprawling compounds housed fifteen thousand workers and their families. Dozens of two-and-a-half-ton Red Flag trucks rolled off its assembly lines every day.

My mother and I went to see the factory director, who was also the head of the Party branch committee, giving him a double authority. Secretary Chen was a bluff, hearty man, very unlike the usual run of polite but insincere officials. I liked him instantly. "I do have an opening in the medical clinic," he told me in response to my request. "I need someone to help with women's health work." He looked me straight in the eye. "You understand that this means you will be involved in family planning activities."

I understood only too well. Women's health was originally a broad topic that included, besides family planning, all the common diseases of women and pre- and postnatal care. But in those days it meant mostly contraception, sterilization, and abortion. Though I didn't relish the thought of having to enforce the one-child policy, by now my envy of women with more than one child had hardened into something akin to resentment. Besides, I was desperate to get out of the sanitarium. Struggling to mask my feelings, I nodded.

"Good," he said. "Your mother tells me that you have already signed a one-child agreement. You will be a good example for the other women, then. We still have a lot of women whose thinking is very backward."

I now had a job offer but, as often happens in China, my original work unit refused to release me. I was known as an excellent nurse. I had even received a special "technical excellence award" in recognition of my nursing skills. My supervisor was doubly loath to let me go. Not only was there no prospect of an immediate replacement, but, as she told me: "I am unlikely to get another nurse as good as you."

My mother took matters into her own hands. She went to see the Party secretary of the sanitarium, Secretary Wang, explaining to him that Wei Xin was in the United States and that I was taking care of Tacheng all by myself. "My daughter finds herself in a very difficult situation," she argued. "You really ought to let her go work in the Liaoning Truck Factory, where she can spend time with her son in the evenings. There is no one else to take care of him."

Secretary Wang refused to consider releasing me unless someone from the factory was willing to swap places.

The following day found my mother again pleading my case to Secretary Wang, this time playing up my medical history. "Chi An has a serious problem with her health," she told him. "As you know, she takes a lot of time off work. Why, she's home for a week or two every few months. You would be better off with someone else." The Party secretary was unconvinced.

Far from being discouraged by these rebuffs, my indomitable mother began a campaign to wear the Party secretary down. She went to his office every day after work. Often he refused to see her, since he knew all too well the purpose of her visit. But she would park herself in his waiting room, refusing to go away. His office had no back door, and whenever he left his office my mother would jump up: "Please reconsider my daughter's case, Secretary Wang!"

The Party secretary took to hiding in his office in the afternoons, waiting for her to leave. However late he stayed, though, Mother stayed later. When he finally bolted for home, she would be there: "Please reconsider my daughter's case, Secretary Wang!"

Two weeks passed before he finally caved in. "Never in my life have I met a woman as stubborn as you!" he shouted at her one evening as he left his office. He thrust a letter at her. She knew without looking that it was his endorsement of my transfer. He waved his hands at her as if he were waving away an unpleasant apparition. "Go now, and take your daughter with you!"

As soon as I had been formally transferred to the Liaoning Truck Factory, my new boss, Secretary Chen, sent me to Beijing for six months of advanced training in women's health. I was assigned to the Beijing No. 4 Hospital, where Tacheng and I took up residence in a dormitory. I worked as a nurse intern in the women's health clinic, learning to diagnose and treat ovarian and cervical cancer, bacterial infections of the uterus and bladder, and other, minor female complaints. I also talked to expectant mothers about diet, fetal development, and the birth process.

But such matters constituted the smallest part of my training. As I had expected, nearly all of my time at Beijing No. 4 Hospital was spent studying family planning procedures—how to insert an IUD, how to perform a tubal ligation, and six or seven different methods for performing abortions. Women's health was now a secondary consideration, as I learned when I was given a short refresher course in IUDs.

IUDs worked by preventing the fertilized egg from implanting itself in the lining of the uterus. They were convenient from the government's point of view because, once in place, they were generally effective until removed. During the last few years a new kind of IUD, easier to insert and more comfortable to wear than the old steel O ring, had come into widespread use. It was shaped like a Y, with two arms and a tail like a kite. Unlike the O ring, which came in several sizes and had to be carefully matched to the size of the woman's uterus, the Y came in only one size, which fit all women. With the arms compressed it passed easily through the cervix. Once inside the uterus, the arms expanded to hold it in place. It was also easy to remove. You simply pulled down on the tail, and out it came. This was the kind of IUD that I had been wearing.

This Y IUD, I discovered to my surprise, had recently been

banned. Its use had given rise to too many overquota pregnancies. Women had been taking matters into their own hands, using the conveniently dangling tail to surreptitiously pull out their unwanted IUDs. Since the Y IUD was not made of metal, it was invisible to X rays, and its absence could not be detected.

The old steel O ring had been brought back into common use, though with one difference. No longer was it matched to the size of a woman's uterus. Only one size ring—large—was now manufactured. This was intended to make it difficult to remove, but of course it also made it difficult to insert, especially on those women who had not yet borne children or who had narrow cervixes. I had no difficulty with my new IUD, but young women often got up off the examination table after an IUD insertion doubled up in pain and cramping. For some the discomfort continued for days or even weeks, or gave rise to infections of the uterine lining or fallopian tubes. When I complained about this new policy I was treated to a barked lecture from the clinic supervisor: "Our goal is to prevent all illegal pregnancies! The woman's comfort is a secondary consideration!"

Even some of my prenatal training took on a new and more ominous meaning in light of the overweening emphasis on population control. I learned at the women's health clinic to detect pregnancies by palpating the cervix, whose softening is one of the first signs that a woman is pregnant. But in these times the detection of pregnancy was not a prelude to prenatal care, as the doctor who taught me this skill made clear. "The earlier you are able to detect pregnancy," he told me, "the easier it is to convince the recalcitrant to abort."

My first assignment directly concerned with abortion was to interview pregnant women who were brought into the clinic. I was in charge of taking down each woman's medical history, but the only thing that really concerned the clinic director was how far along she was, as this determined the kind of abortion procedure that would be used. At the same time I was to try and obtain her consent for the procedure she was about to undergo. The abortion would be performed in any case, I was told, but it was easier on everyone concerned if the patient first gave her permission. No one wanted to have to drag a kicking and screaming woman to the operating table if it could be avoided.

Unmarried women, who usually came in alone, needed no convincing. They answered my question with a quick whisper of assent and went quietly to the operating table, eager to be relieved of their burden of shame. There were not many of these, for most Chinese women were still virgins on their wedding night. Most of the women I saw were married, however, and, on the whole, much more difficult to deal with. Many had been subjected to weeks of high-pressure tactics and had only reluctantly come around. More often than not, they arrived at the hospital in the company of one or two unsmiling officials from the Women's Federation. "Hurry up and finish what we have started," I was urged more than once by such escorts, "before she changes her mind and gives us more trouble."

At the time I saw nothing unethical about my assignment. Following my own forced induction into the ranks of one-child mothers, I had repressed my earlier qualms about the morality of the new policy. It made good economic sense to me that China had to control its population in order to modernize. But at the same time I remained generally sympathetic to what these sad-faced women were going through. Had I nourished the slightest hope that one day I might be permitted a second child, I would have been more so. As things were I was convinced that I was doing them a kindness by helping them to accept, as I had, the inevitable.

I was very good at this kind of manipulation, for I set out to make friends with each new patient. While pretending to record her medical history, I would chat with her about her job and her family. Once she began to relax a little in my company, I would bring the conversation around to the question at hand. "Well, you appear to have exceeded your allotted number of children," I would begin in my most sympathetic manner. She would answer yes. "I, too, once conceived an overquota child," I would confide to her. "I, too, had to undergo remedial measures. I know it is a difficult thing to do. But it is necessary for the sake of our fatherland. Are you willing?"

Many were already defeated and, when the question was put to them, would nod wordlessly, tears streaming down their faces. Others I was able to persuade. "You'll have another chance to have a baby in a few years," I would say soothingly. I didn't really believe this, for the one-child policy was getting stricter and stricter, but the desperate women to whom I was speaking sometimes did.

A few, when I asked if they consented to the operation, burst into bitter laughter. "Why ask me?" one scoffed. "I don't have any choice. The population control workers in my unit have been after me for months. *'Fanxing, fanxing!'* they ordered me. 'Reflect on your mistake!' Only if I undergo 'remedial measures' will they stop pressuring me and my husband."

From time to time we would get a "pleader," as they were scornfully referred to by the clinic staff. These women were the toughest to deal with, for they begged shamelessly and unceasingly. "Please spare the life of my child!" these women would cry out. "Please allow my baby to live. My husband and I want this baby very much." Some even got down on their knees and began knocking their heads on the floor in supplication. "This is our last chance to have another child. Please . . . I beg you!"

Their pleas for mercy rang out like accusations and left a bitter taste in my mouth. My usual arguments were ineffective with pleaders, and I was reduced to pleading in my turn. "Please don't make things even more difficult for us," I would say. "We are only following orders. We don't have any more choice than you do. We have no way to escape our responsibilities." Despite my best efforts, I was frequently unable to induce these women to accept calmly their child's fate. Some went into the operating room still begging, making everyone uneasy and uncomfortable.

At least where these pleaders were concerned, my sympathy soon gave way to irritation. Why couldn't they understand that we clinic workers were not personally responsible for our actions? The doctors were only following orders. I was only a minor functionary. Besides, I, too, had been compelled to have an abortion. I, too, had only one child. Why should anyone be allowed to have more children than I? I hardened my heart against such women and began rebuking them.

"Why do you insist on having a second child?" I asked them. "Don't you know that it isn't fair to those who have only one?"

Some time later I was "promoted" from interviewer to first-trimester abortionist. When, for the first time in fourteen years, I picked up the suction device, my hands were trembling. When I set to work, even the smallest cry of pain or grief from the woman made my jaw clench and my heart palpitate. But the pace of my work was grueling—the one-child campaign was even then growing more intense—and left little time for reflection or remorse.

I quickly settled into the habit of haste and became numb to all considerations except speed. I became an expert at performing suction abortions quickly and cleanly, sometimes evacuating as many as two dozen uteruses in a single day. As for the women, I neither conversed with them nor heeded their cries. They meant nothing to me. My only concession to my former squeamishness was that I steadfastly refused to check the collection bottle after I finished. This hardly mattered. So expert had I become that, even without visual confirmation, I was always certain that I had gotten all the parts.

No one was happy with the endless round of sterilizations and abortions they were required to perform. Although no one spoke out openly against it, there was an undercurrent of dissatisfaction, especially among the older doctors and nurses. People in China often disguise their opinions in the form of jokes, and there was lots of gallows humor going around about the one-child policy. Once I and several other nurses were having lunch when Doctor Wan, a kindly old obstetrician who also worked in the clinic, stopped by our table. "Nurse Yang, have you ever considered what is going to happen at the end of your life?" Doctor Wan said to me. He spoke in a bantering tone of voice, but his smile didn't reach his eyes. "When one day you are sent to the netherworld, you will have lots of little hands clawing at you."

The image made my skin crawl. I knew that Doctor Wan was really expressing his opposition to the way the one-child policy was being carried out, though for my part I wasn't about to say anything that might be taken as a criticism of the government. "I wouldn't do this if I had any other way to fill my rice bowl," I said crossly, momentarily losing my composure. Then, after an effort to smile that must have pulled my face awry, I flung his accusation back at him. "In any event, Doctor Wan," I said, "I've only been doing this work for a short time. You will have many more little hands clawing at you than I will."

Doctor Wan's smile disappeared and he gave me a piercing glance. Then he pointed at a doctor sitting at a table a short distance away. "Doctor Yin over there will have much more to account for than I," he said, speaking slowly and with great gravity. "He enjoys doing the late-term abortions." My gorge rose, and I had difficulty eating the rest of my lunch.

The final phase of my training involved assisting at late-term abortions. Under clinic rules such abortions, performed on women five or more months pregnant, could only be performed by doctors. Several methods were in common use. Doctor Wan, whom I assisted on several occasions, used the expulsion method, which was considered to be the safest for women. An expandable rubber bulb was introduced into the uterus and then filled with sterilized water. The extra pressure on the uterus usually caused contractions to begin within an hour or two, resulting in the expulsion of the baby a short time later.

The major drawback of this approach, as far as we on the clinic staff were concerned, was that these babies were usually born alive. Even those of only thirty weeks of gestational age often lived for several hours after being discarded in a waste receptacle in the operating room. Older babies lived even longer. It was upsetting for all of us to see a four- or five-pound baby boy or girl thrown into a trash can still alive, and to hear the muffled sound of his or her crying for the rest of the day.

To avoid this kind of unpleasantness—for no one had the stomach to kill a baby after it had opened its eyes—most doctors terminated late-term pregnancies by means of a traditional Chinese herbal medicine, Trichosanthes kirilowii. This herbal drug was injected directly into the amniotic fluid by means of a hypodermic with a long needle. When the baby swallowed the fluid, as late-term babies do, it poisoned itself. This "poison shot" also induced premature labor, causing the fetus to be stillborn. Nevertheless, it was not without its drawbacks. To be effective the drug had to be administered in such high concentrations that it sometimes caused dangerous side effects in women. Babies who had drunk too little of the amniotic fluid for the drug to be fatal were also occasionally born alive, and we had to endure the sound of their crying for as long as it took them to die.

Not Doctor Yin. His preferred "techniques" were attended by no such embarrassing lapses. First he would induce premature labor. Then, after the cervix had dilated and the crown of the baby's head was exposed, he would inject pure formaldehyde into the fetal brain through the fontanel, or soft spot. The baby would be born dead. On occasions when the cervix refused to dilate fully, he would reach in with forceps and crush the baby's skull. Then he would remove the broken body piecemeal. Even this was considered humane by a nursing supervisor, who spoke of rural clinics where babies were thrown into boiling water and scalded to death or placed in airtight jars and smothered. "As long as you kill the baby while it is still partly in the womb," she explained to me, "it is a legal abortion. Once the baby is born, it becomes murder."

After assisting Doctor Yin with a number of late-term abortions, I had to agree with old Doctor Wan's evaluation of his young colleague: Doctor Yin took a grim pleasure in this grisly business. This was especially true when he was operating on a country woman. Like the army doctor who had likened sterilizing village women to spaying pigs, he had a visceral dislike of the peasantry. "What are these peasants but swine!" he would rant as he worked his forceps. "They live in their squalid villages in the filth and the mud! Their homes are worse than pigpens. Their only instinct is to multiply. It's the only thing these illiterate sows can do. They are dragging us all down, holding China back! The endless children they bear have no chance in life. What child would choose to be born in the midst of squalor and misery? I tell you, Nurse Yang, we are doing this baby a favor! It is better to end its life right now, before it has a chance to experience hunger and pain. Poor wretch."

You can imagine the effect that his rantings had on his patients, none of whom were there voluntarily. As for me, I would just grit my teeth and think about the kind, gentle man who was my husband. Wei Xin, born to a peasant woman in a village, was one of those Doctor Yin would have eliminated before birth. He believed that villagers were "holding China back," yet my husband was in the United States, studying for an advanced degree that would aid China's modernization. *Yes, Wei Xin was born a peasant*, I answered Doctor Yin silently, *but he will surely make a greater contribution to China than you*.

Despite my new conviction—or was it just a rationalization?—that the one-child program was necessary for China, I could not overcome my aversion for late-term abortions, whether performed by Doctor Yin or anyone else. I didn't know which was worse—crushing a child's skull with forceps or throwing a live baby away like so much rubbish. I became increasingly anxious to finish my training and return to the Liaoning Truck Factory.

One night near the end of my stay at the Beijing No. 4 Hospital a shivering young woman was brought in to the women's health clinic. Flanked by two sturdy Beijing policemen, she was a forlorn sight, with her wan, dirt-streaked face and her large belly, enormous in proportion to her slight body. She was not much more than a girl, really, and very close to term.

"We found her crouched in an alleyway," one of the policemen was explaining to the charge nurse. "She doesn't have a residence permit or a ration card, and she won't tell us who she is or where she is from. Probably a runaway from a village somewhere, to judge from her clothes. The sergeant thought it best to bring her here to the hospital first thing, seeing how big her belly is. Even if we knew where she was from, we couldn't send her back in this condition. She might have her brat on the way."

I inwardly agreed, judging her to be at the very end of her ninth month.

"It was good that you brought her here," the nurse said. "We have the authority to deal with such cases."

Beckoning to me, she said, "Take the girl to Number Three Delivery Room and remain with her. The doctors will want to see her in the morning."

I did as told. In the delivery room I took a seat by the door, in case my temporary ward had any thought of bolting. "Where are you from?" I asked after a while, thinking to strike up a conversation and calm down the obviously nervous young woman. "Have you been in Beijing long? Are you carrying a legal child?" The girl gave no sign of having heard me. She sat hunched over in her chair, her pinched face fixed on the floor. For some reason she reminded me of my sister-in-law, Aiming.

Win the trust of those you counsel. I repeated the population control regulation wryly to myself. *The regulations were certainly not written by anyone who had tried to make friends with a girl about to undergo a ninth-month abortion*, I thought. It was going to be a long night. If she wouldn't even talk to me, I could hardly obtain her consent for what was going to happen.

I awoke with a start. I must have dozed off. I looked quickly for the girl, and was relieved to see that she had not stirred from her chair. Then I looked again. The girl was sitting rigidly upright, clutching the chair's sides. Her face was contorted, and her breath was coming in short pants. I flew down the hall to the nurses' station. "You had better summon the doctors," I told the charge nurse. "Our country girl is in heavy labor."

By the time Doctor Wan and Doctor Yin arrived twenty minutes later, I had managed to get the girl disrobed and up on the examining table. With her contractions by now coming every two minutes or so, she had offered only feeble resistance.

I knew exactly what they would do. They would wait until the cervix was fully dilated and the top of the infant's head exposed. A hypodermic syringe would then be filled with formaldehyde. This would be injected, using a five-centimeter needle, deep into the brain through the soft spot. Even before it began its short descent down the birth canal, the infant would be dead.

Doctor Yin took one look under the examining sheet and cursed. "His mother's . . . this sow's baby is already crowning." He motioned to old Doctor Wan, who had prepared the hypodermic. "Hurry up. Give the injection."

The woman screamed as Doctor Wan approached, and the baby's head literally popped out of her body. The baby's arms, trunk, and legs had followed its head in quick succession. He—it was a sturdy little boy—filled his lungs for the first time and echoed his mother's cry. The baby lay in full view on the table; only its twisted white umbilical cord still connected it to its mother. The sight and sound stopped the older doctor short in his tracks.

"No way," I heard Doctor Wan say softly to himself. "There is no way I can do this." He put the hypodermic down as if it had burned his hand and backed away.

"If you won't do it, I will!" Doctor Yin yelled at him. "I'm not going to get a reprimand and a fine for allowing this useless spawn of peasant scum to live." He snatched up the hypodermic and approached the table. He looked down at the red, naked, and crying baby with an expression of disgust. He gripped its head with one hand, and with the other plunged the needle into its skull. The clear, deadly fluid emptied into the infant's brain. "I tell you we are doing this baby a favor," he ranted as he did so. "What child would choose to be born in the squalor and misery of a village hovel? But I have spared him all that." He withdrew the needle.

I waited for the convulsions to begin. Soon, I knew, the infant's body would jerk and thrash in its death throes, and his cries would weaken and cease. But nothing happened. If anything, the little boy screamed all the more vigorously, letting out loud wailing shrieks that seemed to pierce my very vitals.

No one moved for a long time.

Finally, from the corner of the room, Doctor Wan whispered: "The little soul is cursing us."

"Don't be ridiculous," snapped Doctor Yin. "That's rank superstition." But his eyes widened slightly, and he involuntarily took a step back from the baby. "What are these peasants but animals? They drag us all down to their filth and poverty." His voice was now tinged with hysteria.

"He *is* cursing us," Doctor Wan insisted. His voice was louder now and edged with panic. "The little soul won't leave his body. He won't leave until he has cursed us all the way to hell."

"You shut up!" barked Doctor Yin. "There is no heaven and no hell. The first injection didn't take, that's all. We must give it another."

"*You* give it another injection," Doctor Wan hissed. "I wash my hands of this . . . this . . . atrocity. Let his curse be on your head." The door slammed, and he was gone.

Doctor Yin hesitated by the jar of formaldehyde for a few seconds, his hands visibly shaking. Then he flung the empty hypodermic on the floor with a loud oath. "Cursed be you peasants, and cursed be your children!" he shouted as he disappeared out the door.

I was left alone with mother and child. I tried to pray. *Please, God, please.* But the baby's screaming and the mother's sobbing jumbled the words in my mind until I didn't know for whom I was praying—the baby, the mother, or myself—or for what. Then I, too, cried, for there was no other way to pray an unanswerable prayer.

I frantically set to work caring for the exhausted mother, lifting her legs down from the stirrups, sponging her off with cool water, arranging pads to catch the steady flow of blood, finding a pillow for her head. But there was nothing I could do for the baby. I could only keep my eyes averted from its contorted little face. And, as best as I could, I shut out from my hearing the sounds of its cries and whimpers, which only now began to weaken.

The little boy took half an hour to die.

———

I don't know whether the little-boy-who-wouldn't-die—for this was how I came to remember him—had cursed me or not. I do know that the sight and sound of him came unbidden to my mind repeatedly in the weeks that followed. Whenever I assisted in a late-term abortion after that, I would see him sadly looking on. His loud, wailing shrieks had actually driven me out of the operating room during one such abortion. Doctor Yin had taken a pair of forceps to crush the unborn's skull to make it easier to remove. As he positioned the forceps, I saw—or thought I saw—the little-boy-who-wouldn't-die's tiny contorted face. As Doctor Yin started to apply pressure, he opened his mouth and began to shriek. I bolted. After that, I vowed that I would no longer be a party to late-term abortions and found excuses to absent myself from the operating room.

I was relieved when my training ended a short time later and I was able to return to the Liaoning Truck Factory.

15

Childbirth on the Run

LIAONING TRUCK FACTORY was nothing like the workplace I had been accustomed to. The tuberculosis sanitarium had been a pleasant place of quiet wards, covered walkways, and well-kept gardens, where convalescing patients walked slowly about and we on the clinic staff worked at an unhurried pace. The Liaoning Truck Factory, by contrast, was noisy, dirty, and crowded. The huge shops in which the motors and trucks were assembled sat cheek by jowl with rows of gray dormitory buildings, with not a speck of green in between. The clang of the sheet metal presses resounded to the farthest corners of the factory compound, while noxious smoke from the electric arc welders hung like a pall over shops and dormitories alike. I was glad I was living off compound, even though it meant a forty-five-minute commute to and from work every day.

Most of the factory's fifteen thousand employees lived with their families in the dormitories. Like most state-owned factories, the

Liaoning Truck Factory was a paternal organization that provided much more in the way of benefits to its workers than simply housing. Within the high walls that surrounded the compound were schools, shops, restaurants, an activities center, and a health clinic. Housing cost just pennies a month, food in the factory restaurants was heavily subsidized, and the activities center was free. Marriages between young workers were common, a trend encouraged by the factory to ease the shortage of apartments. So complete was the cradle-to-grave safety net that the factory even guaranteed employment to the workers' children when they reached maturity.

The health clinic was also free, but the quality of care provided was low. Worse yet, from my point of view, no effort was being made to meet the special needs of women. I started doing pelvic examinations and was shocked by what I found. Nearly half of those I examined were suffering from chronic vaginal infections. One in three had precancerous cervixes, and polyps, tumors, and warts were common, even among women in their twenties. Far too many Pap smears came back positive, indicating the presence of cancer cells. During my first weeks at the factory I was scheduling women for hysterectomies at the local hospital at the rate of one or two per day.

This epidemic of female disorders stemmed from the ignorance of most factory women about even the most elementary aspects of feminine hygiene. They simply had no idea how to keep themselves clean. They went to the bathroom and wiped themselves back to front instead of the reverse. During the long winter months, because of the cold and crowded living conditions, they went weeks between baths. Their husbands, who were uncircumcised and equally unschooled about matters of personal hygiene, were also part of the problem.

With the permission of the director of the health clinic and the encouragement of Secretary Chen, I tackled these problems head-on. I opened a women's health department (funü zhiliao bu). Here I treated common female disorders, various yeast and fungal infections, venereal diseases, and the like. I also gave prenatal care to pregnant women, as well as providing them with IUDs and other birth control devices after the birth of their babies.

Next door I set up a women's hygiene department (*funü weisheng bu*), which I had equipped with a dozen shower stalls where women could shower and douche (*qing xi*) in privacy. I or an assistant gave lectures on female hygiene to groups of women workers throughout the factory, encouraging them to keep themselves clean, especially in the winter, by douching at regular intervals. I also held sex education and pregnancy classes for newlyweds and pregnant women.

I derived great satisfaction from my work, especially when I began to see dramatic declines in the incidence of various diseases. The combination of better hygiene with the early detection of problems reduced the rate of vaginal infections virtually overnight. By the time I left the factory five years later, only one in eight women had a precancerous cervix, while cases of cervical cancer, at least among the younger women, had become rare.

I was proud of my accomplishments, thinking them an advance for women. And I was not alone in thinking this. Nearly every day women workers would come up to me and thank me for curing them of an infection or for teaching them the basic rules of hygiene. The showers in the women's hygiene department, especially, were a big hit. In the winter the lines outside the cubicles were so long that I had to institute a rotation system, reserving certain days for certain departments. Even so, women disappeared from their posts so often and so long that their male coworkers began complaining about the special treatment the women were receiving. "Why don't you set up a men's health department?" they groused at me, more or less good-naturedly, when I walked by. "We have to wash in buckets of cold water."

At this time the primary responsibility for population control matters belonged to the local branch of the Women's Federation. Every shop and office in the factory had a federation representative, whose job it was to track the menstrual cycles and the contraceptive methods of all young women of childbearing age who worked there. This record keeping was done publicly, by writing each woman's name, means of contraception, and expected date of menstruation on a large blackboard that was hung in a conspicuous place. When her period came, she was required to place a check mark next to her name. Women occasionally lied about the onset of their menses, but of course it was only a matter of time before they were found out. If a woman failed to start her period on schedule, the Women's Federation representative would order her to go to the women's health clinic for an examination.

A positive pregnancy test spelled trouble for a woman with a child. The representative would take the young woman aside for a series of "heart-to-heart" chats. "Have an abortion immediately," she would be told, "and you will receive a cash bonus and a week off work." If the woman did not respond to these inducements within the next few days, the carrot would be replaced by a stick. The woman would be told that she would not be allowed to enter her illegal child's name on the factory's population registers after birth, so that her child would have no medical benefits, no grain rations, no opportunity to attend school, and no chance of factory employment in the future. "For the good of your fatherland, your factory, and your family," she would be urged, "you must 'think clear' about abortion."

If the woman resisted her representative's warnings, activists from the Women's Federation and the Party would step in and lend a hand. The daily chats would take on the character of struggle sessions, as the pregnant woman was attacked for her stubbornness by several activists in turn. There are heavy financial penalties for "illegal" second births, she would be told. If she continued to resist, she would not only lose her annual bonus, but she would have to pay a heavy fine as well. The meetings also spilled over from work to home, as groups of activists visited the woman each night in her apartment. Husbands and mothers-in-law, who were often opposed to the idea of an abortion, would be required to attend these talks. "Do you want China to be backward and impoverished forever?" they would be asked. "Your individual whims in childbearing must be subjected to the interests of society as a whole."

If the woman and her family still stood their ground, the pressure would be turned up a notch. The senior leadership of the Women's Federation and the factory Party organization would enter the fray, determined to break their will to resist. As many as a dozen officials might impose themselves on her and her family at all hours of the day and night, hectoring, blustering, and threatening dire consequences. If she still insisted on having an illegal child, the local Party chief would join in as well. She would then hear, for the first time, the ultimate threat in China's social welfare state: "You will lose your job if you continue to resist remedial measures."

In the beginning my role in the population control campaign was limited to administering pregnancy tests and performing IUD insertions. All abortions, both early- and late-term, were performed at a nearby hospital. I was happy with this arrangement, but it was not to last.

A nationwide census conducted in July 1982 revealed an alarming trend: Tens of millions of babies born after the 1959–61 famine would soon reach marriageable age. Unless something was done, and done quickly, to keep these young people from reproducing, it would be impossible to keep China's numbers in check. The goal of limiting the population to 1.2 billion in the year 2000, officially adopted just two years before, would have to be abandoned. As the end of 1982 approached, high-ranking officials like State Councilor Bo Yibo began calling for even tighter controls on population growth. It was publicly announced that a "family planning propaganda month" would begin on January 1, 1983, and continue until after the Spring Festival. The clinic director privately hinted to me that much more than just a new propaganda campaign was in the offing.

In late December, Secretary Chen summoned me to his office. He told me that, according to a directive jointly issued by the State

Family Planning Commission, the Party Central Committee, and several other ministries, the "propaganda month" program would require the immediate abortion of all illegal pregnancies and the sterilization of every couple with two or more children. Birth quotas were to be tightened still further and, to ensure that these quotas were met, Party branch secretaries at all levels of government would have to sign "job responsibility" contracts. "Factories and villages throughout the province have already been assigned reduced birth quotas for 1983," he told me. "We here at the Liaoning Truck Factory have been told to keep our population increase rate at 0.5 percent. We have been given a quota of 322 babies. Nurse Yang, will you help the Party committee enforce our quota?"

Secretary Chen's idea was to set up a separate family planning clinic and name me as director. This meant that I would receive a promotion and a raise of twenty-five yuan a month. In addition to IUD insertions, which I had been doing all along, I would now do abortions as well. Sterilizations would be performed by one of the clinic doctors, after a period of training in this surgical procedure.

But my most important responsibility would be to ensure that the factory met its birth quota. In the past each department of the factory had been responsible for controlling its own births, but from now on all conceptions and births would be under the centralized direction and control of the family planning clinic. As clinic director, I would have to sign a "baby contract" just like Secretary Chen. If I succeeded in holding births under the allowed number, Secretary Chen and I would both receive a cash bonus and a commendation. If I exceeded our allowance, we would both be fined and criticized. "I have no doubt you will help us meet *our* quota," Secretary Chen said, emphasizing the plural. "I am told that you are not only very persuasive but that you are an excellent abortionist."

It was impossible for me to say no to Secretary Chen's request. I owed him my job, which had freed me to spend precious evenings and weekends with my son. I was also convinced that the population problem in China was so serious that individual desires had to be suppressed for the good of society as a whole. I agreed that those who had more than the permitted number of children were holding China back, besides being secretly jealous of them myself. My old desire to be accepted also came into play, for in this new position I would be working directly for Secretary Chen and the Party leadership. Still, I hesitated to throw myself into this new political campaign with the same fervor with which I had approached the Cultural Revolution. I would faithfully serve Secretary Chen and the Party, I decided, but there would be limits beyond which I would not go. The image of the little-boy-who-wouldn't-die appeared before my eyes. "I will do my best to persuade women to abide by the new quotas," I told Secretary Chen. "And I will perform abortions. But only on women in the early stages of pregnancy. After that they must go to the hospital. . . . I am not qualified. . . ."

Chen agreed to this arrangement and I took up my new post. The pleasant part of my job came in the first week of January. That's when I visited the several dozen shops in the factory and announced the names of the lucky women whose applications to conceive children had been approved by the Party committee. The unpleasant part began in the second half of January and was an unending and often exhausting struggle from then until the end of the year. Identifying the women who conceived children outside the plan was hard enough, requiring me to perform pelvic examinations on all those suspected of being pregnant. Pressuring women who were pregnant with "illegal" children to get abortions was even more time consuming. Even though I had the help of the Women's Federation, there were still dozens of women who remained unswayed by "heart-to-heart" chats. The hard cases were now my responsibility, and there were not enough hours in the day to deal with all of them.

After a few exhausting months of trying to win over these holdouts one by one—only to see their numbers and their stomachs continue to grow—I asked Secretary Chen if we could order them all to attend a single family planning study session. He readily agreed. Our first session was held in April, in an isolated storeroom far removed from both the shops and dormitories.

We used what in Party parlance were "hard and soft" tactics—known in the West as the "good cop, bad cop" approach. Secretary Chen and other senior officials would first frighten the women with harsh threats of dire consequences for failing to abide by the one-child policy. Then, speaking softly and as a friend, I would tell them that I was there to help them. I was an expert at convincing women to abort—I had learned all the arguments during my earlier training at the hospital—and my gentleness helped to break down their resistance. Those who angrily resisted Secretary Chen's bluster often broke down in tears when approached by someone they thought was sympathetic. I would put my arm around them, and they would go quietly to the hospital.

Throughout 1983, each time the number of women awaiting abortion reached twenty or so, I would schedule a study session. The holdouts would be ordered, on pain of heavy fines, to report to the storeroom. To increase the pressure on the women, I obtained Secretary Chen's permission to keep them in custody for as long as they resisted. During the day they would be subjected to morning-to-night study sessions. At night they would be locked inside in the storeroom. They would only be released if they agreed to an abortion.

As the end of 1983 approached, Secretary Chen and I got busier and busier. Under tremendous pressure to meet our quota, we locked up our final group of twenty-three holdouts on December 1. If even one successfully carried her child to term, we would exceed our allotted number of births for the year. Both of us would be fined, and I might lose my new position. I did not want to disappoint my superior any more than he wanted to disappoint his.

It was all I could do to keep up with Secretary Chen, who strode up the narrow alleyway between the workers' dormitories seemingly heedless of the smooth layer of ice that gripped the ground and made walking treacherous. The pipes in the poorly constructed dormitories froze solid in the bitter Manchurian winter, and women simply cast dishwater, bathwater, and worse out of their windows into the alley below. With fifteen thousand workers and their families housed in close quarters, that was a lot of gray water. It was already more than a foot thick, and it was only mid-December. By the time of the spring thaw it would reach five feet in places, as slick as a skating rink.

I chose my footing more carefully than the head of the factory's Communist Party committee, and being a head shorter, this caused me to lose ground with each step. By the time we had passed the last of the dormitories I was ten yards behind. As soon as the snow offered firmer footing, I broke into a dogtrot, heading for a building made of the same discolored gray cement as the others, but much smaller and possessing no windows. This was the isolated storeroom I had converted into a makeshift jail. I had the key in the lock of the thick plank door by the time Secretary Chen walked up.

I opened the door, then stepped through quickly after the secretary, and bolted it behind us. After the glare of the morning sun off ice and snow, the darkness left me temporarily blind. I stood there blinking, trying to keep my expression stern as I peered into the dimness.

The storeroom was small, only fifteen feet wide and perhaps twice as deep. There were rows of plank benches at the far end, directly under the single twenty-five-watt bulb that was the room's only illumination. My eyes swept across the row of young women sitting huddled together on the nearest of the benches, counting as I went. Over the course of the last two weeks sixteen women had surrendered. Only seven holdouts now sat on the benches. With any luck one or two more would break during the course of the day.

Secretary Chen took up a position in the center of the room. He didn't bother to take off his overcoat; it was scarcely warmer inside than out. He began as he had each day for a week: "You all know why you are here. You have violated the one-child agreements you signed. You have gotten pregnant outside the plan. You will remain here until you agree to remedial measures to take care of your problem."

I listened with only half an ear. I knew the speech that the factory's senior Communist gave to holdouts by heart. I was more interested in its effect. I looked searchingly at each of the young women, trying to judge which one was wavering in her determination to bear the illegal child she was carrying. It would be my job to take that woman aside, convince her that an abortion was her only option, and escort her immediately to the hospital four blocks away.

"Most of your comrades have already 'thought clear' about this question. You who remain must also 'think clear.' You must understand that one child is enough."

The women sat with downcast eyes, avoiding my stare. They ranged from Ah Qing, who was eight months pregnant, to Little Hua, who was at least four months along. *All well past quickening*, I thought sourly. Women who had felt that telltale little flutter in their stomachs were always more stubborn. Something nagged at the edge of my consciousness, something of the joy I had felt at my only son's first kick, but I refused to acknowledge it. *You must put your personal feelings aside*, I chided myself. *You must remember that you are working for the common good*. I turned my attention back to the task at hand, trying to concentrate on Secretary Chen's blunt words.

"You must realize that none of you has any choice." His voice was cold and deliberate. "Your pregnancy affects everyone in the factory, everyone in the city, indeed, everyone in the country. You will get an abortion whether you want one or not."

I looked again at the women to gauge the effect of this blow. Ah Qing, who sometimes took care of Tacheng in the factory's day-care center, scowled back at me. I sighed and looked away. The ones you knew were the worst. They blamed you personally for what was government policy. Couldn't Ah Qing understand that I was only doing my duty? Besides, it was selfish of Ah Qing to insist on having this child. She already had one, a well-behaved little girl of five, whom

I had met at the center. Who was she to demand a second when the rest of us, including me, had to content ourselves with one?

"You must realize the seriousness of your situation. Your husbands, your fathers, and your mothers have already agreed that we need to control our population and that an abortion is your only alternative. You are alone in ignoring the needs of the country and the factory. You are alone in your resistance to the Party. You must 'think clear' about abortion."

I kept my eyes on the young women, trying to judge the effect of Secretary Chen's words on each. Several of them were crying now, Little Hua the loudest. Perhaps she was ready, with a little help, to "think clear."

Little Hua started when I touched her on the shoulder. "Come with me, Little Hua," I said gently, "I want to talk with you." Little Hua only sobbed louder but did not resist when I led her out of the storeroom.

Other women capitulated in the days that followed, and finally even Ah Qing ended her resistance. My work was over, at least for 1983. The Liaoning Truck Factory had met its quota—just barely. Over the course of the year, 321 babies had been added to the population registers, one short of the limit. Secretary Chen was pleased with my performance.

In the beginning of 1984, the head of the district birth planning office, Huang Junmei, called an urgent meeting of all the birth planning workers in her district. As the director of the factory's program, I was required to attend such meetings, though I had no liking for Huang herself. With her shrill voice and her penchant for propaganda, she was almost a caricature of a Party activist. I gave her as wide a berth as I could in my work.

Huang was known as an utter fanatic about the one-child policy. Even though the family planning regulations allowed for second children in exceptional cases, or for some flexibility in the awarding of quotas, she seldom gave her consent. One of the many stories told about Huang involved a postal clerk who, after many years of barrenness, adopted one of her sister's daughters. Three months later, to everyone's surprise, the clerk giddily announced that she had at last become pregnant. Huang reacted to this news by telling her that, because she already had one child, she had to abort the second. "This *is* my first child," the clerk objected. "Legally I have no other children because I have not officially adopted my niece. I will send her back to my sister's village, and I will keep my baby." But Huang still refused her request for a quota. Rather than abort, the clerk ran away to Shantung Province, where she stayed with relatives until her son was born. Only then did she come back to Shenyang to face Huang's wrath. But she gave as good as she got. The clerk named her little boy Hen Huang, which meant "hate Huang."

Huang's ferocious ambition was to be selected as the "model birth planning worker" of Liaoning Province, and winning the promotion and prizes that would follow such an honor. In 1982 she had placed second, a near success that led her to redouble her efforts. She had become even more close-mouthed *(kou hen jin)* about quotas over the past twelve months, having allowed only a handful of exceptions to the one-child policy. She had made no secret of the fact that, this year, she was determined to come in first in the competition.

Today she was very unhappy, pacing back and forth across the room, for reasons that became obvious as soon as she began to speak. "I have just come back from the provincial meeting of family planning directors," she said, not bothering to hide the angry, disappointed scowl on her face. "The city of Anshan has been selected as the model birth planning city in the province. And the model birth planning worker for Liaoning Province for 1983 is . . . the director of the Anshan family planning program. She was selected for this honor because she held the birthrate in the city to only one per thousand."

I gasped inwardly. At that time the legal limit for births in the cities was 0.5 percent. We had worked night and day to ensure that no more than five babies were born for every one thousand people at the Liaoning Truck Factory. And the Anshan director had only allowed one birth per thousand people! How had she done it?

Huang quickly dispelled the mystery, telling us that the birth planning workers in Anshan city had not been content with half-measures. All women of childbearing age, with the exception of the few who had been awarded birth quotas, had been subjected to quarterly pelvic examinations. Women pregnant with illegal children had been exposed early and ordered to go in for an abortion. According to Huang, the Anshan cadres gave women a simple choice: "Either go willingly, or we will take you by force."

To illustrate their resolve, she recounted how they had arrested a woman who was eight and a half months pregnant (she had been in hiding up to that point). It had taken four or five birth planning workers to drag her, struggling and crying, through the streets to the hospital. Her husband and parents had followed in tears, forming a kind of funeral procession for the doomed baby, who was promptly aborted. "You might think that this was a barbaric act," Huang concluded. "You would be wrong. The Anshan workers were carrying out the great birth planning program of the Party. Without such determination, how will we ever achieve the Four Modernizations?" She spoke in a tone of open admiration, sure that no one would contradict her.

"If it had been me," a doctor challenged, "I would not have been able to perform the operation. My hands would have been shaking too badly. Inside the woman was crying; outside the relatives were howling. Why can't we make exceptions for such cases, Director Huang? I do not oppose the one-child policy, but I think that we are getting a little overzealous. Early abortions, yes. Up to the fifth month, yes. But after that, no. What will the people say if we continue to act this way?"

After the doctor finished speaking, you could have heard a pin drop. It was rare for anyone to raise questions of ethics. Most family planning workers, not wanting to create doubts about their loyalty, accepted what they were told without comment.

"This is why we can't reduce our birthrate to one per thousand," Huang's caustic voice rang out. "Softhearted people want to make exceptions to the policy. There shall be no exceptions during the coming year. Not one!"

"But there are tragic cases," another family planning worker said with some embarrassment. "For example, I have a woman whose only son was born with spina bifida. He is now four years old, severely handicapped, both mentally and physically. Under such circumstances, perhaps the quota can be relaxed a little bit . . ."

The district head cut her off. "Don't even think about it," she snapped. "Do you want me to be criticized for exceeding my quota? This year we are going to hold the birthrate in our district of Shenyang down to 0.1 percent. We will match, if not better, Anshan's record. All quotas will be reduced by 80 percent. And there will be no exceptions."

"But people will talk. . . . They will say that we are too strict," several people grumbled under their breath.

"What does it matter what people say about you?" she continued. "At first I was unhappy about the little boy named Hen Huang—" She scowled as a titter went through the audience. "But then I thought, *What does it matter?* The use of force is a necessary administrative measure. Vice Premier Deng Xiaoping has instructed us: 'In order to reduce the population, use whatever means you must, but do it! With the support of the Party Central Committee, you will have nothing to fear.' "

As the months went by, the dark side of the family planning program was in evidence as never before. Urged on by Huang, and struggling to meet their new, drastically lower quotas, many activists in Shenyang did not hesitate to resort to coercion. In some units, abortion posses "escorted" expectant mothers to clinics as soon as they were discovered to be pregnant. Rumors of women bound, gagged, and aborted were rife. The provision of China's family planning law forbidding the use of force was simply ignored.

I thought that the use of physical force on helpless women was shameful and instead continued to rely upon the "hard and soft" tactics that had worked so well in the past. It was tough going. Huang had slashed my baby allowance from 322 to a mere 65, and more women were getting pregnant outside the plan. Many were young women with no children, who were especially stubborn in their resistance. Secretary Chen's threats left them angry and rebellious rather than cowed and shaken. It was unfair not to allow them at least one child, they often yelled at me. I was constantly on the edge of exhaustion. I no sooner finished with one storeroom study session than I was compelled to start another.

I had my own confrontation with Director Huang a few months later, over the question of a special birth quota. A young woman in my factory had been unable to conceive a child despite three years of trying—and three successive birth quotas. Her problem had finally been diagnosed as an ovarian tumor. When surgery was performed not one but both ovaries were discovered to be diseased. The right ovary, which was completely enveloped by a large tumor, was removed. The left ovary, which had a small, benign tumor, was left alone, for the sake of the female hormones the undiseased portion would continue to produce. In two or three years, the surgeon declared, it too would have to be removed. In the meantime it would be quite impossible for her to conceive a child.

Hearing this, I had listed her on the population control registers as a *bu yun*, a "barren" woman, and revoked her birth quota. Several months later, to everyone's utter amazement, she had gotten pregnant. The doctors declared it a miracle. Her fellow workers offered their congratulations. I went to offer my personal best wishes and found her delirious with joy.

The problem was that I had no remaining birth quotas for 1984. Not only that, but I had already announced who was to receive quotas in 1985. I had no choice but to take my dilemma to Director Huang. Normally, because she was so close-mouthed where quotas were concerned, I would not have bothered petitioning her for a special quota. It would not have been worth the trouble. But this was not a case of asking permission for a second child, which she was sure to reject. The woman in question had no children. Nor would she, with only one diseased ovary remaining, ever conceive another. Her situation was so unusual that it cried out for a kind and sympathetic response.

I had no sooner finished explaining the purpose for my visit than Director Huang exploded. "What are you saying?!" she burst out. "This year's quota for the entire district is already used up. Next year's quota has already been assigned."

"I was hoping that you would allow me to borrow a birth quota from the year after," I said timidly. "We will willingly make do with one less quota in 1986 for this woman."

"Absolutely not," she replied curtly. "If I allow you to borrow from your 1986 quota, other people will ask to do the same thing. How will I be able to do my job? I can't 'relax my mouth' even for an instant. This is my answer to your request: You tell that woman that there is no hope, no hope at all."

Defeated, I went back to the factory. I had no heart to tell the woman that our request had been denied, asking her Women's Federation representative to give her the bad news instead. She spent many weeks confined in the storeroom before I and others were able to convince her to have an abortion.

Even though I understood the one-child policy, I had always had certain mental reservations about the inflexible way it was being carried out. Now, seeing the suffering caused by Huang's ruthless insistence on meeting unrealistic quotas, my doubts deepened. I was tired of confronting expectant mothers with the unwelcome news that they must abort. I was sympathetic to the claim of the childless that they were entitled to at least one child. I became disgusted by the implicit dishonesty of my efforts to win the trust of women for the sole purpose of subjecting them to my will.

Even my refusal to use overt force, I now decided, was a kind of sham. If a woman walked the last one hundred yards to the clinic under her own power, I had considered her to be choosing an abortion of her own free will. Like the Party, I always preferred a woman to "volunteer." Yet how could her act possibly be considered voluntary? Was a prisoner who walked to the gallows consenting to his execution? What about the weeks of imprisonment and mistreatment I had subjected them to beforehand? I was as willing to threaten, lock up, cajole, and browbeat these poor women into submission as anyone else. By pretending otherwise, whose conscience was I salving? In reality I was no better than Director Huang. In fact, by imposing herself on these women, she was shortening their mental torture and might even be said to be doing them a kindness. At least she wasn't trying to turn them into accomplices in the killing of their own children, as I was.

I had no one I dared share my thoughts with. I could not possibly put my reservations in a letter to Wei Xin, for fear that it might be opened and read. I did mention my doubts over one or two of the more difficult cases to Secretary Chen, though with a caution born of the political struggles of the Cultural Revolution, I kept my general criticism about the inflexibility of it all to myself. Even so, I think he began to suspect my reliability. I did not even feel comfortable confiding too much in my mother, though I did tell her about the barren woman. She sighed and remarked on the joy that had surrounded pregnancy and childbirth in the old days. *Compared to the fear and unhappiness that it brings in the present*, I thought bitterly.

Only my happy and guileless little boy, Tacheng, gave me solace—when I was able to forget all the other sons and daughters who had been taken from their mothers.

I worked closely with the members of the Women's Federation, who were my partners in enforcing the quota system, and got to know many of them well. My best friend, a young woman named Ah Fang, came from their ranks. She was the federation's representative in the factory's small upholstery shop, which made seat covers and cargo tarps for the trucks.

Ah Fang and I had a lot in common. My husband was absent overseas; hers, a purchase agent for the factory, was on the road at least three weeks out of every month. Her only child was a boy Tacheng's age; both children would begin elementary school in the fall. I often brought Tacheng over to her apartment in the evenings. While Ah Fang and I talked, or I was off busy with the women in the storeroom, Tacheng and her son played together.

Ah Fang and I were like sisters. I shared news of my difficult cases with her and even hinted at my misgivings about the population control policy. For her part, Ah Fang confided in me her secret longing for a second child, a damning admission for an official of the Women's Federation to make. Not that I took her confession all that seriously. If you took a poll of the younger married women at the factory, probably three-quarters would say the same thing. Which is why, at any given time, we had upward of a dozen expectant mothers incarcerated in the storeroom. Even I, when I permitted myself to think about it, felt a twinge of longing for the little girl I would never have. Whatever Ah Fang's private feelings, though, I was sure that she would never openly violate the policy she was charged with enforcing.

One morning I arrived at the health clinic to see a wan-looking Ah Fang standing in line for sick call. I hurried over to find out what was the matter. She mumbled something about headaches and fatigue. I told her to take care of herself and get plenty of rest, then hurried off to open my own clinic.

I stopped by Ah Fang's apartment a few nights later to see how she was doing. I didn't stay long, for she had gotten out of bed to receive me and was dressed only in her nightgown. She told me that she still felt weak but was hoping that the month-long medical leave she had been given would enable her to recuperate. I voiced concern over the length of her leave, since her original complaint had not sounded all that serious to me. The doctors weren't sure what the problem was, she responded vaguely. I dropped by to see her a few more times over the next few weeks, but my visits seemed to tax her so much that I gradually stopped going. Besides, she didn't seem the least bit happy to see me. Her medical leave was extended and then extended again. Whatever mysterious ailment she was suffering from, it didn't seem to be getting any better.

Three months went by. Then one day a member of the street committee in charge of Ah Fang's dormitory building came to see me at the women's clinic. "I think you ought to give Ah Fang a pregnancy test," she said without preamble. "No one believes that she is seriously ill. We see her on her balcony hanging out her laundry to dry every day. We think that she has been staying home to hide her condition."

All at once everything clicked into place for me. Ah Fang's mysterious illness. The loose nightgowns when I visited. Her coolness toward me. I dropped everything and went to see Ah Fang at once. I had intended to ask her to come in to the clinic the following morning for an examination, but as soon as I laid eyes on her I knew there was no point. Even in her nightgown I could tell that Ah Fang was at least five months pregnant.

Had I been able to read Ah Fang's heart, I would have ordered her arrest and imprisonment on the spot. But I softened in the face of her tearful assurances that she had been meaning to come in for remedial measures. She had truly been ill, she said, and just needed a little more time. It was an unlikely story, but I gave my friend the benefit of the doubt, knowing that if I reported her condition she would lose her position with the Women's Federation. I would not make her pregnancy public, I promised her, on condition that she took care of her problem in the near future. Though I didn't really believe that she had been afflicted with anything except morning sickness, I was certain that I could talk her into doing the right thing.

I spent several evenings over the next few weeks sitting in the living room of Ah Fang's modest factory apartment, gently prodding her and her husband in the direction of an abortion. I was positive that she was about to come around. She would nod as I spoke, giving me the impression that she agreed with everything that I was saying.

All our conversations ended the same way: "You must take care of your problem," I would urge. "I'll check into the hospital in a day or two," she would respond. "Just give me a little more time."

In the meantime Ah Fang was swelling alarmingly. She was noticeably bigger from visit to visit. Finally I lost patience. If you don't do something about your problem, I told her, I am going to have to order you to attend the next study session. Ah Fang just looked at me with an unreadable expression and asked when it began. "Next Monday," I said as I left. "Remember: No more extensions!"

The following Monday morning I personally went to fetch Ah Fang to the study session, only to discover that she had disappeared. Her husband, a round-faced man with a shock of prematurely gray hair, claimed that he had no idea why she had left or where she had gone. But I knew. Like my sister-in-law and the mother of Hen Huang, Ah Fang had chosen "childbirth on the run." As to where she had gone, I was certain that she had fled to another city or, even more likely, was hiding out in the home of a relative nearby.

Ah Fang was gambling that, away from the Liaoning Truck Factory where she was known, she—and her condition—would escape notice. And she was probably right. Authorities in other units and towns were only vigilant in preventing births among the women on their own population registers. They had no incentive to prevent illegal births by outsiders, since these were not counted against their own allowances. Large cities like Beijing regularly swept the streets for pregnant vagabonds, but many smaller towns did little or nothing. More birth quotas were blown by women in hiding than anything else, which is why Director Huang constantly harped on us to keep pregnant women under surveillance lest they run away. Unless I could somehow find out where Ah Fang was hiding, I knew I would not see her again until she had given birth.

I was upset with myself and angry at Ah Fang. I had allowed my feelings for Ah Fang to blind me to her determination to carry her child to term. Worse yet, she had cynically abused our friendship by using it to manipulate me. Yet, upon reflection, I had to admit that it served me right. Had my own actions over the past year been any less calculated than hers? I had self-consciously and for my own ends set out to win the trust of dozens of women only to betray it. Ah Fang had simply beaten me at my own game.

It was difficult to admit to Secretary Chen that a pregnant woman was missing on account of my misjudgment, but at least he took the news calmly. The fury of Director Huang, on the other hand, knew no bounds, especially when she found out that Ah Fang was already six months pregnant. She ordered me to do everything I could to find Ah Fang before it was too late, on pain of a fine and demotion.

Though Ah Fang was safely out of reach, her husband was not. He received the brunt of the onslaught that followed. Secretary Chen, the head of the Women's Federation, and I missed no opportunity to pressure him to reveal his wife's whereabouts. Each day he had to report to Secretary Chen's office for a lecture. Each evening I visited him in the company of several officers of the Women's Federation. At his shop's twice-weekly political meeting, he was repeatedly criticized by his boss. The message to Ah Fang's husband was always the same: "You are going to be fined, criticized, and even fired if you do not cooperate with us. You must tell your wife to return for remedial measures."

Ah Fang's husband shrugged off our threats. Not only did he feign ignorance of his wife's whereabouts, he claimed that she had abandoned him and their young son. I did not believe him for an instant. He was not nearly as practiced at dissembling as Ah Fang. When he said these things he looked away and his voice rang hollow. I knew he knew where his wife was hiding. But what could I do? I wanted to lock him up in the storeroom in Ah Fang's place, but Secretary Chen would not allow this because he was a man. The weeks slipped by.

I racked my brain for some hint of where Ah Fang had gone. Then I remembered that she was very fond of a sister who lived not far from Shenyang in a rural commune. Often, when her husband was traveling, Ah Fang would go and stay with this sister over the weekend. I and four members of the Women's Federation set out late the following evening, having made arrangements with the county police chief to pick up a couple of patrolmen on the way.

We arrived at the village after midnight as we had planned, a time when even the village dogs were asleep. We found the house where I suspected Ah Fang was hiding, and then I gave the go-ahead to the patrolmen. The quiet of the night was instantly shattered by the sound of their shouting. "Public security department!" they yelled, pounding on the door, "Open up!" A few seconds later a bewildered man opened the door and tried to ask what we wanted. The patrolmen pulled him outside while I and the other members of the Women's Federation rushed into the house. We discovered Ah Fang still in bed. She tried to escape, but she had no chance against the five of us. We rolled her up tightly in her quilt and carried her out to the truck.

I didn't want to give Ah Fang another opportunity to escape, so I had her taken directly to the storeroom, where I locked her up with a new group of a dozen or so holdouts. The other women in this group behaved as I had come to expect. Separated from their husbands, bullied into submission, so distraught that they were often unable to eat and sleep, I led them one by one to the clinic as they wept. Not Ah Fang, who sat as unsmiling and dry-eyed as a wooden Buddha, her gaze fixed defiantly on me. Secretary Chen and the other "bad cops" missed no opportunity to badger her into accepting an abortion, but Ah Fang was unmoved by their threats.

Finally only Ah Fang and I were left in the storeroom. Even Secretary Chen did not come any more. He had wasted too much time already on the Ah Fang case, he told me. From now on I would bear full responsibility for a successful outcome.

By this time Ah Fang was farther along than any woman I had ever had in detention. I judged her to be only a couple of weeks away from giving birth. I redoubled my efforts, trying every approach, every opening, I could think of. But the reserved, untalkative Ah Fang of the past few weeks had disappeared. In her place was an angry, assertive young woman who scornfully rejected my counsel to accept the inevitable, who dismissed our past friendship as unimportant, and who angrily disputed everything I said about the population control program. Ah Fang, herself an expert in the art of persuasion, was not about to let herself be persuaded. She had an answer for everything.

"You know China has a population problem," I said once.

"It is not 'China' that will take care of this baby," she retorted. "I will. My husband and I can afford to feed and clothe him."

"But the cost to society—"

"According to the population control regulations, the fines for having overquota babies are intended to pay for the additional cost that society will incur. I will pay the fines."

"But you and your husband could be fired from your jobs. Then how would you pay?"

"So the state imposes heavy fines for having children and then makes it impossible to pay them. Isn't that a contradiction?"

"No exceptions to the one-child quota are allowed. You know that."

"I know that the policy is unnecessarily strict. Even if every couple had two children, China's population would still stop growing."

And so it went, in one long, fruitless conversation after another.

I did find out, during the long hours that we were alone together, what had really happened. As I had suspected, Ah Fang's pregnancy was premeditated. Her husband had opposed the idea of a second child, but Ah Fang had gone ahead on her own. She had found a midwife who, for a fee of twenty-five yuan, was willing to commit an illegal act: removing the ring-shaped IUD that had been inserted following the birth of her first child. "It took her a long time to hook the IUD, and coming out it was painful," she recalled. "But it was worth it."

Several months later she got pregnant. Her husband was flabbergasted by the news but quickly agreed that an abortion was out of the question. Instead they decided that, when the pressure to end the pregnancy grew too great, Ah Fang would go to live with her sister. "I would still be at my sister's if you, my best friend, hadn't betrayed me," Ah Fang concluded bitterly. "And one more thing. If you intend to abort my baby, you will have to bind me hand and foot and carry me to the hospital."

I quailed before the fierce gleam in her eye, remembering how she had fought when we surprised her at her sister's house. I was not willing to use force, and she knew it.

I knew then, if I hadn't known before, that Ah Fang had decided to have this baby at all costs. It would be impossible for me to convince her to do otherwise. I went again to Secretary Chen to ask for help, but he only repeated that I would be held personally responsible for the outcome of the case. "And if she goes into labor before she agrees to remedial measures," he added ominously, "have her taken to the hospital. They will know what to do."

A few mornings later I saw Ah Fang stiffen in pain and knew that it was time. After the contraction had passed, she looked at me imploringly. "Chi An," she pleaded. "Please don't call anyone. Help me deliver this baby. We were once friends. We can always say that I gave birth during the night when no one was here. No one will be able to blame you."

Ignoring her pleas, I rushed out of the storeroom to inform Secretary Chen. Ah Fang, already in heavy labor, offered only feeble resistance as we pulled her up onto the back of a truck and took her to the maternity ward of the hospital. Members of the Women's Federation rushed her into the delivery room, but I lagged behind. In truth, I couldn't bring myself to witness what was going to follow. Instead, tormented by my betrayal of my friend, I waited outside. The hours passed with agonizing slowness. Images of the little-boy-who-wouldn't-die came back to me, and the sound of a baby's cry echoing down the corridor made me jump. Ah Fang was finally wheeled out again, looking as pale as a corpse, her once-huge stomach flat under the sheet that covered her. I trailed along behind her gurney, physically exhausted and emotionally drained by the episode, as though I had been on the operating table alongside her. She looked at me briefly, her face expressionless, and then looked away. Words of consolation died in my throat.

Secretary Chen was pleased, congratulating me on the excellent work I had done and promising me a large bonus for the year. Director Huang also begrudged me a brief compliment, though she was more pleased by the fact that Ah Fang had not only been aborted but sterilized at the same time: "She at least will not cause us anymore trouble in the future."

This whole episode left me sick at heart. My doubts about the way the one-child policy was being shoved down people's throats came to a head. I had seen enough. No, more than enough. I could not in good conscience enforce a Party policy I no longer believed in, and I was not interested in winning kudos from my superiors for browbeating other women. My sympathy was for those, like Ah Fang, who were denied the right to bear the children they were carrying. I desperately wanted to leave everything connected with population control behind me and do nothing but women's health work—helping women instead of hurting them and their unborn children. But there seemed no way out of my dilemma unless I left the factory altogether.

In 1984, despite her best efforts, Director Huang once again came in second in the birth control competition, losing for a second time to Anshan.

16

Coming to America

THE WEEKS AFTER Ah Fang's forced abortion and sterilization found me still engaged in endless self-recrimination. The thought of seeing my onetime friend again filled me with dread, and whenever I left my clinic I anxiously scanned the walkways to avoid a chance encounter. I did not run into Ah Fang, who I later heard had a long and difficult recuperation from her surgery. Again and again, though, I chanced upon other women I knew from the close confines of the storeroom. With each encounter, my gloom deepened. I was overcome with remorse at the thought of all the hundreds of women I had driven to despair. Just as the little-boy-who-wouldn't-die had brought home to me the suffering of infants, so Ah Fang's futile resistance made real to me the damage I was inflicting on women. So many women. So much sadness. *There are already too many women who hate you in this world,* my conscience constantly reminded me, *and too many little souls who will be clawing at you in the next.*

I impetuously came to a decision. I would no longer force women to become unwilling accomplices in the abortion of their own children. I would no longer brutalize women in the name of population control. I would find a way to distance myself from this dreadful work forever.

This was far easier said than done. I could not simply announce one day that I was quitting the one-child program, resigning my post in protest as Western officials sometimes did. Cadres in China served at the pleasure of the Party. Any attempt to publicly opt out of population control work would, in all likelihood, be taken as an attack on the Party and could land me in jail. Nor could I, holding such a key position, just fade into the background. I would have to continue doing my job well enough to avoid the suspicion that I was just going through the motions. At the same time, I would have to displease Secretary Chen sufficiently that he would decide to reassign me. I would have to allow an illegal baby or two to live and thereby exceed next year's quota.

The more I thought about my dilemma, the more I came to regret having ferreted out Ah Fang's hiding place. Had her child survived birth it would have put the factory over its quota. By now I would have been relieved of my duties at Director Huang's insistence. I could have gone back to my work at the women's hygiene clinic, helping women instead of hurting them. Instead I was stuck harassing pregnant women for another year. The thought depressed me.

Then I received a letter from Wei Xin, containing the exciting news that it was now possible for Chinese spouses to get exit permits and visas. "The wife of a close friend of mine arrived here just last week," he wrote. "Perhaps you can get permission to come to the United States, too."

I immediately seized upon this idea as the solution to my problem. If I were able to join Wei Xin, who had at least two more years of study to obtain his doctorate, it would put me half a world away from the one-child policy. Nor would it be just a temporary reprieve. Once in the United States, I would improve my English enough to take courses in nursing administration. Perhaps I would even be able to get a college degree. When Wei Xin and I returned to China several years hence, I would be too valuable to waste on the one-child policy, or so I imagined. I hoped to be assigned to teach in a nursing school. Even if I was forced to return to the Liaoning Truck Factory, there was always the possibility that the one-child policy would by then have been relaxed, or that I would not have to resume my former responsibilities.

Secretary Chen initially frowned on my request for a two-year leave of absence. Only after Wei Xin and I wrote a letter promising that I would return to the factory after my time abroad did he reluctantly agree. Even then he wanted to make sure that my IUD was still in place. I burned with resentment when he asked—no, told—me to join the line of women workers waiting for their regular three-month X rays. *Do you think that I, a population control official myself, will have my IUD secretly removed and conceive an illegal child while I am abroad?* I silently fumed.

I knew the X-ray technician well, for I had worked closely with her to detect illegal pregnancies. "I hear that people have large families in America," she joked as she swung the blunt green cone into position in front of my groin.

I was not amused. "One child is enough for me," I replied testily. She flipped the switch, sending a pulse of radiation through my body to strike the film at my lower back. I saw the result the following day: The O-ring was still in place, its crisp white image stark against the small black-gray fist that was my uterus, brighter even than the fuzzy light gray discs of my spine. Only after Secretary Chen saw the X-ray report form did he approve my leave.

It took half a year for me to beg and bribe my way through the rest of the maze of government offices that had to approve my plans. Background investigations delayed the issuance of my passport for several months, and my exit visa was held up for a time when it was discovered that I wanted to take Tacheng with me. No one at the provincial department of foreign affairs came right out and said so, but I knew that they were concerned that if I were allowed to exit with my only child, I would never return to China. I thought their fears foolish. There was no doubt in my own mind that Wei Xin and I would return to our fatherland.

At last I was ready to go. Not even the parting from my mother at the Beijing Airport could dampen my joy at my release. I was leaving the sorrows of the one-child policy behind and had no thoughts about anything except joining my husband in the United States.

Wei Xin was waiting for Tacheng and me at the International Arrivals lounge when we landed at Kennedy Airport in New York. As soon as we cleared customs, he came running up and threw his arms around us, giving Tacheng and me a big bear hug. I was startled by this un-Chinese demonstration of public affection. Tacheng, who had not seen his father since he was a small boy, was totally unnerved. His welcoming *Ba Ba* (Dad) died on his lips, and he struggled to free himself from the unwanted embrace of this overly exuberant stranger.

I felt a little awkward being face to face with Wei Xin again, wondering how much he had changed during our years apart. We had written each other a mailbag full of letters but, with a ten-minute conversation costing upward of thirty dollars, phone calls had been few. Wei Xin and I exchanged pleasantries as we walked to his car, but our conversation was halting and unnatural. Even the sound of his voice, once so familiar to me, took some getting used to, since he now mixed a lot of English words into his sentences. From the safety of my far side, Tacheng silently studied his father. Apparently he was not entirely reassured by what he saw and heard. "Mommy," he piped up anxiously as we were about to get into the car, "are you sure this is my true dad?" Wei Xin and I both laughed, breaking the ice, and I assured Tacheng I was not mistaken about his father's identity.

I was impressed that Wei Xin had a car—a 1973 Plymouth Duster—for in China motor vehicles were a luxury reserved for important leaders. But when Wei Xin got behind the wheel I began to have qualms. Driving in China was restricted to a special class of trained drivers. "Are you sure you know how to drive this thing?" I asked anxiously as Wei Xin turned the key in the ignition. He smiled and roared off down a freeway ramp. Cruising at sixty miles an hour down a six-lane expressway surrounded by cars and trucks was a new and terrifying experience. I was used to riding buses that crawled through the streets of Shenyang at twenty-five or thirty miles an hour. We seemed to be moving at an impossible speed, even though Wei Xin stayed in what I later learned was called the slow lane. By the time we arrived at the State University of New York at Stony Brook, which would be my home for the next two years, I was a nervous wreck and exhausted to boot.

Wei Xin received $850 a month from the Chinese government to cover his room, board, and incidental expenses. While this had more than covered things when he was living alone, there were now three of us. To earn extra money, Wei Xin began tutoring undergraduates in mechanical drawing, a skill he could teach by demonstration, improving his hesitant English in the process. We were still constantly short of cash. I spent my first few weeks on campus living in the women's dormitory (Tacheng slept beside me on the floor) until we could save enough for the first month's rent on a student apartment. By my way of reckoning, the rent—$650 a month—was a staggering sum, more than a hundred times as much as the rent on my mother's apartment in Shenyang. Once we moved into the apartment, I immediately wanted to rent out the second bedroom and the living room to other Chinese students. Wei Xin vetoed the idea, telling me that the university administration had become much more strict about subletting since thirteen Chinese students had been discovered sharing a single apartment the previous year. The original tenant had even rented out the closets as sleeping cubicles, charging $50 a month for a space barely large enough to lie down in. We finally did bend the rules a little, though—and saved $150 a month—by renting a bed in Tacheng's room to a visiting scholar. We kept expenditures on food, clothing, and sundry items to an absolute minimum. Our budget for frivolous things like entertainment was zero.

For me, my first weeks in the United States were like arriving on another planet. The first time a supermarket clerk said "thank you" to me, I was amazed, because clerks in China never used those words. Once I stood in anxious bewilderment outside rest-room doors that read GENTLEMEN and LADIES, two words that were not yet in my vocabulary. I had just decided to chance "gentlemen" when the door swung open and a man stepped out, saving me great humiliation. My English, which was very limited, often caused me embarrassing moments. Before leaving China I had memorized an English phrase book, but my accent was atrocious and the hundred or so sentences I knew were just enough to get me into trouble. The first time I said, "How are you?" the reply came back, "Fine. And how are you doing?" *How am I doing* what? I thought in confusion, feeling my face turn red.

Tacheng, whom we promptly enrolled in public school, was soon chatting happily with the neighbor children in English. Though I was eager to improve my English, I was disheartened to learn from Wei Xin how high the tuition rates were for foreign students. While Wei Xin's education was free, since he was on a full government scholarship, mine would cost us a whopping $2,400 a quarter. A single five-unit course (such as English as a Second Language) would set us back a month's rent. Wei Xin offered to tutor additional undergraduates to bring in extra money, but I couldn't let him do that. His tutoring was taking almost two days a week from his doctoral studies as it was. I decided to postpone my formal education for a couple of quarters and find a job instead. *Why enroll in an expensive course*, I told myself, *when I could learn English on the job?*

This plan fell through. My spoken English was so awful that no one wanted to hire me. Even the local Chinese restaurant refused to take me on, probably for fear that my incomprehensible utterances would drive customers away. I gave up looking and stayed home with Tacheng, whose English, picked up from his playmates, was already more fluent than mine. Eventually I found a way to earn a little money at home. I knitted sweaters on a piecework basis. The middleman, who was Chinese, would stop by once a week to drop off new yarn and pick up the sweaters I had finished, for each of which he paid me $40. Since it took me twenty hours to complete a sweater, I averaged only about $2 an hour. Still, it was better than nothing. Day after day I sat in front of my TV set, knitting needles clicking away, trying with only limited success to puzzle out what the characters on the soap operas were saying.

Later I provided in-home day care to small children, mostly the sons and daughters of our American neighbors. This paid much better than knitting sweaters and gave me opportunities to practice my English as well. Fortunately I had no major emergencies. I would have had trouble calling 911 and making myself understood.

I was eager to get on with my education, but our financial situation simply did not permit it. Wei Xin assured me that once he had earned his Ph.D. and begun his eighteen months of practical training, I would be able to go to school full-time. I made grandiose plans— by Chinese standards—to get a master's degree in nursing administration as I changed the diapers of my small charges and put them down for their naps.

My main recreation that first summer took the form of long early-morning walks around the tree-lined campus and into the surrounding hills. I would get up in the feeble light of predawn, leaving Wei Xin still asleep in bed, have a quick bowl of rice congee, and set out in the gray-blue light of daybreak. Away from the central quadrangle of classrooms and buildings, the campus was one beautiful garden, all piney woods and limpid ponds. After the windswept, deforested plains around Shenyang, it seemed like a "peach orchard," as we practical Chinese call paradise. At this early hour I could walk for a mile or more and not encounter another human being, an impossible feat in China, where people were coming and going at all hours of the day and night. While people were sparse, wildlife was incredibly abundant; rabbits, ducks, and squirrels were everywhere.

As the months went by, despite my difficulties with English, I began to feel more and more at ease in my new surroundings. I was happy to be out of the business of browbeating expectant mothers, but my sense of well-being stemmed in equal part from my growing realization of how independent Wei Xin and I were in our new life.

I had come to the United States thinking of Wei Xin's university as his unit, but he quickly set me straight. "If you don't show up for class at a Chinese university," he told me, "they send someone to check on you. Here you pay your own tuition, and it is up to you to get to class. In America people have to take care of themselves." And it was true. Though we lived in a university apartment, we had almost no contact with university representatives. Despite Wei Xin's warning that the university was cracking down on subletting, no one ever inspected our apartment to see if we were abiding by the new rules. There were no street committees to come snooping and prying around, and our neighbors left us pretty much alone. Americans didn't impose themselves on you, I discovered, but they were ready to help when you asked them to.

When I mentioned my slow progress in learning English to a neighbor, for example, she introduced me to an elderly lady who offered to tutor me for free. Agnes, as she insisted I call her, was a retired nurse in her early seventies. Confined to a wheelchair and in generally poor health, she was nonetheless a happy, cheerful person, and I enjoyed our weekly visits.

Every Tuesday afternoon I would take the bus over to Agnes's house. We would sit down over tea and cookies and she would begin to talk, rattling on about the weather, the seasons, or this or that American custom. In the beginning, strain as I might to follow what she was saying, I caught only about one word in three. I remember one blustery day in November when she spent the entire afternoon trying to tell me the story of Thanksgiving. All her talk about Pilgrims, Indians, turkeys ("fire chickens" in Chinese), and religious freedom went right over my head. Only after Wei Xin, Tacheng, and I ate our first turkey at her house did it begin to make sense.

Then it would be my turn to tell her, in my best broken English, tales of life in China. In the beginning I stuck to innocuous topics, but after we had gotten to know each other I spoke with her about my personal experiences in the famine, the Cultural Revolution, and even in the population control campaign. She had heard of China's one-child policy but was shocked to learn that women in large numbers were being coerced into abortions and sterilizations. "Those poor women. Those poor women," she kept saying over and over as I spoke. After that she worried that I might be forced back into population control work after Wei Xin and I returned to China. She encouraged me to follow through on my dreams of getting an advanced degree and gave me a box full of her old nursing textbooks to bone up on.

With a caution born of the Cultural Revolution, I had always instinctively veiled my thoughts from others. Almost all Chinese did the same, afraid that if they said anything critical of the regime, they would be secretly denounced to the authorities. But in America, where the very air seemed to breathe freedom, different rules had come into play. Wei Xin and his friends frequently engaged in heated and critical discussions of Party policy, apparently unafraid of being persecuted on their return. Such openness was infectious. The day soon came when I broke into the conversation to attack the one-child policy as inhumane and ill-conceived. It was a liberating experience. Our newfound candor did not alter our plans to return to China, but it did give real meaning to the word *liberty*. I was not yet fluent in American English, but I had begun to appreciate the value of American-style freedom of thought and speech.

To save money I bought rice and noodles in bulk, vegetables only in season, and only enough meat, fish, and milk for Tacheng. A growing boy, he needed the extra protein; Wei Xin and I could get by on rice, vegetables, and tea. Even with all my economizing we ate better than we had in China.

Despite the improvement in my diet, by the middle of 1986 my chronic indigestion had returned, accompanied by the now-familiar symptoms of bloating, cramping, and nausea. I returned to my earlier regimen of tiny meals and avoided all foods high in fiber. I didn't want to get seriously ill, much less be hospitalized for an intestinal blockage. Medical care in the United States was incredibly costly for those without insurance. I had no insurance. Wei Xin and I had decided not to spend the one hundred dollars a quarter necessary to have me insured through the university.

As the months went by, I felt a growing heaviness in my midsection. Despite my careful diet, the swelling and pain in my abdomen grew steadily worse. Soon I could no longer carry the small children for whom I was caring. Running, or even walking at a brisk clip, brought on what seemed to be stomach cramps. Even standing for long periods of time was uncomfortable, because it felt as if something were pressing upon a nerve. I spent my days sitting down or walking slowly, keeping my back slightly bent to lessen the pressure. I could no longer sleep on my back—my favorite position—for the same reason. I had to sleep on my stomach. I drank a lot of hot tea, which, along with regular doses of aspirin, seemed to ease the discomfort a little.

Wei Xin was awarded his doctorate in December 1986. We immediately moved from New York to San Diego, where he had gotten a job with an engineering firm called Scott Turbines. Under the terms of his visa, he was allowed eighteen months of practical training in his field before returning to China. After renting an apartment near a college campus, I did two things: I enrolled in an English course, and, taking advantage of the fact that we now had medical insurance, I went in for a thorough physical examination. The old diagnosis of an intestinal narrowing was incorrect, the doctors concluded. In reality my problems were caused by a large and possibly malignant tumor between my stomach and small intestine. In years past it had pressed against my small intestine, preventing the passage of food and mimicking an intestinal blockage. Now that it was larger, it was also pressing against the nerves of my spine, leaving me in constant pain.

The operation to remove the tumor went without a hitch in February 1987. The surgeon excised a growth the size of a grapefruit, which laboratory analysis revealed to be benign. I made a speedy recovery. Within a few weeks I was a new person, able to eat anything and everything. For the first time since I was fifteen years old and in nursing school, I was totally healthy.

———

In May my period was late, which surprised me. I had always been very regular, one lunar moon almost to the hour. *Except when* . . .

No sooner had the thought flashed across my mind than I dismissed it. *I can't be pregnant*, I reminded myself. *My IUD was still in place when I left China.* The insult of the X ray that Secretary Chen had demanded I take still rankled even two years later. I thought of the little stainless-steel device, coiled up inside my uterus.

The following weeks passed slowly. The slightly full feeling that usually heralded the onset of my period refused to either release itself or go away. *What if the tumor has returned*, I worried, *or what if* . . . *I am only thirty-eight, too young for menopause, but not too young for* . . . I never allowed myself to complete the second thought, but it nagged at me nonetheless.

I fell into the habit of studying my body each time I got out of the shower. The apartment we had rented had a full-length mirror in the bathroom. Until now my innate sense of modesty had prevented me from looking at my naked body. "Americans are so narcissistic," I joked with Wei Xin. "Whoever heard of a full-length mirror in the bathroom?" Now I unblushingly examined my slender body from every possible angle. My stomach didn't look any different. But it *felt* slightly swollen inside. Or was there a slight swelling, a hint of a curve that hadn't been there before? I couldn't be sure.

I, who always told Wei Xin everything, did not tell him that I had made an appointment to see a gynecologist.

As he was doing the ultrasound, the doctor had turned to me, smiling, sure that he was the bearer of good news. "There is no sign of an IUD, but there is every indication of a baby. I estimate that you are about eight weeks along."

I kept my face expressionless, as I had learned to do in the presence of authority, but I felt as though I had fallen into a well. *I am pregnant—despite being thirty-eight years old; despite wearing an IUD, which is somehow missing; despite my plans to go to nursing school as soon as my English improves; despite my intention to return to China to help my backward country—despite everything, by accident, I am pregnant.*

I saw a look of chagrin spread slowly over the doctor's face. He was talking more briskly now. I forced myself to pay attention to his words. "I hope you realize that you still have viable options," he was saying. "You can get an abortion."

I had no idea what "viable options" meant, but the word *abortion* came through loud and clear. It had been one of the first English medical words I had memorized, in order to be able to tell my American friend Agnes about what was happening in China. "Thank you," I said. "I . . . I know about abortion."

I left the doctor's office quickly, and was halfway home before I realized that no one was going to report me to the authorities—not the doctor, not my husband's university, not the American government. Here no one cared if I had a second child, or a third for that matter. Only in China did they care, but China was an ocean away. I could keep the baby if I wanted. I felt an odd and unpleasant sense of emptiness, as though I were weightless and the least breeze would change my course.

In bed that night, with Wei Xin asleep at my side, I wrestled with my newfound sense of freedom. It was a fiction, I decided, a tempting, distracting, seductive fiction. I might be free to have a second child in America, but I could not take two children back to China. Not without subjecting us all to heavy penalties and jeopardizing our family's future. And I was definitely going back to China. The thought that I would not do my duty was unworthy of someone who had been an official and would be again someday after my return. I would do what the Party expected, what I had demanded from so many other women: I would end this unexpected, irregular, illegal pregnancy.

I repeated the word *abortion* to myself. Like many English words I had learned in books and on television, it had no depth and no resonance. So unlike the Chinese *duo tai*, I thought, which meant to rip out the fetus. *Abortion* . . . I fell asleep with the foreign word on my lips, comforted by its shallow, harmless sound.

I called a clinic the next day and made an appointment for the following Friday, the first available day. Now that everything was decided, I tried to avoid thinking about what I was about to do. The first couple of days I had wanted to tell Wei Xin, but there never seemed to be a good time. He was putting in long hours at his engineering firm, wrestling with a foreign language and a generation and a half of practical advances in his field of mechanical engineering that China knew nothing about. Or Tacheng would be present. In the end I resolved not to bother him.

Conversations with my husband grew shorter and shorter. Much of the time I was silent, and when Wei Xin tried to talk to me I avoided his eyes. I had no choice. The secret I was carrying welled up inside me each time I opened my mouth, until it threatened to spill out. Afraid that I would share everything, I shared nothing. On the appointed day I told Wei Xin that I was going shopping.

I was three months along, so the abortion would be by suction. One of the clinic aides gave me a booklet to read, but many of the English words were still unfamiliar to me. I found I lacked the patience to puzzle through it, and tossed it aside. *I don't really need to read it anyway*, I thought to myself. *I have performed the procedure hundreds of times myself.* I knew that a tiny vacuum hose would be inserted into my vagina, and that it would suction up the fetus. I knew about the dangers of infection and of excessive bleeding.

Now that I was lying on the examining table with my legs on the thigh rests, I wished that I had told Wei Xin what I was about to do. I thought of him, of how much I loved him, though of course I would never say so out loud, as I saw these syrupy, sentimental Americans doing all the time on TV and in the movies. Authentic affection between a husband and wife could only be cheapened by being expressed, my Chinese mind told me. It had to be shared over the course of decades, over the course of a lifetime.

If only Wei Xin were here to share this, too, with me, I thought as the aide lifted up the examining sheet that was draped over me. I felt a soft sponge leaving a trail of warm liquid across my stomach and thighs. I wouldn't want him in the same room, or course, with what was about to happen. The aide held my wrist lightly, taking my pulse. But if he were nearby, in the waiting room next door, what a comfort that would be. I tried to imagine him sitting there, poring through one of the textbooks that he always carried with him these days. A blood pressure cuff went around my left arm, tightened, and released.

But if Wei Xin were here, would he approve of what I was doing? The thought caught me off guard and left me confused. I began arguing with myself. *Of course he would approve; how could he not approve?* Distracted, I only half heard the doctor come in, the murmur of his instructions to the aide. *He would agree that I am doing the only sensible thing. How can we go back to China otherwise?* The touch of another hand on me, this one firmer, more commanding, brought me out of my confusion. *So, it is beginning.* I wanted to let go, to let the tenseness drain out of my body.

The question stabbed at me once again. *What if Wei Xin did not approve?* I squeezed my eyes tight against the accusing thought, but it thrust its way into my brain again and again. *What if Wei Xin wanted this baby?* The question hammered against my skull, reverberating through the calm and quiet in which I was trying to hide. The hands on me, which had seemed so careful and soothing a minute before, were now rough and intrusive.

Frantic, I tried to relax, to lean into the doctor's ministrations, to give myself and my body up to them, but it was no use. I could not be alone in this decision, as if I had no mate, no partner, no husband, no family, no responsibilities to anyone except myself. *This is Wei Xin's child, too,* I suddenly realized.

It was Wei Xin who gave me strength. *He would want this child!* I tried to sit up. With my legs in the stirrups I could not, but I found my elbows and propped myself up. Over the examining sheet I saw the doctor holding the suction tube in his hand, looking startled. The aide sought to soothe me, to restrain me, to lay me back down, but

I reared up onto my hands. "It's all right," the aide was saying. But it wasn't all right. It could not be all right. Not without Wei Xin. Not without our baby.

"Please, no . . . no," I heard myself pleading. "I don't want an . . ." But now that word, that smooth, shallow, painless English word, had deserted me.

I kicked my legs out of the stirrups. The sheet fell to the floor. I was naked before the surprised doctor and his assistant, and I didn't care. I was fighting now, fighting for my child, my husband, our life. The aide tried to stop me, but I rolled off the table and crouched on the floor. "Don't touch me!" I shouted. "We want the baby. We want the baby."

The doctor looked at me in reproach at my change of heart—a look I knew all too well from my own work with "pleaders"—and began peeling off his rubber gloves. I realized that I had won. There would be no abortion.

"I am pregnant," I said simply. "I went in for an abortion, but I couldn't go through with it."

Wei Xin did not disappoint me. His face lit up instantly. "Perhaps we can get permission from the authorities to have a second child," he said quickly. "After all, we are in America now. Perhaps they will make an exception to the one-child policy."

17

"Fix Your Problem"

I HAD WRITTEN to Gong Chang, the head of the population control office of the Liaoning Truck Factory, the following day to see if the one-child policy applied to couples living outside China. Her answer had left me shaken. "Please think carefully about our country's one-child policy and how much you want this baby before making a decision," she had written. "Don't come back until you do."

Gong is correct, I told Wei Xin emphatically. Whatever the authorities in China order me to do, I must not return before giving birth. Remaining in America for six more months would be a problem. The baby was not due until February, while our American visas would expire two months from now, in October. We would have to try and get an extension from the Immigration and Naturalization Service.

That we would return to China after the birth of our baby both Wei Xin and I took for granted. But we scarcely knew what to expect. What kind of punishment would we face for violating our one-child agreement? Just how harshly would we be treated?

While we wrung our hands over what awaited us in China, I received a second letter from the factory:

August 1987

Comrade Chi An:

I reported your pregnancy to Director Huang, who is in charge of the district birth planning office. I asked for her opinion on whether you would be permitted a second child because you were living overseas in America. Her answer was that second children are absolutely banned for state employees, no matter where they might be stationed.

She went on to say that factories are judged by how successful they have been at preventing second births. If the Liaoning Truck Factory has even one woman who has a second child, then all promotions and salary raises will be put on hold for a year or more. All of us, from the lowest staff member to the director of the factory, will be punished.

In addition our factory is being considered for a special government contract. If approved, it will mean raises and bonuses for everyone. Everyone here is very excited. But if we exceed our birth allowance by even one baby, we will lose this contract.

The women responsible for bringing this on her comrades will be dealt with severely. She will be ineligible for a bonus, a cost-of-living allowance, or overtime. Moreover, she will be placed on probation for at least two years, more if she is a member of the Party.

There will also be a heavy fine. In cases where families fled to avoid remedial measures, they were fined up to five thousand yuan when they returned with their "illegal" second children already born. Many of the families did not have enough money to pay these heavy fines, even though they sold all their furniture and other belongings. It is hard for them to live.

This is her answer. How can you afford such heavy political and

*financial losses? Whether your child was conceived in America or China
makes no difference. Second children are absolutely banned.*

*I hope that you do not lose any time and take care of this problem
as soon as possible. The earlier you take care of it, the easier it will be
on you and your health.*

> *To your health!*
> *Comrade Gong Chang*
> *Population Control Office*
> *Liaoning Truck Factory*
> *Shenyang City, Liaoning Province*
> *People's Republic of China*

After receiving this letter, my anxiety over what awaited us was
replaced by fear. Not over the fine. Five thousand yuan, the equivalent of about five years' income in China, no longer sounded like a
large sum of money to me. Wei Xin was making three times that
much every month now. Even if Director Huang doubled the fine,
we could easily pay it out of the small savings we had accumulated
since Wei Xin started working. For the same reason, I shrugged off
the threats having to do with my bonus, cost-of-living allowance, and
overtime. Finances would be tight, but we would survive.

What kept me awake at night were the paragraphs about the special government contract about to be awarded to the Liaoning Truck
Factory. "If we exceed our birth allowance by even one baby, we
will lose this contract," the letter had read. "The woman responsible
for bringing this on her comrades will be dealt with severely." I did
not want to be that woman.

Many couples at the factory already blamed me for the loss of a
child. If they were to lose their bonuses and raises as well, and all
because I had insisted on having the second child that I had denied
them, who knew what they might do? Someone might seek to avenge
their child's death. An eye for an eye, a baby for a baby. My newborn would not be safe in the factory nursery, or anywhere else for
that matter.

This was not just a wild, irrational fear. Stories of revenge slay-ings were not uncommon and were sometimes even carried in the official press. Shortly before I left China, a man was executed for hacking to death the seven-year-old son of a population control worker. He had waylaid the boy one morning as he was walking to school. The man had been distraught over his wife's late-term abortion some weeks before, an abortion that had been ordered by the dead boy's father.

"Maybe we shouldn't go back," I blurted out to Wei Xin one day after rereading Gong's latest letter for the tenth time. My words seemed to hang in the air. Even to speak about uprooting ourselves from our native soil seemed a betrayal of the fatherland. We were bound to China by an unbroken chain of generations stretching back many thousands of years. Exile meant the rupture of that chain. But then, we reflected, so did the loss of the child I was carrying to some cruel act of revenge. In our minds the past warred against the future.

In order to stay in the United States, Wei Xin reminded me, we would have to apply for and be granted political asylum. This was not a step to be taken lightly. Nothing we could do, not even having a second child, would infuriate the Beijing authorities more. Merely applying for asylum, if our act became known, would mark us as traitors. No one knew better than I that it was impossible simply to opt out of the system.

There was no guarantee, of course, that the Immigration and Naturalization Service would view our request for asylum favorably. We were being threatened with persecution not because of our reli-gious or political beliefs but because of our desire for a second child. These were unconventional grounds for asylum, and we had no idea how the INS would rule. If we were ultimately denied asylum and deported back to China, we would pay a heavy price.

We also worried about putting our families in jeopardy. Even if we were granted asylum, our parents, brothers, and sisters and their families would remain in China. The Party operated on the principle of guilt by association, and our relatives might be punished in our place, especially if a new political campaign broke out. China seemed calm at the moment, but one never knew when the next "leftist wind" would spring up.

These risks notwithstanding, we decided to go ahead. With the help of a well-known immigration attorney, Marshall Whitehead, we filed the necessary forms with the INS requesting political asylum. We were not permanently severing all ties to China, we reassured each other. Our refuge in the United States would be only temporary. After the policy failed or the government fell, we would go back. In the meantime, our children's safety and well-being would be assured.

Then I received a letter from my mother. Short, almost terse, it was very unlike the long, gossipy letters she usually sent. "Cadre Gong Chang from the Liaoning Truck Factory and another family planning worker have been visiting me every night for the past two weeks," she wrote. "I have also been visited by Director Huang of the district birth planning office. They tell me that you have gotten pregnant in America. They also said that if you don't get an abortion, your factory will not be selected as an outstanding unit in the field of population control. If this happens, there will be unimaginable consequences for our entire family. This is a very serious matter. You must take care of your problem. Mother."

I did not for an instant believe that the opinions Mother voiced were her own. Her strategy for surviving political campaigns was never to take a stand on principle. "There is no point in trying to reason with Party hacks and political activists," Mother used to tell me. "They will struggle you until you have no opinion at all. Just say what they want you to say, write what they want you to write, and be done with it." I had no doubt that the letter I held in my hand had been dictated to Mother by the population control officials standing over her.

While its contents were a fraud, the letter did prove that my mother was now a target. Unable to pressure Wei Xin and me directly, Director Huang had shifted her efforts to a surrogate. The thought made me sick with worry. Mother had never really recovered from the shock of Father's death and the terror of the Cultural Revolution. She had been plagued with high blood pressure and periodic bouts of depression ever since. It was for health reasons that she had retired in 1982, one year before reaching the legal retirement age of fifty-five. Like the ancient Taoists, she had retreated from a world whose ways she found intolerable and now preferred to spend her days quietly with her grandchildren. Now, because of my illegal pregnancy, she was being denied the peace and tranquillity she craved.

My concern deepened when my oldest brother, Liang-yue, wrote to tell me that mother was suffering from anxiety and depression. "She cannot eat or sleep for worry over what will happen to you if you come back with a second child," he reported. "Mother's health is not so good, you know, and since the visits began she is worse. Her blood pressure is up, and she is beginning to have headaches. Please fix your problem soon for her sake. Liang-yue."

Wei Xin was of the opinion that Director Huang had put my brother up to writing this letter. "What difference does that make?" I responded testily. "Mother's suffering is real." I was determined to have this child at all costs. But what if the cost was a paralyzing stroke to my mother?

I did not know from day to day how I would feel in the morning. One day I would stand my ground, thinking about the child forming in my womb, imagining its features, or its tiny fingers and toes, or it sucking its thumb. *I will never abort*, I told myself fiercely. These were my strong days.

The next morning I would open my eyes frantic with worry about my mother. *If only there were some way I could take the pressure off her*, I frequently thought. But I knew there was only one thing I could do that would help. I put one hand on my swelling stomach and the other on my throbbing head. Both ached.

My nights were troubled. Often the little-boy-who-would-not-die was a part of my dreams, sometimes laughing and playing, other times howling with that last desperate cry of his. Sometimes his face would disappear and be replaced by a familiar one, which I would soon recognize as my own, or Wei Xin's, or, most disconcerting of all, my mother's face.

"We must obey the Party's order!" I found myself yelling at a sleepy Wei Xin early one morning after a particularly bad nightmare. "Think of what will happen to my mother if we don't," I continued in a softer voice. In my mind's eye, I saw my baby waver and blink out of sight, like a mirage that disappears when approached.

Seeing my desperation, Wei Xin decided to resort to subterfuge. He wrote my mother and told her that I had obeyed my superiors: I had gone in for an abortion. The next time Mother was visited by Gong Chang and her cohort she showed them this letter, and the nightly visits ceased for a time.

Then Wei Xin made a serious tactical error. Worried that we would not be granted political asylum after all, he tried one last time to obtain permission to have a second child. He wrote to his university, hoping that his colleagues there might be more forgiving of our situation than my factory. He put the question hypothetically—"What if my wife became pregnant in America?"—but it made no difference. The Liaoning Truck Factory found out about the letter, and the pressure was on Mother, and on Wei Xin and me, once again.

Before Gong Chang had been trying to talk me around to having an abortion. Now, obviously under pressure from Director Chen and Secretary Chen, she out and out ordered me to. An "extremely urgent letter of warning" came by express mail (at a cost of some sixty yuan):

September 25, 1987

Comrade Chi An:

How are you? After explaining the birth planning policy to you in our last letter, we were sure that you would fix your problem right away. But from your husband's recent letter to Shenyang University we know that your pregnancy continues.

We have been severely criticized by the district birth control office and ordered to send you this extremely urgent letter of warning.

Birth control is one of our nation's basic policies. The "one-couple, one-child" policy is known to every family and every individual throughout the land. You are an official as well as a medical worker. It is hardly necessary to repeat this slogan to you. You have not been out of the country that many years. If you bring a second child back, you and your husband will be seriously punished.

Let me give you an example that deserves your serious attention: Recently, a woman at the Zhuangliu Grain Store ignored official warnings and had a second child. As punishment both the woman and her husband were fired from their jobs and put on probation for one year. During this period they are receiving only thirty yuan [about five dollars] a month for living expenses. They have been ordered to pay back the subsidy they received for the health and nursery school care of their first child. The officials in charge of both the husband's and the wife's place of employment and their superiors had their bonuses withheld for several months.

Right now the Liaoning Truck Factory is working on a major, government-sponsored expansion. We have successfully passed all the necessary evaluations and reviews. But if our birth control program allows even a single second birth, our factory will not be permitted to advance. All of the strenuous efforts of our fifteen thousand employees toward this goal will have been in vain. Moreover, our whole factory will be disqualified from any production contests, and the bonuses and benefits of all employees will be negatively affected. From the factory director, to the department heads, to the cadres in charge of the birth planning program, we will all be punished.

The consequences for you are unthinkable. You would be condemned by all the staff and line employees of the factory. How could you bear the losses you would cause and suffer?

You should seriously reflect on these consequences and come to a speedy decision to fix your problem. You must not delay! If you have real difficulties [getting an abortion in the United States], return to China immediately.

We expect you to report your actions to factory officials as soon as you receive this letter, so that we may report them to higher authorities. There is no time to waste.

> *To your health!*
> *Comrade Gong Chang*
> *Population Control Office*
> *Liaoning Truck Factory*
> *Shenyang City, Liaoning Province*
> *People's Republic of China*

It was around this time that I began to suspect that I was being watched. A middle-aged Chinese man had begun loitering in the vicinity of our apartment, and once or twice I even saw him when I was out shopping. It was common knowledge among visiting Chinese students and scholars that the government had recruited agents from among their number. Every campus had its informers, who filed reports with the nearest Chinese consulate on the opinions and activities of their fellow students. One spoke freely only in the presence of trusted friends.

At first Wei Xin pooh-poohed my fears, but a series of "heavy-breathing" phone calls and a car full of Chinese strangers parked in front of our apartment building two days running convinced him that I was not imagining things. If these clumsy efforts were designed to spook us, they succeeded. Wei Xin and I decided to move out of our apartment near the college campus. With the help of the classified ads, we found a house in a distant suburb that was available for a modest rent. A week later, in the middle of the night, Wei Xin loaded up our meager belongings and drove Tacheng and me to our new home. We broke off contact with our few Chinese acquaintances and got an unlisted telephone number. It will not be easy, Wei Xin tried to reassure me, for the Chinese government to track us down. The strangers did disappear after our move, but not my fear that they would find us again.

Not long afterward another express mail letter from the factory arrived, this time at Wei Xin's work address. It was the bluntest of them all:

October 1987

Comrade Chi An:

Have you received our last express mail letter? Have you taken any action as a result?

The factory officials are anxious to know whether or not you have done as ordered, since your actions affect the benefits of all employees in the factory as well as the factory's future. The punishment for this violation is very severe. We strongly advise you not to risk it.

If you cannot have this abortion done abroad, then the factory director orders you to return to China immediately. Any further delays, and you will be punished according to the law.

There is nothing ambiguous about our order! Make up your mind immediately!

> *To your health!*
> *Comrade Gong Chang*
> *Liaoning Truck Factory*
> *Shenyang City, Liaoning Province*
> *People's Republic of China*

Also enclosed was another note from my mother. "I was visited by Director Huang," Mother began without preamble. "She says that if you have your baby, she will be forced to resign her position as director of the district family planning office. This doesn't matter, she says, but you should understand that the workers in the Liaoning Truck Factory will never forgive you. Abide by the population control regulations. Come back on a plane and fix your problem here. Mother."

The pressure was back on Mother—and on me. While I anguished over what to do, yet another letter arrived at Wei Xin's office. The return address was unfamiliar to me, but I recognized the handwriting as my mother's. It read:

Dear Chi An:

Disregard my other letters. They were written under pressure. I want you to have this baby. When Director Huang ordered me to write you that you should return to China for an abortion, I did as I was told. But inside I was on fire with anger. She is treating you exactly like a pig to be shipped to the slaughterhouse.

In my heart I want to have another clever grandchild. I want you to add one more to the next generation of our family. I am also worried that your health will suffer further if you have a late-term abortion. You have always been sickly. Don't worry about my health. I am fine.

One more thing. Do not come back to China at all after the birth of the baby. Don't come back, lest my grandchildren suffer. Stay in America and start a new life. I repeat: Whatever happens, don't come back.

Mother

P.S. I am mailing this letter from a friend's for reasons you will understand.

By the time I finished reading Mother's letter I had tears in my eyes. If I still nourished the slightest resentment toward my mother for the things she had said and done to me as a child, I forgave her now. In her willingness to suffer for the sake of her unborn grandchild, my mother had fully redeemed herself. She was taking a certain risk in even mailing such a letter, since international letters were often opened by the authorities.

Reassured that Mother supported us without reservation, Wei Xin and I recommitted ourselves to staying in the United States. We were on tenterhooks as we waited to see if our request for political asylum would be granted.

Whatever happened, for us there was no going back to China.

18

I Have a Daughter

A FEW DAYS before Christmas 1987, Wei Xin, acting on the advice of Doug Scott, an American friend, placed a call to Steven Mosher. Steve was a China watcher well known for his reports on China's population control program. During a yearlong stay in a Chinese village in 1979–80, he had witnessed the arrest and forced abortion of several dozen young women, many of whom were six or more months along. With his insider's knowledge of the dark side of the one-child policy, we were hoping that he might be willing to serve as an expert witness on our behalf. Perhaps his testimony would convince the INS that our fears were not groundless: Even though security officials would not be waiting for us at the airport with a gun or a rope, we *would* face severe persecution if we went back.

Steve listened to Wei Xin describe the letters and threats we had received, shocked to learn that relentless Chinese birth control officials would try to enforce their policies on a couple living in the United States. He agreed to submit a deposition on our behalf and then offered a bit of parting advice. "If it appears that the INS is going to deny you asylum," he told Wei Xin, "we should take your case to the American people. I'm sure they would be sympathetic to your plight."

"Only as a last resort," I heard Wei Xin say quickly. "We have family in China, you know, and they are already under a great deal of pressure." I was even more adamantly opposed to publicizing our story. Publicly admitting that we had applied for asylum would once again bring the wrath of the authorities down on my mother. It is out of the question, I declared to Wei Xin.

Our attorney, Marshall Whitehead, explained to us that we would be breaking new ground in our application for political asylum. Under the provisions of the 1980 Refugee Act, foreigners were entitled to permanent sanctuary in the United States only if they could demonstrate "a well-founded fear of persecution" based on race, religion, social group, or political opinion. He was confident that he could demonstrate that we would be persecuted if we were forced to return to China. The threatening letters we had received were proof positive of that.

The problem was that we did not fit neatly into one of the existing categories of dissidents. We were not being singled out for forcible abortion or sterilization because of our race, religion, or political opinions. Neither was the right to conceive and bear children, which the Beijing regime wanted to take away from us, generally recognized as a fundamental and universal human right. Our hope was that in deciding whether or not to grant us refugee status, the Immigration and Naturalization Service would not look to the narrow, textual meaning of the law but its broad humanitarian spirit. If our application was denied, we would face deportation.

The first INS hearing did not go well. The attorney for the service, John Bottle, argued forcefully before the judge that granting Wei Xin and me permission to stay in the United States would "open the floodgates" to a vast torrent of illegal Chinese immigrants. To us this dire prediction seemed to ignore both geography and politics. China is separated from the United States by the vastness of the Pacific Ocean, not by a mere river, like Mexico. Moreover, the Beijing regime keeps close tabs on emigration. How could millions of my countrymen get out of China, across the Pacific, and into the United States? To Steve it smacked of a modern-day version of the old, irrational fear of a "yellow peril."

The immigration attorney also tried to convince the judge that the one-child policy was merely, in his words, "social policy." Because it was applied uniformly across China without singling out any particular group, he argued, it had no political implications. Those who resisted the policy should not be eligible for asylum; they were merely social malcontents, not true political dissidents.

Wei Xin and I regarded the INS position as native, if not downright disingenuous. In China *any* dissent from *any* official policy was an act of political rebellion. In the case of the one-child policy, the regulations clearly stated that those who interfered with family planning work would be treated as "counterrevolutionaries." By refusing an abortion, Wei Xin and I had engaged in an act of political dissent.

Later, the U.S State Department also weighed in to the controversy. According to Marshall Whitehead, the diplomats manning the China desk were vehemently opposed to granting us asylum, although their rationale for doing so was even murkier than the INS's: We were to be sacrificed to the Seoul Olympics.

The 1988 Olympic Games were by then less than nine months away, and North Korea had threatened to launch a wave of terrorist attacks in the South to disrupt them. According to the diplomats, the only country that could restrain the "wild-eyed" North Koreans was China. But the Chinese would exert themselves on behalf of America's South Korean allies, they argued, only if the United States stayed on their good side. If it became known that we or any other Chinese had received political asylum, China would be greatly upset, with potentially disastrous consequences for the games. Whatever the merits of our case, geopolitics took precedence.

Wei Xin couldn't believe that the U.S. State Department actually believed such loosely woven logic. Neither could Steve, who told us that most Asian specialists considered the then Soviet Union, North Korea's major arms supplier, to have more influence over North Korea than China. Besides, he added, Beijing had its own reasons for wanting the Olympics to be a success—namely to improve relations with South Korea—and Chinese officials were already privately urging Pyongyang to back off from its threats.

State Department officials, it was apparent from their arguments, felt themselves to under considerable pressure to placate Beijing. Almost nothing angers China's leaders more than the Western practice of granting asylum to political dissidents, for it causes them to lose face in the eyes of the world. When the United States granted asylum to the Chinese tennis star Hu Na in 1984, Beijing was up in arms. The intensity of the Chinese reaction shocked the State Department, which seems to have decided that having friendly relations with Beijing was more important than helping dissidents. Whatever the reason, it was generally known among the Chinese student population that the U.S. State Department frowned on asylum applications, which it more often than not denied.

In January, Whitehead told us that he expected the INS to hand down its ruling in our case any day. He made it clear that he was not overly optimistic about the outcome. Fearing the worst, Wei Xin prevailed on me to allow Steve to go ahead and publicize our case. Although apprehensive for my mother's safety, I reluctantly agreed.

My third pregnancy, at least in its early stages, was much easier than my first two. The morning sickness that had made me so miserable never materialized. I was no longer working outside the home or even taking care of perschoolers, so I got plenty of rest. Best of all, an ultrasound at six months had revealed that I was carrying a girl. What a tremendous boost to my spirits this was!

As my due date of February 8 approached, though, my sense of well-being gradually vanished. The baby was growing rapidly now, taking up more and more room. She pressed downward on my bladder, sending me scurrying off to the rest room every hour or two. Unable to get a good night's sleep, I was constantly exhausted. My feet and hands began to swell up the way they had during the great famine so many years before; I had developed a case of pregnancy-related edema. My body felt pendulous and overripe, like fruit that has been too long on the branch.

Nights were even worse. The baby was quiet during the day as I moved about, but as soon as I settled down for the night she started turning somersaults. What with her constant flip-flopping and my weak bladder, I never fell into a really deep sleep and was constantly dreaming—or rather having nightmares. I would sometimes see myself back in China in the storeroom, scheming to win the consent of the pregnant women incarcerated there. Other times I would be in the operating room, assisting at a late-term abortion. The babies were always born dying. I awoke with their cries ringing in my ears, my heart racing, my hands clammy with sweat.

The days passed in dreary succession, each one longer than the last. With Wei Xin at work and Tacheng off at school, I was home alone much of the time. Having only recently moved, I hadn't gotten to know any of the neighborhood women, all of whom worked outside the home. Nor did I have much companionship in the evenings. Tacheng had discovered Nintendo, while Wei Xin would usually be found sitting in front of another monitor, attacking some complex engineering problem with computer simulations.

Solitude was a stranger to me. I had grown up immersed in an endless ocean of humanity, where even at night the coughs, moans, and furtive whispers of sleeping crowds could be heard. Even after we moved to the United States, we had our share of visitors—Wei Xin's classmates, the students he was tutoring, our neighbors. Now, in the midst of the most frightening, tumultuous period of my life, at a time when I craved company, I found myself isolated in an empty house three times the size of my mother's apartment in Shenyang, in a suburb that was practically deserted during the day. I often sat staring out the living room window at the silent world without, hoping to catch sight of another human being. But only an occasional motorist would drive past, a head dimly visible through the glass of the windshield.

My thoughts turned increasingly inward, and my fears began feeding on themselves. I anguished over our decision to go public, knowing that the harassment of my mother would now resume. How much pressure would the Beijing authorities bring to bear on my mother when they learned that we had applied for political asylum? My approaching labor and delivery also filled me with dread. What if something went dramatically wrong at the last minute, as it had with Tacheng? What if Beijing found some way to harm me and my baby?

I spiraled downward into an emotional abyss of alienation and guilt, powerless to halt my descent. My occasional spasms of regret over my past work as a family planning enforcer lengthened into one long ache of remorse. Not an emotional person by nature, I found myself in tears a dozen times a day. The slightest provocation was enough to set me off: a careless word from Wei Xin, some small act of rebellion by Tacheng, the cry of a newborn on television.

Yet, as much as I feared that something would go wrong during the birth process, I became increasingly eager to get it over with. It seemed the only way out of the abyss into which I had fallen. Once I have given birth, I told myself, things would be different. The authorities would quit harassing my mother. I would be able to put the horrors of the past behind me. The new baby would help me to let go of my guilt and focus on the future.

I had wanted to deliver this baby naturally. My obstetrician had examined the ragged scar of my previous incision and cautioned against the attempt. The possibility that my uterus would rupture during the final stages of labor was too great to chance. Like Tacheng, this baby would have to be born by cesarean section. My obstetrician did agree to wait until the onset of labor, just to make sure that the baby was ready to come into the world. At midnight on February 1, 1988,

I felt my first light contraction. A few hours later, while Wei Xin waited anxiously outside, I was being prepped for surgery.

The anesthesiologist had me sit bent over double in a chair, my baby pressing uncomfortably against my diaphragm, while he probed with a long hypodermic needle for a gap between my lower vertebrae. Once he had the needle in the proper position within the dura mater—the membrane surrounding the spinal cord—he injected an anesthetic. A few minutes later, now prone on the operating table, I felt my body go numb.

When the obstetrician made his first incision I felt no pain at all, only a pulling sensation. Neither could I see anything, for my lower body was curtained off. But the pulling was enough to trigger the memory of Tacheng's birth. *Something is going wrong!* my mind screamed at me like a frightened child. An unreasoning fear gripped my chest, making it difficult to breathe. I felt as if I was suffocating.

Something is going wrong! it screamed again. An unbearable pain from deep within my gut rose up into my throat. I tried to flinch away from it but couldn't move.

Something is going wrong! I shut my eyes tight against the voice in my head, telling myself that this was a phantasm of my fears. I fought to control my ragged breathing.

Something is going wrong! I heard the obstetrician utter a sharp oath. Fear choked my throat, and the pain in my gut grew so intense I wanted to die. *Beijing has found some way to harm my baby!* I thought hysterically.

"I'm sorry, Chi An," my obstetrician said a few seconds later from behind the screen.

What was wrong with my baby? Then another thought: *I have taken so many women's babies away from them. Why should heaven allow me to keep mine?*

The sound of a baby's full-throated cries out through my fog of despair. For the next few minutes I clung—like a shipwreck victim to a bit of flotsam—to that sound as it rose and fell. The cries moved farther away, and I vaguely knew that my newborn was receiving her postnatal checkup.

Then the cries came closer again, and my pediatrician moved into my limited field of view. "It's a girl," she said, bringing a little pink bundle down to my eye level. "A healthy baby girl. About seven and a half pounds, I'd guess." I looked at my daughter's tiny, crying face. My eyes fastened on an inch-long gash on her left cheekbone just below her eye.

My obstetrician's face appeared from behind the screen. "My scalpel slipped a little," he apologized. "But she's basically fine."

Two hours later, after I had been moved from the recovery room to a regular hospital ward, my baby was brought to me. As Wei Xin looked on, I stretched out my arms to take her from the nurse, suddenly aware of the significance of the moment. It was for the sake of this tiny human being that I had endured so many months of long-distance blackmail and personal torment. I drew my infant daughter close to me, thankful that Wei Xin and I had chosen to defy the authorities, exulting in our triumph.

I studied the serious little face looking up at me, the small eyes with their black irises, the thatch of straight black hair. She had inherited her little snub of a nose from me, I decided. Her high cheekbones and her well-shaped mouth, resembling a wild strawberry, were her father's contribution. The deep cut on her face, masked as it was by a flesh-colored bandage, was scarcely noticeable. "You are safe now, my little 'illegal' daughter," I whispered. "Whatever happens now, no one can ever take you away from me."

By the time I returned home from the hospital, the first article written by Steve about our case had appeared in *Catholic Twin Circle* magazine. It closed with an appeal for concerned readers to petition the INS on our behalf. A surprising number did. Steve showed me some copies of letters that had been mailed to him:

> *I am writing in support of the petition for political asylum by [Chi An] and her husband. From the evidence in the . . . article it is painfully clear to me that our country must accept this couple into*

our protection. If they were to return to their homeland, they would be punished with a fate worse than death: ostracization and utter poverty. The Communist government in China has shown its cruel face in yet another way to the Free World. This poor family would be punished beyond human decency because they wanted to have [children]!

Please don't let this happen! Accept their petition for the sake of their freedom and personal rights, and show the Communists that the Free World has taken notice of their inhuman treatment of not only the unborn and newborn, but of mothers and families as well. We cannot as a nation sit idly by as such atrocities occur throughout the world.

> *Chris Heath*
> *Costa Mesa, CA*

We have given refuge to the boat people, the Mexicans from across the border, and to so many other hopeful people. Why can't we help this young Chinese family find a safe place here in this beautiful, free country of ours? All they are asking is to save the life of their unborn child. Abortion and infanticide should not be a "must" for this or for any couple. Please look favorably on [their] application for asylum. God bless you.

> *Lucille Smith*
> *Hopkins, MI*

I am writing in support of the application of [Chi An] and her husband for asylum in the United States. I am the mother of four children (two stepchildren and two natural children), and my husband and I feel that they are all gifts from God. A family should not be punished for accepting the responsibilities and joys of parenthood. Life is precious.

Thank you for your consideration in this matter.

> *Susan Stancher*
> *Springfield, WV*

I was moved to tears of gratitude by these letters, even as I struggled to understand what had motivated their authors to write. Why should these people, strangers all, care what happened to us and our baby? What did they hope to gain from such an act? I had grown up in a culture where only people who knew you well—kinfolk, coworkers, classmates, or close neighbors—exerted themselves on your behalf, and even they expected favors in return. And yet hundreds of Americans from across the country had taken the time to petition their government on our behalf. I did not know what to make of such generosity of spirit. "The American people have good hearts," Wei Xin and I told Steve wonderingly.

"Do unto others as you would have them do unto you," Steve replied. "Americans would not like to have their government forcing them to abort *their* unborn children," he added, "so naturally they sympathized with you."

This "Golden Rule," as he told us it was called, had a familiar ring to it. *The Analects of Confucius* contained a similar precept: "Do not do unto others what you would not have them do unto you." But the more I reflect on the two formulations, the more I realized how different they in fact were. Confucius had merely forbidden people to wrong one another, not encouraged them to perform positive acts of charity. Living under such a rule, no wonder so many Americans had written letters on our behalf—and with no expectation of a return.

The awareness of what others were now doing for me convicted me anew of what I had earlier done to others. Not just once but a thousand times I had broken both this new rule and its Confucian variant. I had done to other women what I did not want, and had finally not allowed, to be done to myself. The horror I had hoped to leave behind me in China came back to torment me anew. *What good is your regret?* I sneered at my reawakened conscience. *How does it help the troubled and despairing women, now forever barren, whom you tortured, aborted, and sterilized?*

I abandoned myself to the care of my tiny daughter in the weeks following. Holding her in my arms, I could finally let go of the memory of the other little girl or boy who had been taken from me twelve years before. But the joy that my "make-up" baby brought to me was not untempered by sorrow. She was both balm and wound, consolation and accusation, for her very presence seemed to speak to me of all those other children who were absent, who would never be. I had won my struggle to give birth, but how many hundreds of women had lost theirs? I was able to hold my daughter, but how many others would never hold theirs? *What right do I have to this child*, I thought bitterly, *after what I have done?*

One day Wei Xin, looking rather abashed, told me that he wanted to go to church. "I know that we were taught by the Party that all religion is superstition, but a lot of my friends at work go, and I would like to find out what it's all about. Besides," he said wryly, "if the Communist Party is against it, maybe we should be for it."

Wei Xin's suggestion came out of the blue. There were no Christians in either of our families. My parents had been atheists, while Wei Xin's had been Buddhists. I had been force-fed Communism, which was virtually the state religion of the People's Republic, since I was old enough to talk. I was not about to submit myself to some new cult, however pleasant sounding its rules. I didn't know whether the benevolent heaven of Chinese folklore existed or not, but trying to find out had never seemed to me to be worth the trouble. I thought Wei Xin foolish for even suggesting that we make the attempt.

It was by appealing to my concern about Tacheng, who would be entering the sixth grade that fall, that Wei Xin convinced me to go. As far as I could tell, he was receiving no ethical instruction in the public schools at all. Teachers in China placed a heavy emphasis on learning right from wrong, even if it was confounded with Marxist ideology, but all that was missing here. Wei Xin told me that it was in America's churches, not in her schools, that such things were taught.

Walking through the doors of Saint Michael's Catholic Church the following Sunday, I had a strong sense of trespassing on forbidden ground. Attending services in China was either discouraged or entirely banned. I had never before been inside any religious edifice, unless one counts the Buddhist temple I had helped a horde of fanatical Red Guards demolish during the Cultural Revolution. The only Christian church I knew of in Shenyang had been converted into a warehouse in the fifties by the government.

I looked over the hundreds of people present with interest. Mixed in with the Anglos were Mexican Americans, Filipinos, Korean Americans, African Americans, Vietnamese, even a Chinese family or two. No one had ordered these people to come. Like Wei Xin and me, they were all here because they wanted to be. As we sat down I was struck by the realization that this was the first time I had ever taken part in a meeting not organized by the Communist Party for its own purposes. But for what purpose had these people voluntarily gathered here? To practice the Golden Rule? To improve themselves? To socialize? To adore the deity of love?

I understood almost nothing of what followed. It hadn't occurred to me that there would be so much chanting and singing, so much standing and kneeling, and so much invoking and summoning in a religious service. I followed as well as I was able, which was hardly at all. I caught only the odd phrase. "As it was in the beginning, is now . . ." What was in the beginning and is now? "Holy, Holy, Holy."

I was fascinated by the painful figure on the cross that hung over the altar. *Why would anyone worship a dead God*, I thought to myself. Chinese god images were always robust and happy—fat, laughing Buddhas without a trace of suffering in their features, or sturdy figures of Guan Gong, a famous general whose body carried no scars from his numerous military victories. Of course they were also easy to dismiss as mere excrescences of human desires—happiness and success embodied in little wooden divinities. But the idea of a dead God was simply absurd. Surely the fact that this man had been killed proved that he wasn't God at all. *Who would want to kowtow before a defeated creature*, I thought, *unless he was not a mere creature at all but the Creator? But then why had he allowed himself to die?* It was almost beyond belief, certainly beyond the human imagination. The wildest dreams of human beings, I was sure, could not have begun to conjure up a dead God. Perhaps there was something to all this after all.

I remembered the hundreds of women I had forced to have abortions, how they had writhed and screamed and cried. And I remembered my own abortion, and how I had writhed and screamed and cried. If this tortured figure was God, then surely he understood the pain and suffering that I had felt and caused. Was there in his death some larger meaning?

From the time I was a small girl, I had been eager to help others. It was for this reason that I had become a nurse. At times, I had allowed myself to be twisted by selfishness into acts that I regretted, but my one true desire was to serve, to love. How could I have gotten to be thirty-eight years old and not realized this? That I had hurt and injured others was a failure of love.

Wei Xin and I enrolled in adult classes, Tacheng in catechism. Months later I made my first confession—and felt at peace with myself for a long time. The little hands that had been clawing at me could no longer reach me in the new place where I lived. My mind laid the little-boy-who-wouldn't-die to his rest. From now on the only baby's cries that would wake me in the night were those of my newborn daughter.

I was forgiven, but justice demanded that I do more. I would spend the rest of my life doing good to others—a goal I happily adopted, for it corresponded to my own deepest wishes. I did not know which way the scales of justice would tip when I had completed the course; I could only try to weight them in favor of mercy. In caring for others, I would be atoning for my past crimes. But how could I help women still in China? I resolved to begin by telling my story to Steve, however painful that might be, so that he might write it.

19

Asylum!

MARSHALL WHITEHEAD, our attorney, had cautioned us not to raise our expectations too high. But it was still a shock when, on February 29, 1988, he called with the news that the INS had turned down our application for asylum. As we had feared, immigration officials had seized on a narrow interpretation of the law, arguing that resisting Beijing's family planning policies did not amount to "political dissent" and was therefore not sufficient grounds for asylum. The State Department had not hesitated to second the INS's decision, dismissing our concerns about persecution with a form letter. Whitehead told us that the INS would be initiating deportation proceedings, as our U.S. visas had already expired. Only the U.S. attorney general, who has final jurisdiction in asylum matters, could overrule the INS.

When Steve found out what had happened, he encouraged us to fight for asylum. He would help by taking our case to Washington and to the American people. He first published articles in the *Wash-*

ington Post and *Human Events*, two publications widely read in the nation's capital. Then, a couple of months later, the *Post* article was picked up by the *Reader's Digest*. In a new postscript, Steve appealed to the vast readership—estimated at more than 27 million—of that publication to write letters to the U.S attorney general. Letters poured in to the Justice Department by the thousands.

The articles attracted the attention of Robert Hill, director of the Asylum Policy and Review Unit in the Justice Department. His office had been set up two years before to avoid a repetition of the so-called Medved incident, in which a Soviet sailor trying to defect to the United States had twice been forcibly returned to his ship, his appeals for political asylum falling on deaf ears. Hill's job was to review asylum decisions made by the INS and to intervene when necessary. Although he did not personally have the authority to overrule the INS, the attorney general and his deputy did, and they often followed his recommendations.

Hill decided that our case was worth a closer look. After a brief tussle with the INS, he was able to have the deportation proceedings put on hold while he investigated further.

To establish the well-founded fear of persecution required by law, Hill needed affirmative answers to two questions: Now that our child had been born, would we still be persecuted if we were returned to China? Could our refusal to obtain an abortion be considered an act of *political* dissent?

As soon as Hill read the letters that Gong Chang had written to me, he realized that the answer to his first question could only be yes. There, in black and white, Wei Xin and I had been threatened with everything from heavy fines to house arrest to loss of our jobs. Gong's letters also left no doubt that, because of the loss of bonuses, I would be the butt of universal scorn and contempt at the factory. Our two children would suffer as well, since they would be denied medical benefits and educational opportunities restricted to one-child families. They would be pariahs in a society of only children, discriminated against by the government at every turn.

The answer to the second question—Was our refusal to obtain an abortion an act of *political* dissent?—was less self-evident to Hill. But one conclusion was beyond question: By giving birth to a second child, we had not only violated the one-child policy, we had disobeyed a direct order from our Party superiors. If we returned to China now, we would be treated as dissidents or, in Communist Party parlance, counterrevolutionaries. Hill knew we harbored no illusions on this score, and concluded that our refusal to abort was properly viewed as a calculated act of political dissent. If we and the Beijing regime were both in agreement about our dissident status, he reasoned further, surely the U.S government should recognize it, too.

Hill fired a memorandum up the chain of command, strongly recommending that Wei Xin and I be given sanctuary in the United States. When the State Department and the INS got wind of his action, they were furious. In the face of their combined opposition, neither Hill's immediate boss nor Acting Deputy Attorney Harold Christianson was willing to move on his proposal. Nor were they willing to pass it up to Attorney General Edwin Meese for a final decision. Hill was stymied by the resistance of his superiors. He had done all he could, short of going outside of normal channels and taking our case directly to the attorney general. And if he did this, it might well cost him his job. Hill had reached an impasse.

Mother was once again a target. I had long worried what the Beijing regime would do to my family once it became known that Wei Xin and I had applied for political asylum in the United States. Now a short letter arrived from my mother containing the unbelievable order: "Return to China at once!" Later I was to find out just how much pressure had been brought to bear on her.

Mother began receiving visits from Director Huang within days after we had gone public. Huang's message was always the same: We know your daughter has applied to the U.S. government for political asylum. By doing so she is causing China to lose face. She must withdraw her application and return to China—or else.

Mother had handled Director Huang's threats and bluster much better this time around. She took heart from the news of the safe arrival of her newest granddaughter. Huang was only a district-level functionary of the city government, she told herself, nothing to worry about.

Then came the afternoon that Director Huang appeared on her doorstep in the company of a tall man in a well-tailored Mao suit. Huang never introduced the official by name, saying only that he was from the provincial government, but from the deference that Huang paid him Mother concluded that he was of high rank. For the first time in many months, Mother felt fear.

On the surface the unknown official was very polite, although he was unable to mask completely the overbearing manner of one who is used to command. "We have come to *zou fang,*" he said, implying that he was merely paying a courtesy call on the family of a student who was studying overseas. He called Mother "Teacher Yang" and asked after her health and financial circumstances.

Wei Xin has been overseas for six years, my mother thought suspiciously as she answered his questions, *and not one single official has ever stopped by to see how we were faring in his absence, much less one as senior as you. What are you really here for?*

"We have heard that your daughter has given birth to a baby girl in America, Teacher Yang," he said finally. "We are very happy for you. We have come to offer our congratulations." Then, smoothly, without a pause: "Did you know about the birth?"

"I wasn't sure," Mother responded noncommittally, unsure where this was leading. "How do *you* know?"

"We have received information from Beijing—" Director Huang started to say. The official gave her a sharp glance, and she instantly subsided into silence.

"Director Huang asked me some months ago for a special quota for your daughter," the official continued softly. "Unfortunately, it was impossible for me to say yes right away. You understand why. The province has set a ceiling for births. We have to keep the pressure on." He pinched his thumb and forefinger tightly together to illustrate his point. The gesture made my mother shudder.

"I cannot *suibian songkou*—open my mouth lightly. The ceiling, you know. But I was very sympathetic to your daughter's special circumstances. I was planning on approving her request at the appropriate time. Isn't that right, Director Huang?"

Director Huang nodded, a puppetlike jerk of her head. *This official is very, very senior*, Mother thought. She knew that such people were not to be trifled with or trusted. Their words were sweet to the taste but turned sour in your stomach.

"I have come to bring you good news: I have decided to award Chi An a birth quota. This means that Chi An's second child is now legal, and that she won't be punished in any way. She can keep her old job. In fact"—he gestured expansively—"we will not even ask her to return the only-child award money. She can keep it."

Mother had fought to keep her incredulity from showing.

"I really do hope that Chi An comes back to China with her child," he said, smiling broadly. "I really would like to see the little tyke." *I'll bet you would*, Mother thought. *You'd like to see her back in China in your clutches.*

"Teacher Yang, I have a favor to ask of you. I want you to write a letter telling your daughter to return. Tell her that she will not be punished in any way." The friendly expression never left his face, but it was clear from his tone that this was an order.

Mother was surprised at how small her liver—the Chinese seat of courage—had become. This unknown official's polite words and imposing presence were more threatening than Director Huang's bluster and threats had ever been. She had not hesitated to obey, dashing off a letter and handing it to the official. He read it quickly, nodding his approval. He would mail it himself, he told Mother, folding the letter and putting it in his pocket.

The rest of the day Mother's thoughts were in turmoil. The official may have been attached to the provincial government, but he was acting on orders from Beijing. Promise Yang Chi An and Wei Xin anything, he had been told, but make sure they come back to China. Everything he said had been a lie. There was no birth quota for the

new baby. There was no pardon for Wei Xin and me. Our punishment would be more severe than ever if we actually came back. We
had caused too many people to lose face. Beijing would seek revenge.
The unknown official would seek revenge. Director Huang would
seek revenge. Officials always did.

"Chi An can never come back!" Mother had shouted at Liang-yue
as soon as he walked through the door that evening. "She must stay
away!" It had taken a long time for my brother to calm her down.
He soon let us know, in a note mailed by relatives, not to come back
under any circumstances.

Wei Xin and Steve talked often during the summer of 1988, although there was precious little good news to relay from either Washington or China. We told him what we knew about Mother's encounters
with officialdom. He told us of the impasse faced by Robert Hill.
Still, Steve tried to keep our spirits up by reminding us of the thousands of Americans who had written letters on our behalf. "Hang in
there," he encouraged us. "If the INS decision is going to be over-
turned, it is going to be because of the innate decency of the American people and their attorney general."

But by late July it appeared that time was running out for us.
The INS notified us that a deportation hearing had been scheduled.
Even more disheartening, the attorney general submitted his resignation to the president. In three weeks Meese would step down. His
deputy, Harold Christianson, the man who had earlier declined to
intervene in our case, would become acting attorney general. Faced
with this circumstance, Robert Hill decided to take a calculated risk.
He would push a memorandum on our case right to the top.

On August 4 Hill's recommendation on our case went home with
Meese in his night mail. The following day, in one of his last acts in
office, the attorney general signed a memorandum addressed to the
commissioner of the INS. It directed that nationals of the People's
Republic who express a fear of persecution on return to the People's

Republic of China (PRC) because they refuse to abort a pregnancy or resist sterilization may be considered for asylum. Steve called to read us the text.

"If such refusal is undertaken as an act of conscience," Attorney General Meese had written, "with full awareness of the urgent priority assigned to that policy by high-level PRC officials and local party cadres . . . [and] of the severe consequences which may be imposed for violation of the policy, it may be appropriate to view such refusal as an act of political defiance sufficient to establish refugee status . . . [T]here is evidence to support the assertion that such an act is viewed by PRC officials as 'political dissent.' "

In a second memorandum Meese had written: "I have determined that the following nationals of the People's Republic of China have demonstrated a well-founded fear of persecution upon return to the PRC and . . . am today directing that asylum be granted to these individuals and to their families present here with them."

Wei Xin's name was at the top of the list! When we heard the news Wei Xin and I hugged each other in the very un-Chinese fashion to which we had become accustomed. Tacheng, whose English was by now better than his Chinese, was dancing around with the exuberance of a typical American schoolboy. I held my rosy-cheeked daughter close to me. "This is your country now," I told her with mock seriousness. "It was yours from your first breath, and now no one can ever take it away from you." She cooed happily in response, oblivious to the amount of high-level concern her existence had caused.

The PRC Embassy in Washington immediately issued an angry protest but got nowhere. Meese's decision was irrevocable. The pressure on my mother ceased soon after, as the authorities in China realized that there was no way they could strongarm us into coming back.

Even today Beijing continues to deny that its controversial population control program relies on coercion. Yet the facts tell a different story. The "technical policy on birth control" remains very much in force. It mandates IUD insertion for women with one child, sterilization for couples with two children, and abortion for women pregnant outside the plan. Couples who violate this policy are threatened and persecuted.

I left China disgusted with a government that tries, by the cruelest of methods, to dictate the number of children born to its citizens. On whose authority does the state deny couples the right to conceive and bear children in accordance with their own notion of happiness?

China is a very poor country, senior Party officials argue, and people cannot be allowed to have as many children as they want. The logic seems self-evident: Ten people cannot eat their fill from a rice pot intended for two. There had been a time when I would have agreed. Even after I had rejected forced abortion and sterilization, I remained convinced that my fatherland's population was the number one obstacle to its prosperity.

I no longer believe that to be true. I have since learned that the enormous wealth of the United States was created by individuals, not by the government. I have also come to realize that most of the countries of the developed world—Japan, Taiwan, and much of Western Europe, to be exact—are more densely populated than China. Despite this "overcrowding," none of these countries has declared war on its own people the way China has. Quite the opposite. Many of these countries suffer from labor shortages, and their governments encourage births. Until recently they even imported foreign workers. *Why is it,* I asked myself, *that only poor countries are defined as having too many people?* Could it be that what is mistakenly called overpopulation is really just underdevelopment? Could it be that China doesn't have a people problem so much as it has an economic one?

In my experience the Chinese Communist Party has produced little but misery in its four-plus decades in power. The state-owned sector of the economy, created by the Party in the fifties to lead China to socialism, is long bankrupt. (The Liaoning Truck Factory has run at a loss for years.) Tens of millions of my countrymen have been starved to death in famines. Tens of millions have been tormented in repeated political campaigns. Again and again large sectors of the population—the capitalists, the landlords, the intellectuals, the students at Tiananmen Square—have been singled out and persecuted for problems largely of the Party's own making.

I see now that China's continuing ills—its poverty, hunger, health problems, housing shortages, transportation problems, lack of education, unemployment, overcrowding, resource depletion, soil erosion, and environmental degradation—are in large part the direct result of nearly a half century of Party misrule. How convenient for the authorities to have a prestigious foreign theory—overpopulation—that allows them once again to shift the blame onto the Chinese people.

The Party is again making use of this ploy in the one-child campaign, in effect holding women and children responsible for all of China's problems. In the West there is a name for such deception: It is called blaming the victim.

I watch the corners of my tiny daughter's mouth move upward in a smile as she sleeps. How different her memories will be from mine! "Your face is Chinese," I tell her silently, "but you will grow up with an American mind. All the things that are such toil for your father and me, the maddening grammar of the language, the holidays that come at the wrong time of the year and for mysterious reasons, the demanding choices and freedoms of this vast and outlandish country, will be as nothing to you. You will grow up dreaming in English, clapping your hands at garish Christmas trees, squealing for joy when you find funny-colored eggs at Easter, and dressing up like a ghost at Halloween and asking strangers for candy. You will grow up free and proud, doing what you want to do and not what the state decides. You and your big brother will grow up to know freedom, not persecution. You will leave your ancestors behind, and even your parents will be struggling to keep up with you." As though that thought gives her pause, her tiny eyes with their dark irises blink up at me.

"You should still listen to your old parents," I tell her with mock sternness. "Even if they do talk funny."

I smile anew at the name Wei Xin and I have chosen for our daughter, for it is more than just a name. We have named her Mei, which is the way we Chinese say America, the land of her birth. It is a Chinese blessing bestowed on her birthplace.